PSYCHOLOGICAL CONCEPTS APPLIED TO PHYSICAL EDUCATION AND COACHING

PSYCHOLOGICAL CONCEPTS APPLIED TO PHYSICAL EDUCATION AND COACHING

REUBEN B. FROST
Springfield College

ADDISON-WESLEY PUBLISHING COMPANY
Reading, Massachusetts · Menlo Park, California · London · Don Mills, Ontario

This book is in the
Addison-Wesley series in physical education

*To my wife, Jean
and to
my children
Mary, Margaret, Kathryn, Barbara,
Helen, Dorothy, Nancy,
Richard, Karen
and Herbert*

PREFACE

The importance of basing teaching and coaching methods on sound scientific principles has gained, in the last several years, increasing acceptance. The application of psychological as well as physiological principles to the improvement of performance in sports has received greater and greater emphasis. Coaches and physical education teachers have expressed a real need to know more about principles of motor learning, about growth and development, about the role of emotional phenomena, about motivation for peak performance, about interpersonal relationships, and about character traits of pupils and athletes.

It is the purpose of this book to present generally accepted psychological principles and apply them to the furtherance of health and fitness, the teaching of physical education, and the coaching of sports. Theoretical concepts are considered and their utilization illustrated. Incidents and experiences are selected from interviews and correspondence with athletes, coaches, and physical education teachers. Pertinent literature in the field has been reviewed, and the findings related to the observations and personal experiences of those who work daily and intimately with pupils, athletes, and fitness devotees.

Several of the chapters are liberally sprinkled with quotations drawn from personal interviews. These lend a realism to the presentation and add interest to the material. Teachers, physical fitness leaders, coaches, and athletes from the high school level through the professional ranks have contributed their thoughts and suggestions. The author has drawn from forty-two years of personal observations, experience in coaching several major sports, teaching physical education at all levels. It is believed that this combination of sources will add appreciably to the validity, the interest, and the value of this book.

The author wishes to express his deep appreciation to the many individuals who contributed so immeasurably to this enterprise. To the athletes, physical education leaders, and coaches who gave so generously of their time and of themselves, the writer extends sincere thanks. He is grateful to the many authors and publishers who have granted permission for the use of quotations and other materials. Special appreciation is extended to Miss Eleanor Atherton, who so meticulously read and typed the manuscript, and to John D. Lawther, who assisted with ideas and criticisms.

The hundreds of athletes whom the author has coached and the many colleagues with whom he has worked have furnished a background of experiences without which this book would have been impossible. The review of the manuscript by Jean E. Frost, the author's wife, helped to eliminate errors, clarify meanings, and improve the quality of the presentation. The opportunity to observe intimately and regularly the author's ten children has contributed to a greater depth of understanding of growth and maturation as it proceeds from birth through adulthood. To all of the above, and many more who must go unnamed, the author expresses his affection and sincere appreciation.

Springfield, Massachusetts   R. B. F.
December 1970

CONTENTS

1 PHYSICAL ACTIVITY AND MODERN MAN

*What a piece of work is man! How noble in
reason! How infinite in faculties! In form and
moving how express and admirable! In action
how like an angel! In apprehension, how like
a god!*

Shakespeare

1.1 THE COACH AND THE PHYSICAL EDUCATION TEACHER NEED ANSWERS

Physical education teachers and coaches deal with the development of
man through the medium of physical activities. They are concerned
with the building of strength and endurance, the teaching of intricate
skills, the development of personality, the adjustment of one person to
another, and with game tactics and strategies. Coaches are also very
much interested in identifying and developing those character traits
which make for winning individuals and winning teams.

As these leaders work toward the achievement of their various
goals, questions, one after another, keep presenting themselves. What
are the principles involved in emotional reconditioning? Are there any
motivational techniques which will help a person break unhealthful
habits? How can coaches assist players to best prepare themselves
psychologically for a contest? How can athletes be motivated to really
strive to reach their highest potential? What are the differences between
teaching children and teaching adults? What can coaches and physical
education teachers do to assist individuals in the development of
desirable character traits and a sound sense of values?

Questions are asked about the structure and function of the
human body, about perceptual development, about the learning of
movement patterns, about teaching and coaching methods, about the
relationship of personality traits to athletic prowess, about activity
needs and self-expression, about sociological aspects of sports, about

1

mechanical and physiological principles involved in the learning of skills, and about many other tangible and intangible things.

Answers to these questions, if answers there are, must come from those who have conducted research in these or related areas or from persons who have had long and intimate experience as athletes, coaches, or physical education teachers. One may learn about developing endurance by studying exercise physiology, about the mechanical principles of jumping from physics, about the interaction between students from sociology, about the development of values in a philosophy or religion class, and about performance techniques from master teachers. Where questions regarding motivation are concerned, much can be learned by talking to participants, high-level performers, and experienced coaches. To obtain additional scientific information concerning motivating, motor learning, emotional involvements, perceptual development, and theories of personality, one had best appeal to psychology. It is in the field of psychology that many of the difficult and sometimes intangible behavioral matters are studied. Needs and drives, feelings and emotions, reflexes and reaction time, anxiety and aggressiveness, feedback and perception, principles of transfer, and many other psychological phenomena which need to be understood by the master physical education teacher and the coach may thus be investigated both formally and informally.

1.2 MAN: A COMPLEX ORGANISM

Man is much more than bone and muscle, blood and lymph. He is an unbelievably complex and marvelously effective living organism. Among other things, he possesses both the capacity and the desire for movement. His movement is dependent on his skeletal muscles, his nervous system, his circulatory system, his ductless glands, and many other components of his body; they are, in turn, dependent on movement for their continued vigor, health, and development. Ray Wunderlich, in an article entitled "Hypokinetic Disease," expressed it this way:

In summary, movement is primary for all physical and mental development. It provides sensory data. It broadens the perceptual horizon. It stimulates function and structure of all bodily organs. It is the means by which an individual learns about himself in relation to his ambient environment.[31]*

Man has needs, urges, and drives, upon which are dependent his survival both as an individual and as a race. One of the most

---

*Numbers in brackets are keyed to the references at the end of each chapter.

fundamental needs and urges is the need and the urge to move. The desire for approval of one's peers, of one's teachers and coaches, and of one's parents can often be satisfied through participation in physical activity and skill in movement. Self-esteem, self-expression, self-discovery, and self-realization can come about through play, participation in dance, engaging an opponent in a game of tennis, or competing in a vigorous team sport. Tensions and anxieties can be relieved through physical activity of the right kind and intensity.

Man organizes Olympic Games and fights wars; he builds dynasties and drops atomic bombs; he constructs computers and heals the sick; he dissents, demonstrates, and sometimes riots; he explores space and worships God. He lives, works, plays, and interacts with others. He is concerned about love and comradeship, about anger and hate, about integrity and authenticity, about the ultimate meaning of things. Man has many dimensions: intellectual, physical, social, emotional and spiritual, to mention a few.

Glenn Olds, in an address to members of the Eastern District Association for Health, Physical Education, and Recreation, put it in these words:

But man, like love, is a many splendored thing, and his education, like his nature, must be responsive to his complexity. As Aldous Huxley has reminded us, man is an amphibian. He is a child of nature, subject to her laws and processes, yet he transcends her in the promise of his freedom and the capacity for self-determination. Man is an embodied spirit, fixed in space and time through his body; yet he is free to explore and inhabit the whole spaceless, timeless world of mind and meaning.[24]

1.3 MAN: A TOTALITY

We must not forget that man is a unified and integrated organism. Biological, psychological, and sociological evidence supports this concept. Any experience to which this organism is exposed affects all aspects of its development. The whole *is* more than the sum of its parts. The total person is taught and the total person learns. Learning is a matter of the totality of responses of the whole organism. To discover how an individual behaves, one must observe the reactions of the total person. This concept of "wholeness" has important implications for physical education teachers and coaches. Kenneth Doherty gives two examples:

... holism is wary of speaking of a muscle injury. For an injury is always to the person as a whole; it has a muscle or physical aspect to be sure, but it also has a mental-emotional aspect whose healing is just as crucial and often more difficult than the physical. As one more illustration, fatigue is often dealt with in purely physical terms, as work decrement, or as the accumulation of waste chemicals from activity; holism considers it a psychophysical complex out of which we can abstract certain mental-emotional aspects or certain physical aspects. But holism does its utmost to be clear that the abstraction is not "the" thing.[13]

1.4 PRACTICAL CONSIDERATIONS

And yet, as we teach and as we coach, we must also bear in mind the following equally important and very real considerations:

1. While it is true that the whole organism is affected by all experiences, it is *not* modified in the same manner or to the same degree by different kinds or lengths of such exposures. Two identical individuals will no longer be identical after one has participated in a wrestling program for two hours a day for six months and the other exposed to violin lessons for the same time periods, even though other factors are rigidly controlled and exactly the same.

2. In all education, analysis is as important as synthesis. Many great discoveries have come about as a result of separating the whole into its parts for closer observation. The splitting of the atom, the microscopic study of blood, the study of the isolated frog muscle, the post-mortem examination of cancer cells and the analysis of movement are but a few examples. Doherty emphasizes the necessity for such "separateness" in the following passage:

In our society, "separateness" is absolutely essential. To deny this is to deny the values of science; in fact, to deny the values of words and thought itself. We must at times consider the "body" as though it were the entity-body; and the mind as though it were the entity-mind. We must perform isometric training as though it developed muscle fibers only, and interval training as though it developed the heart and capillaries directly and alone.[13]

3. As teachers we must be aware that there is a limit to the magnitude of the whole which can be meaningfully handled by human beings in practical situations. Some types of "whole" may be beyond the capacity of human beings to act upon or to comprehend. No human being can think effectively about mathematics, history, literature, and philosophy all at the same instant. No person can grasp all the details of a complicated physical skill the first time he encounters it. The units of learning must be of a magnitude appropriate to the individual's previous background and his present capacity.

4. For ages man's intellectual, emotional, spiritual, as well as physical development took place with movement and physical activity being almost the sole content of educational programs. Education now occurs during physical education classes, during wrestling matches, during choir practice, during lectures, and while playing in the back yard or listening to a radio.

It is clear that every experience to which man is exposed has an effect on his total being and that this fact must be considered in planning and conducting practices, in preparing lesson plans, and in individual instruction and guidance. It is also evident that in our attempts to educate we must first look at our goals, our aims and objectives, and then at the methods, tactics, and activities which will be the most effective in their attainment.

1.5 THE EDUCATIONAL PROCESS

Our faith in the future rests on the belief that it is possible to improve man individually and the society of which he is a part. Education should strive to do both. Parents are hopeful that their children will be exposed to teachers who will effectively guide them in their self-discovery and toward their self-fulfillment and self-realization. This kind of education will provide for maximum organic and neuromuscular development, the releasing of the powers of intellect and reason, the enrichment which comes from happy companionship and joyous interaction, and the discovery of the self and the resources available in times of stress. If the education is complete, it will generate a commitment to worthy cause, a concern for others, and a philosophy of life that manifests itself in a spirit of equanimity and stability under the pressures of living in today's world.

1.6 GOALS AND PURPOSES

Physical education and athletic programs should continue to hold forth the following as their aims and objectives:

1. Providing an environment which leads to maximum health and normal growth.
2. Developing adequate strength, endurance, agility, and speed.
3. Developing general coordination and the motor skills needed for daily life (e.g., walking, standing, lifting, pushing, dodging, running, climbing).

4. Improving the power of perception and understanding through a natural and progressive development of the highly organized nervous system and a sound supporting organism.

5. Developing the ability to perform well in a variety of sports, in gymnastics, in dance, and at the same time fostering appreciation for these activities and the habits and attitudes which will lead to continued participation during childhood, adolescence, and adulthood.

6. Providing opportunities for self-expression through movement exploration, rhythmic activities, aquatics, games, and contests, and other similarly rewarding activities.

7. Satisfying needs for belonging, self-esteem, and approbation of superiors through the development of competencies in games, dance, and sports.

8. Providing a means of social interaction where individuals can learn to know and to understand one another and to live together in healthful and wholesome ways.

9. Providing opportunities to lead and to follow, to cooperate and compete, to share responsibilities, triumphs, and defeats. It is through such experiences that friendships are made, self-reliance is fostered, and character molded.

10. Testing the individual physically, emotionally, and morally through participation in vigorous and demanding competitive activities in the course of which hidden resources must be called out and courage, determination, and self-confidence may be discovered and developed.

11. Satisfying the needs for fun, relaxation, and the satisfaction of accomplishment, which are so necessary for both mental and physical health.

12. Achieving that self-fulfillment which comes through optimum growth and development, challenging and exciting physical and emotional experiences, and through teamwork in accomplishing goals and experiencing success.

1.7 EDUCATION THROUGH PHYSICAL ACTIVITY

Coaches and physical education teachers who can bear in mind the objectives of physical education as they go about their business of teaching sports and trying to win games are indeed educators in the truest sense. They must of necessity be conscious of their responsibilities toward the individuals with whom they work and be aware of the fact that, as they assist a pupil who is trying to perform a feat of strength or skill, or as they talk to a player about tactics and strategy, they are also affecting him in many other ways. They should be alert to the fact that any experience to which an individual is exposed can modify his total behavior and effect changes, both temporary and permanent, in the many dimensions of his being.

1.8 THE SPECIAL ROLE OF THE COACH

Coaches are physical education teachers. They are working with the development of individuals through physical activity. Their techniques, their methods, their words and their acts will have a modifying influence on the athletes with whom they deal.

Coaches do, however, work under a peculiar set of circumstances, have problems and enjoy pleasures which are not common in physical education classes, endure pressures and experience satisfactions which are somewhat unusual, and teach in situations where nonacademic people of all descriptions become deeply involved. In addition, they must mold a group of boys or young men into a team and present them before spectators time after time as they compete with similar groups from other communities. Their work is in a sense being publicly evaluated many times during each athletic season.

There are many wonderful things about the life of the coach. His life is enriched by the intimate relationship with his athletes which comes from shared experiences and adventures. The pleasant memories which crowd in upon the thoughts of a coach are not easily put aside. The pleasure of teaching sport in an active, stimulating environment is a common source of satisfaction to coaches. The camaraderie which exists in "the great athletic fraternity" and the pleasures of getting together at banquets, tournaments, conference meetings, and other athletic affairs are not easily forgotten. Most important of all, it is very rewarding to a coach to see a former player enter the adult world as a fine doctor, a successful business man, a great teacher, or in some other way make his contribution to the betterment of the society in which he lives. It is pleasant to feel that part of this success might be attributable to his influence as a coach. Finally, the satisfactions that come from working day after day in a life's work which one loves and to which one can give oneself completely cannot be taken lightly.

Coaches often operate in the glare of the spotlight. Fans, parents, students, alumni, and representatives of various news media scrutinize their every move. Scoreboards and sports pages publicize wins and losses as successes and failures. Each athlete's mistake becomes the responsibility of the coach. Friends and enemies magnify out of all proportion the importance of victory and defeat. Employers and administrators often reflect the attitudes of the publics for whom they work. The coach, perhaps more than any other faculty member in an educational institution, holds the center of the stage. This is particularly true of the "pressure sports," and therefore the amount of public attention on a coach may differ from one situation to the next.

For some coaches, including some of the most successful ones, winning can become an obsession and coaching an unbearable problem. During a losing streak, the coach may become critical of himself, his players, members of his family, his colleagues, and others. Because of the stresses and responsibilities attendant upon coaching and the travel which goes with it, many coaches lose sleep, have difficulty eating, and become irritable. Coaches feel that they are being judged on their win-loss record alone and tend to use the same yardstick when judging themselves. Because of the tensions and strains of coaching, only a relatively small number have lengthy careers as coaches of "pressure sports." John Lawther explains this phenomenon in these words:

When a coach grows so old either in mind or in body that he no longer enjoys the trips with his boys, the foster-parent responsibility, the play and enthusiasm of youth, he should change his profession. When the coach becomes old beyond the level of enjoying the adolescent enthusiasms of his boys, when their immature chatter bores him, when he becomes critical and unsympathetic toward their opinions, their ideas, and their likings, he is no longer an effective coach. This statement seems to be a little more applicable to team games than to individual sports. He may even be more mature, better educated, more realistic, a greater student of humanity than he was in preceding years, but he is out of touch with youth. He will be a less successful sports teacher. He shares too few kindred feelings, emotions, joys, and objectives with his boys.[20]

It is important that a coach try to develop a philosophy which will help him recognize and accept his role. The responsibilities involved, as well as the human frailties and strengths, make the world of sports not only frustrating at times but also exciting and challenging. He may need to reflect on the fact that unearned praise comes as often as undeserved blame, and that others who are not so personally involved do not really take the games as seriously as their words and actions after a contest would lead one to believe. A coach who is magnamimous enough to make allowances for the actions of others under intensely emotional situations, who can give himself unstintingly to the team effort, who

Coaching Is an Intense Business

"Each athlete's mistake becomes the responsibility of the coach." *By permission,* Coaches Dunn and Meadors, Springfield College.

can place victory and defeat in the proper perspective, and who then can be deeply and sincerely concerned about the effect of the experiences on the players, is in the final analysis the most successful coach and the truest educator.

1.9 PHYSICAL EDUCATION AS A CAREER

Those who choose physical education as a career, and who do not coach, will also find in their lives a mixture of pleasure and pain. They may be revered as exemplars or stereotyped as "muscle men." They may glory in the freedom to move and the escape from the ivory tower. They occasionally experience frustrations resulting from too little influence on faculty decisions and a lack of power in campus politics. They find satisfaction in the enthusiasm of their students and the development of new abilities and skills; they may, however, wonder why the news media pay so little attention to them and their work and wonder if they themselves have a mistaken notion as to its importance. Physical education teachers usually put in long hours, many of which are outside the regular school day, and they usually get little or no extra compensation.

Elementary school physical education teachers often feel that others look condescendingly on them and their work. Those in high school physical education are sometimes dissatisfied because their professional associations appear to be run by college people. And college physical educators often feel discriminated against because college policies sometimes make it difficult for them to attain promotion and rank. Teachers of physical education also find that there are both pupils and parents who object to showers, who consider physical education anti-intellectual and physical activity in school a waste of time. Special attention and effort must be directed at such individuals if they are to be effectively motivated.

On the other hand, most children tend to "love Gym" and it is easy to become enthusiastic and deeply involved when teaching sports and dance. Teachers in these areas also seem to retain, in a greater than average measure, their youthful spirit and zest for living, and enjoy their many opportunities for intimate communication and serious counseling with students. For those who are more deeply interested in the more strictly intellectual aspects of physical education and who have special abilities along these lines, there are numerous challenging tasks in graduate teaching and in research.

Clearing the Bar

"There is no limit to the possible accomplishments of athletes, coaches, and physical educators." *By permission*, Jack Ernst, Washington State University.

1.10 COMMUNITY DEVELOPMENT

There are those whose concerns are with the problems of human relations and society in general. They, too, will find many challenging opportunities. Physical education activities can be an excellent medium for fostering understanding among people and often serve as an integrating factor in our culture. Differences in race, color, and creed can be transcended by the common loyalties and enthusiasm found in sports, by the recognition of an individual for what he does, and by emphasis on team and squad performance. Barriers to communication have been lowered and lasting friendships formed through programs of athletics. The sharing of personal adventure and experiences makes for an intimacy which forms the basis for understanding and respect. Sports have been found to serve as a focal point for group loyalty and as a medium for developing community pride and initiative. Because of the spontaneous and informal nature of sport, it can often be used as an opening wedge in starting new programs for youth or adults in a given community.

1.11 HORIZONS UNLIMITED

There is no limit to the possible accomplishments of athletes, coaches, and physical educators. They may set new records, organize international games, discover new dimensions of man, coach athletes to All-American status, assist young men and women to become fine citizens, or teach children how to run and play. All these are important. To achieve such goals and to exert the greatest possible influence, it is necessary to have both commitment and knowledge. It is important to know the anatomical and physiological mechanisms and principles involved. To work most effectively with the development of man and the community of which he is a part, one must also be aware of the best motivational techniques, the role of the emotions, the principles of motor learning, the personality factors affecting behavior, the most effective ways of bringing about the transfer of skill and response, and the many other factors which directly or indirectly influence man's actions and his relations with others.

As Earle Zeigler has said,

Ours can be a proud profession, if each of us strives to help people realize all the values that life has to offer.[32]

REFERENCES

1. American Association for Health, Physical Education, and Recreation, *Knowledge and Understanding in Physical Education.* Washington, D.C.: AAHPER, 1969

2. American Association for Health, Physical Education, and Recreation, *Values in Sports,* Report of a joint national conference, Interlochen, Michigan, June 17-22, 1962. Washington, D.C.: AAHPER, 1963

3. Arsenian, Seth, "Development of values with special reference to college years," *Values in Sports,* Report of a joint national conference, Interlochen, Michigan, June 17-22, 1962. Washington, D.C.: AAHPER, 1963

4. Bonder, James B., *How to Be a Successful Coach.* Englewood Cliffs, N.J.: Prentice-Hall, 1958

5. Brown, Roscoe C., Jr., and Bryant J. Cratty, *New Perspectives of Man in Action.* Englewood Cliffs, N.J.: Prentice-Hall, 1969

6. Bucher, Charles A., *Foundations of Physical Education,* St. Louis: C. V. Mosby, 1952

7. Bucher, Charles A., and Myra Goldman, *Dimensions of Physical Education.* St. Louis: C. V. Mosby, 1969

8. Cooper, Kenneth H., *Aerobics.* New York: Bantam Books, 1968

9. Cousy, Bob, *Basketball is My Life.* New York: Lowell Pratt, 1963

10. Davis, Elwood Craig, and George A. Logan, *Biophysical Values of Muscular Activity.* Dubuque, Iowa: William C. Brown, 1961

11. Dean, Everett S., *Progressive Basketball.* Englewood Cliffs, N.J.: Prentice-Hall, 1950

12. Dinkmeyer, Don C., "Psychology in athletics and physical activities," *Journal of Health, Physical Education, and Recreation,* Vol. 17, No. 7 p. 407

13. Doherty, J. Kenneth, "Holism in training for sport," *Anthology of Contemporary Readings,* Howard S. Slusher and Aileen Lockhart, editors. Dubuque, Iowa: William C. Brown, 1966, pp. 86 and 90

14. Garrison, Karl C., and Stanley J. Gray, *Educational Psychology.* New York: Appleton-Century-Crofts, 1955

15. Garrison, Karl C., Albert J. Kingston and Arthur S. MacDonald, *Educational Psychology.* New York: Appleton-Century-Crofts, 1964

16. Graubard, Stephen, and Gerald Holton, *Excellence in Leadership in a Democracy.* New York: Columbia University Press, 1962

17. Hilgard, Ernest R., *Introduction to Psychology.* New York: Harcourt, Brace, and World, 1962

18. International Olympic Committee, *The Olympic Games.* Lausanne, Switzerland, 1962

19. Kistler, Joy, "Student opinions as to values derived from physical education," *American Academy of Physical Education, Professional Contributions,* No. 3: 1954, pp. 71-72

20. Lawther, John D., *Psychology of Coaching.* Englewood Cliffs, N.J.: Prentice-Hall, 1951, p. 4

21. Loader, W. R., *Sprinter.* New York: Macmillan, 1961

22. McCanley, Swayne E., "Opinions concerning values received from physical education," *Texas Association for Health, Physical Education and Recreation Journal,* Winter Issue, 1969, pp. 6-7

23. Nixon, John E., and Ann E. Jewett, *An Introduction to Physical Education.* Philadelphia: W. B. Saunders, 1969

24. Olds, Glenn A., *Somato-Psychic Education,* address delivered at the First General Session of the 41st Annual Conference of the Eastern District Association for Health, Physical Education, and Recreation, April 3, 1960

25. Rhoda, William P., "Student attitudes and opinions toward the university service course program for men," *Physical Educator,* 1958, No. 15: pp. 141-142

26. Rockne, Knute K., *Coaching.* New York: Devin Adair, 1931

27. Slusher, Howard S., *Man, Sport and Existence.* Philadelphia: Lea and Febiger, 1967

28. Tricker, R. A. R., and B. J. K. Tricker, *The Science of Movement.* New York: American Elsevier, 1967

29. Tyler, Ralph W., "Human potential in a dynamic environment," *School Health Education Study,* Airlie House Conference, June 9-11, 1968

30. Weiss, Paul, *Sport: A Philosophic Inquiry.* Carbondale, Ill.: Southern Illinois University Press, 1969

31. Wunderlich, Ray C., "Hypokinetic disease," *Academic Therapy Quarterly,* Vol. 2, No. 3, 1967, p. 188

32. Zeigler, Earle F., *Philosophical Foundations for Physical, Health, and Recreation Education.* Englewood Cliffs, N.J.: Prentice-Hall, 1964, p. 294

2 GROWTH, MATURATION AND PERCEPTUAL-MOTOR DEVELOPMENT

Everything ripens at its time and becomes fruit at its hour.

Divyavadana
Indian Wisdom

2.1 HEREDITY AND ENVIRONMENT

In the process of educating, whether as coaches or teachers, it would be helpful to know which characteristics, abilities, and traits are inherited and which may be influenced or modified by educational experiences. These matters, however, are quite difficult to determine, for as Anna Espenschade and Helen Eckert have said,

Each individual receives from his parents the greatest gift of all—that of life. Through the parents come also a multiplicity of hereditary factors which determine to a great extent physical appearance and maximum potential. Environment from the moment of conception modifies and interacts with heredity to shape the individual and to control the extent to which the maximum potential will be realized. It is difficult, if not impossible, to assess the relative contributions of heredity and environment.[15]

Anatomical characteristics are generally inherited, and yet we know that environmental influences, nutrition, health habits, and activity patterns will affect a given organism in many ways, including the development of organic structures which influence strength, endurance, agility, and intelligence. Not only does the physical structure of an organism to a great extent determine how the organism functions, but the activities of the organism also influence its growth and development.

When we study the behavior of human beings we should recognize the influence of both hereditary and environmental factors and at the same time attempt to discriminate between those things which can be

15

modified and those which must be accepted and for which adjustments must be made. For it is important, in today's competitive world, not to waste time trying to educate by ineffective methods. It is for this reason that a knowledge of accepted psychological concepts is so relevant to the work of the physical education teacher and coach. As Henry Lindgren says,

What teachers know about effective teaching is to a large extent psychological. Teaching and learning are, as we have said, psychological processes, and the teacher who understands them is in a better position to develop the kind of procedures and techniques that will lead to effective learning. With this kind of understanding, he can develop expertise and competence in dealing with educational problems in a professional way.[27]

Growth, development, and maturation manifest themselves in many ways. As the child becomes adolescent and the adolescent moves into adulthood, a number of different changes are occurring simultaneously. With the passing of time a young girl becomes taller, her intellectual capacity increases, and her emotions become more controlled. Meanwhile her desire to associate more with her peers and less with her parents becomes more pronounced, and her sense of responsibility appears more consistent and reliable. These changes and an infinite variety of others often occur at the same time. It is impossible to separate them into two groups, those which are genetically determined and those which are environmentally induced. In general, biological structural similarities are inherited, and there is every reason to believe that this is true of every minute characteristic of a cell, whether the cell be in the nervous system, the circulatory system, the endocrine glands or other parts of the organism.

Since the behavioral characteristics of man are in part influenced by hereditary factors, it would be helpful for physical educators and coaches to become acquainted with parents and relatives so as to more effectively deal with players and pupils. In most instances parents are responsible not only for those traits which are genetically determined but also for the early environment of the child. We must be careful, however, not to attribute too much to heredity, for, as Ernest Watson and George Lowrey state,

Since a new combination of genes is formed with every child, there may be great diversity among siblings or between parents and the child. However, in general it may be stated that the child will show genetic characteristics similar to those of his relatives if he comes from a distinctly superior or inferior family. But there is no such thing as certainty in predicting the characteristics of children from knowledge of the family, with the possible exceptions of some of the congenital anomalies previously mentioned in which the mode of inheritance is known.[37]

2.2 THE PHENOMENON OF GROWTH

Growth begins immediately upon conception and proceeds almost explosively in early embryonic life. While the growth and development of a child before it is born does have an important bearing on later health and ability to function, it is not a purpose of this book to dwell upon this early part of the life of the human organism. It will suffice at this point to say that movement of the human organism begins in the mother's womb, that prenatal influences are important in the final realization of an individual's potential, and that perceptual development and the ability to learn motor skills may well be affected by what happens both before and during birth. Watson and Lowrey summarize this notion in these words:

Growth and development have progressed to a considerable degree before birth. All the organ systems are well established by the second fetal month and at no time after birth is growth as rapid as during the prenatal period. Through an understanding of fundamental embryology a better concept of congenital anomalies is obtained as well as an appreciation of future trends in growth and development. We have seen that most of the vital reflexes are well established and prepared for the initial shock of extrauterine existence. Behavior depends upon functional and morphologic development and is influenced by regulating growth mechanisms which determine the pattern of behavior both pre- and postnatally. Behavior may well be a better criterion of the degree of maturity than physical measurements during the neonatal period.[37]

Both heredity and environment affect the rate and extent of growth. People of a certain race tend to remain small even when they are brought to environments where there is a taller race. The people of Southeast Asia and the South American Indians are examples. Small parents generally have small children, while large parents have large children. Where both parents are long-legged and slender, the children tend to grow in a similar way. Endomorphs tend to reproduce endomorphs, and ectomorphs tend to reproduce ectomorphs. Coaches should understand this and not expect a tall basketball center to come from a family where the ancestors are small, or a heavy-boned, thick-legged athlete to be born of slender, petite parents. Nevertheless, good health habits, an ideal diet, adequate activity and rest, freedom from handicaps and disease, and a home environment which is reasonably serene and free from tension, are factors which can lead to faster and more extensive growth.

Erling Asmussen emphasizes the fact that children and adolescents are growing faster, taller, and heavier than they did a quarter of a century ago. He reported in Tokyo (1964) that height and weight of modern children show a steady average increase at all ages, and physiological functions related to sexual maturity develop earlier. He summarizes data from many countries and then concludes:

From all available data it thus seems that a tendency exists for the population to reach a greater height and to mature sexually at an earlier age than before. Several possible explanations for this phenomenon have been offered: industrialization and urbanization; rising world temperature; more and better physical education, to mention a few.[5]

Espenschade reported a survey in Oakland, California, which showed that eighth-grade girls are on the average one inch taller and four pounds heavier than were girls of the same age twenty-four years ago. Boys have increased their average height by 1.8 inches and their average weight by ten pounds[13].

Watson and Lowrey dealing with the same subject, but emphasizing height-weight relationships, say[37],

Recent studies have shown a general trend toward increase in height and weight in all civilized countries with each succeeding generation . . . This trend is noted within the first few months of life and is very striking in school age children. There has been a slightly greater increase in weight in proportion to the increase in height. Meredith has selected samples showing this relationship in boys, all aged 14 years, from 1877 to 1938. Appended to this is a 1954 study from the state of Michigan.

	Height-inches	Weight-pounds
Boston, 1877	57.7	87.1
Milwaukee, 1881	59.1	89.7
Several states, 1924	61.2	99.5
Los Angeles, 1938	63.2	109.8
Michigan, 1954	63.6	116.4

Growth proceeds rapidly during infancy and childhood, slows down a bit when children are in the lower grades, and then speeds up again before the onset of puberty. Girls generally enter this stage at an earlier age than do boys. Secondary sex characteristics appear at this time, and behavioral changes may also be expected.

Muscle mass increases throughout the period of growth, but is dependent on the specific kind of activities performed for the degree of its development. Bones change from cartilage to osseous tissue as the child grows, and completion of the calcification process indicates that the growing period has ended.

The volume of blood increases, but not in direct ratio to the magnitude of the growth. As the circulatory system develops, there are also changes in the blood pressure, and in the rate and rhythm of the heart beat. The rate and depth of respiration may be irregular during infancy, but level off during childhood. Early in life breathing is maintained by the diaphragm, but later the thorax also plays an important role.

The nervous system grows and matures during infancy and early childhood. Neurological integration occurs relatively early in life. The disappearance of some of the original reflexes is balanced by the appearance of a few new ones. Sensory organs are usually quite well developed at birth, and early maturation usually completes their association with nervous centers in the brain. The eyes are almost completely mature by middle childhood. The digestive system changes only slightly in function and nature during the developmental period. The kidneys mature, and some changes occur in the position of the stomach, liver, and intestines during the first few years after birth[37].

We have been discussing physical changes during growth. Other adaptations, equally important, are occurring simultaneously. In the words of John Anderson,

The most obvious fact about children is the fact of growth. The infant becomes a child, the child becomes the adolescent, and the adolescent becomes the adult. But this process is not merely a change in size. It also involves changes in almost every relation within and without the human being. We might call attention to the child's strength, speed, and skill, to his growing intellectual capacity, the changes in his interests and activities, to his movement from the dependency of infancy to the independence of adult life, to his growing maturity and responsibility, and so on and on. We deal then, as we observe the child change before our eyes, with a wide-spread and far-reaching series of relations.[4]

The adolescent spurt of growth usually occurs between the ages of ten and sixteen in girls and twelve and eighteen in boys. The pituitary, the adrenal, and the thyroid glands, as well as the pancreas, are all involved and increase in size during the early years of adolescence. Growth is rapid and extensive; it is accompanied by changes due to sexual maturation, and generally brings about both a need for, and a desire for, more food and more activity. Fortunately there also appears to be an increased immunity to disease and a tolerance for more strenuous living at about this stage of development.

The physiological mechanisms involved in adolescent growth are not, however, very clearly understood. This is pointed out by Roswell Gallagher in the following words:

The major physiological characteristic of adolescence is its rapidity of growth. The factors initiating this extensive and highly accelerated process, which is known as the adolescent spurt (and for which there is no counterpart in childhood or adult life), are not fully understood. It is presumed that stimuli from the hypothalamus cause the pituitary to secrete gonadotropic hormones and that an increase in sex hormones and of adrenal androgen then follows. However, what begins this process, how its rate and extent and timing are affected, and what forces influence the receptivity of various end organs to these hormones are not known.[17]

2.3 INDIVIDUAL DIFFERENCES

Although the sequence of developmental and maturational events follow approximately the same pattern for most individuals, there are wide differences in timing. This fact and the temporal variations in the onset of the adolescent growth spurt have important implications in the teaching or coaching of young boys and girls. Unless the pupils are aware that all young people of the same age do not reach puberty at exactly the same time, they may have diffculty adjusting to the fact that some among them suddenly grow away from the rest or mature physiologically at an earlier age than others. Boys and girls often become worried about these things and seem particularly concerned when they fear their sexual growth is retarded, and they often become sensitive, withdrawn, and emotionally upset.

Differences in the rate of maturation may also be accompanied by differences in motor ability. To give one example, Wilton Krogman, in his study of Little League ball players, found that not only were there wide individual differences in the maturity of boys of the same chronological age but also that the better players were advanced in physiological maturation[26].

Differences between the sexes must also be given consideration. While there were many instances in the past where these differences were over-emphasized, the differences must nevertheless not be entirely ignored. Anatomical and physiological differences do make it unwise to have coeducational competition in body-contact activities, such as football, soccer, and basketball, after participants have reached the age of puberty. Boys in general do become stronger, rougher, and more competitive as they pass through the adolescent stage of development, and good judgment and common sense must govern the choice of activities in which boys and girls, men and women, should compete with and against each other.

Individual differences in other aspects of growth may also cause problems. A tall boy who grows very fast may become concerned about his clumsiness; a high school junior whose adolescent growth spurt comes late may worry because he is so short. A fifteen-year-old girl is sometimes upset because she thinks she does not look attractive and feminine in a bathing suit; her classmate may become self-conscious because she is so tall. Aggression, depression, despondency, apathy, and withdrawal occasionally result.

Too much can be expected of a large but young boy whose maturational level may not be equal to his growth level. Parents and teachers, as well as pupils, are faced with the problem of dealing realistically, sympathetically, and healthfully with sexual development and all its implications. Coaches and physical education teachers who regularly see the pupils in informal and undressed states have an unusual opportunity to assist youngsters during the trying period of adolescence and young adulthood. They should therefore have a basic knowledge of the process of growth and development and be sensitive to the problems of young people as they pass through these stages and strive toward self-realization.

The total growth period may be unusually extended when for some reason, such as illness, food deprivation or emotional trauma, growth has been retarded. In such instances, while growth may suffer a temporary setback, the organism is usually able to adjust and eventually, although at a little later date, reach the original potential for growth.

Krogman aptly emphasized this matter of individual differences in the following passage:

To grant the child the right to individuality. Philosophically, this guarantees the integrity of the child's own growth progress; practically it relegates "averages" and similar arbitrary framework to the limbo which is long over-due. We now, in effect, no longer demand that the child tread the straight-and-narrow of a mean value (in height, or weight, or any measure); rather we regard the path of growth as a broad human highway, along which he may saunter as his own inner biological impulse to development sees fit; he may saunter to the left (shorter, shall we say), or to the right (taller); he may saunter to one side (slower grower) or to the other (faster). The important point is that in today's growth studies we follow one child at a time; the study marches along as he marches along; he is the one who, within reason, sets tempo, establishes timing, achieves synchrony and integration in the unfolding process. In very fact we are at an "individual-normal" level of operation. This, of course, is not to be construed as a veritable anarchic anything-goes sort of appraisal. It is, rather, in the direction of giving the child every possible "break" in the matter of acceptability of his growth progress.[25]

If one adds to the differences in growth and maturation the individual variations in inherited mental abilities, physical coordination, and personality traits, then the need for patience, understanding, and wise guidance becomes increasingly evident.

2.4 ACHIEVING MATURITY

Maturation is the process of becoming mature. As used here it includes the appearance of personal and behavioral characteristics which occur essentially as part of the process of growth and aging. It occurs naturally and without effort. It is largely controlled genetically but is also affected by environmental conditions. Maturation is characterized by the rather abrupt appearance of abilities and skills, by physiological and anatomical changes in the organism, and by a state of psychological and physiological readiness for an appropriate task. Espenschade and Eckert indicate the difficulty of defining exactly the concept of maturation when they say,

Although no exact definition of maturation has been universally accepted, the term is most frequently used to describe changes which develop in an orderly fashion without direct influence of known external stimuli but which are most certainly, in part at least, a product of the interaction of the organism and its environment. With respect to higher organisms it is certainly true that no adaptive function is at its optimum of perfection from the moment of its inception.[15]

Of importance to all those who deal with problems of motor learning is the fact that the development of the nervous system and the process of neurological organization are, in the normal individual, essentially due to maturation. Perception, reflex action, movement learning, and the growth of motor skill patterns are all dependent upon these developments.

When discussing the changes which are occurring daily in the lives of children, adolescents, and adults, it is difficult, if not impossible, to distinguish clearly among those brought about by growth, by maturation, by development, or as a result of learning. It is important nevertheless for those who are working with young people to know what to expect from them at the various age levels, to be able to read the signs as they move gradually from one stage of their lives to the next, and to be aware of their physiological and psychological limits as they are being motivated to accomplish one developmental task after another. Such changes are outlined in some detail later in this chapter.

2.5 PERCEPTUAL DEVELOPMENT

Perception, or the process of perceiving, consists in the selection, organization, orientation, and interpretation of sensory stimuli. During perception, the object or event takes on meaning, is related to past events and occurrences, and is recorded in man's computer system, the brain. Or, as Alfred Hubbard says,

Perception . . . involves sensing environmental changes, discriminating essential cues, assessing their relative import, and selecting the most appropriate action in terms of our own and our opponent's ability.[22]

Perception, then, is the result of the total sensory input, interpreted in the light of an individual's previous experiences, his cultural background, his environment at the moment, and all the other stimuli, exteroceptive or proprioceptive, which are brought to bear on the perceiving occasion. Associationists would say that, in perceiving, man combines the "residue" of former sensation with incoming stimuli of all kinds and in this way creates new ideas and percepts. "Gestaltists" would state that "insight" is acquired through the formation of a configuration or pattern as a result of past and present sensory input.

The ability to perceive is obviously dependent upon the normal and adequate development of the perceptual apparatus. This would include the sensory end organs, the afferent neurons, the pyramidal fibers, the pons, the mid brain (cerebellum, red nucleus, etc.), and the parts of the cortex which receive and interpret incoming stimuli.

In perception the proprioceptors, which respond to stimuli originating within the body itself, and the exteroceptors, which respond to stimuli arising in the "outer world," bring a continuous stream of information to the central nervous system. Sometimes the sensory stimuli merely carry messages to the spinal ganglion or the spinal cord itself. At this point an adjuster mechanism redistributes the sensory impulse, which may then be relayed to the brain, or it may send a message directly to an organ of response so that action immediately ensues. In the simple reflex arc (receptor to afferent neuron to spinal cord to internuncial neuron to motoneuron to acting muscle), perception, as we understand it, does not occur.

If, however, the sensory stimuli are transmitted to the spinal cord, relayed to the mid-brain and thence to the cortex, and an interpretation or discrimination is made before the message is sent by way of association fibers to the motoneurons and thence to muscles, then perception will have played its role. As Aileene Lockhart said,

All complex voluntarily-initiated learning is perceptual, the only way learning can occur is through the nervous system via the senses, and the only language that is meaningful to the central nervous system is electrical voltage.[28]

Perhaps the important point is that, in motor learning, sensory input and perception are as important as the ability to move easily, gracefully, and skillfully. Perception, like all learning, is an active process. One cannot become a skilled performer or a great athlete unless the perceptual process is functioning smoothly and effectively. The development of both the ability to interpret, to relate, to perceive *and* the ability to move and explore should proceed simultaneously and continuously if the child is to be a fully functioning person. The judgment of speed as an object is thrown in the air, the gauging of distance and velocity as one player passes to another, the combining of handsprings and twists and somersaults, the performance of an intricate dance, the serving of a tennis ball, team play in badminton, and many other patterns of movement require a combination of the ability to perceive and the ability to perform a highly complex motor skill. Perceptual-motor development therefore generally proceeds naturally and systematically as all components of the neuromuscular apparatus receive appropriate attention and care, and undergo developmental activity.

2.6 ORGANISMIC AND BEHAVIORAL CHANGES AT VARIOUS AGE LEVELS

The following summary of characteristics found to be present and changes that occur during the first twenty-six years of an average person's life is presented to assist those who teach physical education and coach. No attempt is made to distinguish between those which are due to heredity and those which may be attributed to environmental influences. Neither is a distinction made between changes which are a part of growth and those which may be classified as maturational or developmental. The purpose is to summarize in one place the changes and behavioral traits characteristic of the various age levels and thus to assist readers to understand the basic factors which influence the behavior of the pupil or athlete in the various stages of his life. Emphasis will be placed on those changes and characteristics which are of greatest concern to physical education teachers, fitness leaders, and coaches.

Birth through age two

1. The child must adjust from prenatal to postnatal life. Respiration, nutrition, elimination, and temperature regulation are involved in these changes.

2. Rapid growth in height and weight occurs at this age. After the first few months the growth of the limbs and trunk proceed much more rapidly than the growth of the head.

3. The development of postural control and locomotor abilities are perhaps the most noticeable among the many changes occurring at this

time. Most children can run and go up and down stairs when they are two years old.

4. The various stages of raising the head and chest, sitting alone, rolling over, hanging by the hands, standing on knees and hands, crawling and creeping, standing alone and walking have, in the normal baby, been experienced by the age of two. There are exceptions.

5. A great deal of neurological organization and maturation of the nervous system occurs during these years. This is the basis for perceptual development and the congealing of movement patterns.

6. There is a great need for a variety of motor experiences. As the infant and the young child moves, "cell-assemblies" are being established in the cortex. Movement learning is occurring, largely through trial and error.

7. Some kinesthetic awareness is obviously present. The "Moro response" is an example of this.

8. The child begins to talk. This involves control of fine muscles, mental association, perception, and symbolic generalizations.

9. Ego-perception begins at this early age. The child becomes aware of himself as an individual.

Ages three through five

1. There is a decrease in the physical growth rate as compared to the first two years. The proportionate gain in height is far greater than that in weight.

2. The bones are in the process of calcification and are relatively soft.

3. Muscular development proceeds especially in the large skeletal muscles. Postural habits are being formed.

4. There is normally a tremendous urge to physical activity. The child is unable to sit quietly for very long, and his attention span is usually quite short.

5. The child needs and desires to explore the many movement possibilities. Climbing, crawling, hanging, jumping, striking, and swinging are beneficial activities at this age.

6. A few skills such as throwing, catching, kicking, dribbling, dodging, and striking may be learned.

7. The child is self-centered and possessive. He is becoming somewhat independent and resents outside interference with the activities of his personal world.

8. The need and desire for interaction and play with others is beginning to manifest itself. Girls and boys need not be separated for physical education at this age. They will benefit from playing together at least part of the time.

9. The child is susceptible to infectious diseases as he comes in contact with children from other environments and before he himself has built up a great deal of immunity.

10. By this time control of elimination and urination has been gained and toilet habits established.

11. Stronger "ego feelings" manifest themselves; the child begins to take pride in his accomplishments, likes to "show off," and is often boisterous and noisy.

12. A sense of right and wrong begins to develop. The child incorporates into his own being some of the values of his parents and develops a "conscience."

13. The child's vocabulary and ability to speak develop rapidly at this age. By the age of five most children can converse with people outside their own family and are ready for school.

Ages six through eight

1. Growth, while it has slowed down considerably, continues at a steady pace.

2. The need for much vigorous activity and a variety of movement experiences is very pronounced. Emphasis should be on the development of coordination, agility, flexibility, and balance. By this time children have usually become reasonably proficient in the fundamental "racial activities" such as running, jumping, climbing, hurling, striking, pushing, pulling, and balancing.

3. Motor skills can be easily acquired at this age. Swimming and elementary gymnastics are good individual activities. Pupils should be exposed to sports and rhythmic experiences. Stunts and other self-testing activities are also good at this time.

4. Boys and girls of this age show considerable self-reliance and independence but also have need for family security and support as well as affection.

5. The importance of being a member of a group is becoming more and more evident. Group loyalties and close friendships begin to develop.

6. There is a need for self-expression through rhythmic, mimetic, and dramatic activities. Boys mimic older boys and men; girls mimic their mothers and older girls.

7. The competitive instinct manifests itself. This is more pronounced in boys than in girls. The need for some activities where this competitiveness can be expressed and where aggression may be released is evident.

8. There is a good deal of inconsistency in both behavior and attitudes. Children are somewhat emotional and unpredictable; their span of attention is short and they feel a need for praise from teachers and parents; their desire to be independent often seems to conflict with the need for security.

Ages nine through eleven

1. Growth proceeds slowly and sometimes almost imperceptibly.

2. Children seem to have limitless energy and need for activity.

3. The quality of movement and the degree of skill are greatly advanced. Previously acquired movement patterns are refined and new ones established.

4. Reaction time, accuracy of movement, and increased bodily control are quite pronounced. Improvement in the ability to perceive is evidenced in many ways.

5. Deeper friendships are formed and children are becoming more and more concerned about the opinions of their peers. They seek new ways in which to express their individuality. The desire for independence increases.

6. Athletic ability is an important way of attaining prestige among peers. (This is more universally true for boys than girls.)

7. This is the "gang age," and both boys and girls want to be with and play with their peers. Much group activity is desirable. Boy scouts, back-yard clubs, teams, and other similar programs are needed.

8. Leadership and followership can be manifest at this age. Personal performance, however, continues to be very important.

9. Concern about sex is becoming evident. In the early maturing boys and girls there may be signs of puberty and other adolescent developments. More girls than boys begin to mature at this level. "Sex modesty" is prevalent. Boys often express antagonism towards girls and want their activities to be separate.

Ages eleven through thirteen (Adolescence)

1. This is the age of the "adolescent growth spurt." There is a great increase in height and weight, in the size of bones and muscles, and in strength. This is generally accompanied by a corresponding increase in appetite.

2. Secondary sex characteristics are developing rapidly. These include:

    a. an increase in the size and weight of reproductive organs;

    b. the appearance of pubic hair;

    c. the development of breasts in the female;

    d. a change of voice and enlargement of the larynx in the male;

    e. the occurrence of menarche in the female.

3. The increased strength, endurance, size, agility, and coordination at this age result in a vast improvement in performance, especially by boys. This is the age for the development of a wide variety of motor skills.

4. Many changes in the cardiovascular system occur at this time. Among them are:

    a. decrease in heart rate (this is more pronounced in the male);

    b. rise in the systolic blood pressure (this is greater in the male);

    c. increase in blood volume and the oxygen-carrying capacity of the blood (this is greater for boys than for girls);

    d. a resultant increase in cardiovascular endurance.

5. There appears to be a greater immunity to disease which makes possible a more active and strenuous life.

6. Boys' interest in sports is often at its peak at this age. Games which are highly organized and challenging are the most popular. Boys are beginning to be willing to work hard and practice long hours to become proficient.

7. Individual differences, both between sexes and between boys and girls of the same sex, become more pronounced. This manifests itself in the rate of growth, in the degree of maturation, in personality traits, and in academic success.

8. Girls grow faster than boys at this age and tend to be both taller and heavier. However this is not accompanied by a corresponding increase in motor ability. Whether because of their increased weight or

because of cultural influences, many girls actually decrease in motor skill at this age. This trend should be studied carefully for both causal factors and effect.

9. The various changes which occur in adolescence are often a source of self-consciousness and embarrassment to both boys and girls. Their interest in and curiosity about sex is very great at this age. Excessive modesty and exhibitionism may both manifest themselves. This is sometimes described as the "age of conflict."

10. "Self-image" takes on increasing importance, and the youngsters are much concerned about their own development as young men and women. Boys are conscious of their own strength and skill, or lack of it; girls are concerned about their appearance and their skills. Both boys and girls begin to worry about acne, perspiration, and other personal problems.

11. Adolescents generally recognize the necessity for rules and even "authority figures" as they participate in group games and competitive sports. This is a good age for the teaching of values.

12. Boys in particular tend to "hero-worship" older boys and men who were great athletes. This should be recognized and utilized by coaches and physical education teachers.

13. Peer prestige and peer approval tend to be more important than the approval of parents and teachers at this age. This is in part dependent upon the particular decision and the circumstances involved. For minor decisions, such as those pertaining to the clothes they wear or the way they talk, adolescents are guided by the opinion of peers. For major decisions, such as their religious convictions or their choice of school, they are influenced to a greater extent by their parents.

14. The sometimes painful process of moving from adolescence to adulthood is beginning. The youngster often rebels at being made to conform as he struggles to become an individual. Ability to perform well in games and sports may lessen the need for other types of nonconforming behavior.

Ages fourteen through sixteen

1. The adolescent (puberty) cycle is usually completed during these years.

2. For many girls, and some boys, sexual maturity is achieved, the growth of bones largely ceases, and adult facial and bodily contours are attained.

3. This is the age at which adolescents are trying desperately to become young men and women and wish to be recognized as such. Emulation of adult activities is one of their goals. Adult privileges are important, and parental authority is often resented.

4. This is also the age when peer acceptance and approval takes on increasing importance. To belong to a team, an "in-group," a girls' chorus, a club, or to be a member of the student council, editorial staff, or athletic board takes on tremendous importance. As stated in one conference, students at this age "would rather be dead than different."

5. Students are becoming narrower and more discriminating in their sports interests. This is the age for the development of fine skill, appreciations, and understanding.

6. Emotional outbursts are fairly common. Attitudes often appear to have little rational basis.

7. Girls at this age are generally very concerned about and interested in boys; boys' interest in girls is more variable.

Ages sixteen through twenty

1. Most young adults are approaching their full growth, although there are wide individual differences. Most girls have matured physiologically by the age of twenty; only few will continue to grow after they are twenty. Young men often continue to grow until they are about twenty-two years of age, and a few do not reach their full growth until after they are twenty-five.

2. This is the age of emancipation. The urge to break away from parental control, the desire to do things and go places with their peers, the desire for recognition for themselves as individuals, the inclination to set their own standards and styles, and the rebellion against authority are at their height at this time.

3. Motor ability, agility, strength, speed, and endurance are often at their peak during these years. Assuming normal health habits and adequate rest, the resilience of young men and women at this age, their energy, their optimism, their zeal, and their desire to be creative are tremendous. Careful and empathetic guidance at this period of their lives cannot be overemphasized.

4. This may be the age of peak physical performance. Many Olympic champions, particularly in swimming and sprinting, are in this age group. Speed, energy, and explosiveness seem to be at their height at this time.

5. Young adults at this age are seeking to find themselves. They need to discover their powers and inner resources, they need a cause to which they can give themselves; they need to believe that what they are doing is worthwhile and will lead to self-realization.

6. Athletes and prospective coaches are very interested in the scientific bases for sports at this time. They are willing to spend endless hours studying and discussing the kinesiological, anatomical, physiological, sociological, and psychological bases for sports and sports performance.

7. Generally at this age basic animal drives compete with adult controls. This is graphically described by Robert Moore in the following paragraph:

The basic drives burst forth suddenly and shock the adult whose short memory is a result of self-protective repression. Masturbation, homosexual experimentation, gang fights, promiscuity, and car thefts are reflections of the animal inside and we are surprised this could have been just a child so recently. The defenses may quickly gain ascendancy and are shown by esthetic and philosophic preoccupation, pursuit of scientific knowledge, hyper-religiosity, and espousal of causes such as civil rights and pacifism. In most young people we see an alternation, sometimes so quick as to be unbelievable. In others whose early experiences gave them less strength for mature defense one or the other picture may predominate with little of the opposite side apparent. We then have the child who shows the impulses without adequate control and is delinquent or the child who shows only defense and is rigidly constricted and hides all creative potentials.[29]

Ages twenty-one through twenty-six

1. Growth, in the physical sense, is usually complete. Exceptional persons who eventually reach great size may continue to grow beyond the age of twenty-six.

2. Endurance, strength, and skill often reach their peak during these years. Professional athletes and many Olympic performers are in this age bracket.

3. Athletic sense, smartness, and "savvy" are gained with experience and study. When these qualities can be combined with highly skilled performance, the peak of athletic performance can be attained. Athletes and sportsmen can therefore look to this age for some of their greatest satisfactions through sports.

4. Control of impulses, that is increased self-discipline, manifests itself at this time. Stability and dependability are increasingly evident.

5. This is the period in life when most men and women are seeking a mate. This may temporarily bring about behavior which is out of character with the general pattern of the individuals's life.

6. Goals for life and patterns of behavior are now usually fairly well established. We can now also expect to find vast individual differences. These words of Moore give us a clue:

No matter how mature the person, this maturity merely reflects the stable equilibrium between basic biological drives and the learned defenses against these drives. Anyone can be stressed to the point he regresses to less mature and more desperate defenses and even to a breakdown of defense and emergence of the drives (or to withdrawal as a last ditch defense).[29]

It must be emphasized again that these changes vary widely in rate and in pattern with different individuals and that differences between individuals increase with age. It must also be recognized that these changes are gradual and that individuals do not move suddenly from one stage of growth to another. Anderson summarizes:

While the changes that occur as the child grows and matures are not striking when observed over very short periods of time, they are very great over a long period. If we are away from a young child a few weeks, he seems almost like a different person when we see him again. As the child moves forward through time and interacts with other persons, it is difficult for us to separate out the specific results of maturing, the specific results of learning, and the specific results of the cumulation of skills and knowledges which remain with the child as his permanent repertoire for meeting life situations. From the studies in which children have been followed over a number of years it is clear that significant progress with age occurs in all skills and knowledges no matter where we dip into the growth process. In personality, in emotional traits, in motivation, and even in such phenomena as responsibility we seem not to find quite as much change with age.[4]

2.7 DEVELOPMENTAL TASKS

The events and occurrences which constitute the growth and development of the human organism have been described as "tasks of the body." Learning to walk, controlling objects in space, participating in sports, reproducing one's kind, transforming food into energy, circulating blood and lymph, fighting disease, or dancing at a party are such "tasks of the body." These may be internal or external, conscious or unconscious. They may be a part of growth, maturation, or development. They may occur slowly and imperceptibly or dramatically and quite suddenly. Robert Havighurst explains it thus:

Even before the human embryo is as large as a finger nail, a tube has formed within it, enlarged at a certain point, and begun to pulsate. Thus the human heart has its beginning. It develops into a four-chambered organ which circulates the blood for 80 years, without a stop in the pulsations which commenced in that tiny tube.

This is one of the tasks of the body—to develop and maintain an organ which is necessary to life. The body does this all unconsciously, and in the right timing and placing with respect to the other body organs.

In addition to the internal and unconscious tasks, the body also accomplishes a series of visible tasks of which a person is more conscious and which affect his feelings about himself as well as the attitudes of others toward him. These visible tasks of the body constitute the process, in part, of growing up and growing through the life cycle.[20]

The body, then, becomes a means by which we develop and live. It serves us as we move through the cycle of life from conception to death. One task leads to another. Activity combines with growth to bring about development. As the organism develops, new tasks present themselves and lead to a higher level of development. Thus the cycle continues, each task serving a purpose and yet at the same time becoming a developmental hurdle which must be overcome. Challenging tasks, making insistent demands on the various functional dimensions of man, lead to the achievement of specific objectives and goals, and in so doing lead to self-discovery and self-fulfillment. Anderson continues:

Thus the growing person builds a series of skills, one after another, in response to the demands made by development or by society. Patterns are built into his nervous system which make it possible for him, under appropriate stimulation, to call forth whatever activity is necessary with a minimum of effort and energy. Hence, an adult is a working bundle of many skills which are ready to function even though only a few may be used on any particular occasion.[4]

Coaches and physical educators should be aware that every motor task makes certain demands, the satisfaction of which are dependent upon growth and maturational factors. Gross bodily coordination makes demands on the organism, inducing a development which then serves as a basis for further development of finer skills. The calling forth of acquired movement patterns to serve a specific purpose often leads to the laying down of a more complex pattern which may in turn be needed later. In the world of human beings this can be important, for, as Havighurst says,

The tasks of the body are especially important to personal well-being in the present-day American society, because our society sets such great store on the physical appearance of its people. Possibly there will be less emphasis on sheer looks as time goes on, and as the proportion of older people in the society increases. But there is not likely to be any decrease in the social emphasis on health, and people will be expected more and more to make the most of their bodies.

Mustering the Courage to Dive

"As the organism develops, new tasks present themselves and lead to a higher level of development." *By permission*, Roger Nekton and Susan Silvia at Springfield College.

Perhaps there will develop a public opinion which blames people for their own ill health, as Samuel Butler suggested in *Erewhon*. In his Utopia Butler said that people might be severely censured if they became ill, because they were expected to know how to keep healthy, and illness could only come through gross negligence.

In any case it appears that the tasks of the body will be better performed at all ages if people accept the help of health and physical education, and if this profession does what appears to be its manifest duty.[20]

2.8 SUMMARY

We see then that people grow, mature, develop, and learn. Each succeeding day sees an individual slightly different from the same individual the day before. Persons become, little by little, prepared to take on more difficult tasks, to perform more challenging feats. Each hurdle overcome, each struggle won, brings about an increase in readiness for the next higher and more difficult goal. Physiological

Security with Expert Assistance

"Each hurdle overcome, each struggle won, brings about an increase in readiness for the next higher and more difficult goal." *By permission*, Roger Nekton and Susan Silvia at Springfield College.

readiness contributes to emotional and social readiness. Intellectual development and other forms of psychological readiness assist in their way with the accomplishment of tasks of the body and ultimate self-actualization and self-realization.

As one contemplates the development of individuals and considers the many factors involved, he can easily become overwhelmed by the responsibilities of teaching and coaching, and yet the opportunities and challenges become clearer, more meaningful, and more real.

REFERENCES

1. Allman, Fred L., Jr., "Competitive sports for boys under fifteen—beneficial or harmful?" *Journal of the Medical Association of Georgia* February, 1967

2. American Association for Health, Physical Education, and Recreation, *Programming for the Mentally Retarded*, Report of a National Conference, October 31-November 2, 1966. Washington, D.C.: AAHPER, 1968

3. Anderson, C. L., *School Health Practices*. St. Louis: C. V. Mosby, 1964

4. Anderson, John E., "Growth and development today: implications for physical education," paper presented at the National Conference on Social Changes and Implications for Physical Education and Sports Recreation, Estes Park, Colorado, June 22-28, 1958, pp. 1, 1-2, 4

5. Asmussen, Erling, "Growth and athletic performance," *Proceedings of International Congress of Sport Sciences*. Tokyo: The Japanese Union of Sport Sciences, University of Tokyo Press, 1966, p. 105

6. Asmussen, Erling, and K. Heeboll Nielsen, "Physical performance and growth," *Journal of Applied Psychology*, Vol. 8, January, 1956, pp. 371-80

7. Breckenridge, Marian E., and E. Lee Vincent, *Child Development*. Philadelphia: W. B. Saunders, 1955

8. Brooks, Fowler D., *Child Psychology*. Boston: Houghton-Mifflin, 1937

9. Bucher, Charles A., *Foundations of Physical Education*. St. Louis: C. V. Mosby, 1952

10. Clifton, Marguerite A., "The role of perception in movement," *The Academy Papers, No. 1*, The American Academy of Physical Education, March, 1968

11. Cratty, Bryant J., *Developmental Sequences of Perceptual-Motor Tasks*. Freeport, Long Island, New York: Educational Activities, 1967

12. Delacato, Carl H., *The Diagnosis and Treatment of Speech and Reading Problems*. Springfield, Illinois: Charles C. Thomas, 1968

13. Espenschade, Anna S., "Child development research: implications for physical education," *Anthology of Contemporary Readings*, Howard S. Slusher and Aileene S. Lockhart, editors. Dubuque, Iowa: William C. Brown, 1966, p. 156

14. Espenschade, Anna S., "Contributions of physical activity to growth," *Research Quarterly*, Vol. 31, May, 1960, pp. 356-64

15. Espenschade, Anna S., and Helen M. Eckert, *Motor Development*. Columbus, Ohio: Merrill Books, 1967, pp. 1 and 78

16. Espenschade, Anna S. "Perceptual-motor development in children," *The Academy Papers, No. 1*, The American Academy of Physical Education, 1967

17. Gallagher, J. Roswell, "Growing up in the modern world," *The Growing Years—Adolescence*, Ann E. Jewett and Clyde Knapp, editors, 1962 Yearbook. Washington, D.C.: American Association for Health, Physical Education and Recreation, p. 5.

18. Godfrey, Barbara B., and Newell C. Kephart, *Movement Patterns and Motor Education*. New York: Appleton-Century-Crofts, 1969

19. Halverson, Lolas E., "Development of motor patterns in young children," *Quest*, National Association of Physical Education for College Women and National College Physical Education Association for Men, Monograph 6, Spring Issue, May 1966

20. Havighurst, Robert J., "Physical education and the tasks of the body," *American Academy of Physical Education, Professional Contributions No. 5*. Washington, D. C.: AAHPER—NEA, 1956, pp. 54 and 62.

21. Hochberg, Julian E., *Perception*. Englewood Cliffs, N.J.: Prentice-Hall, 1964

22. Hubbard, Alfred W., "Perception in sport," *Psicologia Dello Sport*, Proceedings of First International Congress of Sport Psychology, Ferrucio Antonelli, editor. Rome, 1965, p. 125

23. Johns, Edward B., Wilfred E. Sutton, and Lloyd E. Webster, *Health for Effective Living*. New York: McGraw-Hill, 1962

24. Katsuki, Shinji, "Physical growth and development of children in post war Japan," *Proceedings of International Congress of Sport Sciences*. Tokyo: The Japanese Union of Sport Sciences, University of Tokyo Press, 1966

25. Krogman, Wilton Marion, "Factors in physical growth of children as they may apply to physical education," *Professional Contributions No. 3*, American Academy of Physical Education, November 1954, p. 122

26. Krogman, Wilton Marion, "Maturation age of 55 boys in the little league world series, 1957," *Research Quarterly*, Vol. 30, No. 1, March 1959, pp. 54-56

27. Lindgren, Henry Clay, *Educational Psychology in the Classroom*. New York: Wiley, 1967, p. 6

28. Lockhart, Aileene, "Prerequisites to motor learning," *The Academy Papers, No. 1*, The American Academy of Physical Education, March 1968, p. 2

29. Moore, Robert A., *Sports and Mental Health*. Springfield, Illinois: Charles C. Thomas, 1966, pp. 42 and 44

30. Piaget, Jean, *The Construction of Reality in the Child*. New York: Basic Books, 1954

31. Piaget, Jean, and Bärbel Inhilder, *The Psychology of the Child*. New York: Basic Books, 1969

32. Rarick, G. Lawrence, "Exercise and growth," *Science and Medicine of Exercise and Sports*, Warren R. Johnson, editor. New York: Harper, 1960

33. Seils, Leroy G., "The relationship between measure of physical growth and gross motor performance of primary-grade school children," *Research Quarterly*, Vol. 22, May 1951, pp. 244-60

34. Siegal, Arthur S., "A motor hypothesis of perceptual development," *American Journal of Psychology*, Vol. 66, 1953, pp. 301-304

35. Smith, Hope M., "Motor activity and perceptual development," *Journal of Health, Physical Education, and Recreation*, Vol. 39, No. 2, February 1968

36. Tyler, Ralph W., "Human potential in a dynamic environment," School Health Education Study, Airlie House Conference, June 9-11, 1968

37. Watson, Ernest H., and George H. Lowrey, *Growth and Development of Children*. Chicago: The Year Book Publishers, 1958, pp. 27-28, 29, 44, 194-196

3 THE ROLE OF EMOTIONS

The emotions have always been of central concern to men. In every endeavor, in every major human enterprise, the emotions are somehow involved.

Robert Plutchik, 1962

3.1 EMOTIONS DEFY ACCURATE ANALYSIS

The study of emotions is beset with problems and difficulties. There is far from universal agreement on a satisfactory definition. Many theories have been presented only to be challenged and rejected. Results of animal experimentation have only limited application to humans. The degree or intensity of the the emotion varies greatly and yet must be carefully considered. Almost all behavior is the result of "mixed" emotions. Introspective reports, while yielding considerable information and insight, are not entirely reliable. Valid and reliable measurement is as yet quite limited. There are vast individual differences in the quality and intensity of emotional states and in the effects of the emotions on behavior. Finally, emotions are an intangible and internal kind of phenomena which are difficult to investigate scientifically and to express in words.

3.2 THE IMPORTANCE OF THE ROLE OF EMOTIONS

And yet emotions are tremendously important in physical education and in the realm of sport. Emotional arousal is necessary for peak performance. Frustrations and disappointments are inevitable in competitive activities. Anxiety and stress, as well as joy and fun, are a part of athletics. Anger and fear do rear their heads as people clash in combative and body-contact activities. General emotional excitement surrounds and is part of almost every sports situation. The cheering of the spectators, the music of the bands, the barking of the vendors, and the partisanship of parents and friends, all add to the aura of excitement and stimulate in most individuals an emotional response.

Emotions are involved in healthful living, in self-expression, in leadership, and in the development of values. An understanding of emotions is also important in the study of psychosomatic disease. Our thinking, our motor learning, our decisions are affected by our feelings and our mental attitude. As Lyle Tussing so aptly states,

Emotions give a richness and fullness to life; but if they have too great a hold on the individual, his behavior may become irrational. It appears that emotional expression results from inner forces that have their origins in the neural and endocrine systems. From these sources, the influence spreads throughout the body and affects the entire human being. In the production of emotion there appears to be a fusion of complex sensory experiences with patterns of behavior already established, which are either inherited or learned.[29]

3.3 WHAT ARE EMOTIONS?

Before we can proceed with the analysis of the role of emotions in physical activity and sports, it is necessary to define the term emotion, and to indicate what we intend to include in our discussion of its manifestations and effects. Emotions result from the perception of some "happening." Feelings and sensations follow this perception as physiological processes occur. It is difficult to determine which precedes the other. Succeeding events may accentuate or inhibit both the physiological behavior and the emotional state which is observed and felt. Emotion is described also as a state of physiological and psychological imbalance. In this state the human organism seeks to return to equilibrium or homeostasis. The nervous system, the endocrine system, the circulatory system, the digestive system, and all the others are involved in bringing about this return. Thus the emotion-stimulating occurrence or situation initiates the physiological responses, which accompany the sensation or feeling, and at the same time triggers the mechanisms which either prepare the body for subsequent action (fight or flee) or cause it to return to a state of equilibrium.

Fear, love, and rage are the three "classical" emotions. There are, however, many more. Jealousy, hate, disgust, sadness, relief, joy, elation, anxiety, despair, ecstasy, amazement, expectancy, grief, and loathing are others which have been listed by various psychologists under the heading of "emotions." Many of these are related, and emotions can be classified and categorized for better analysis. It is not

To Balance is Fun!

"Emotions give a richness and fullness to life . . . ." *By permission*, Mrs. Paula Hamada Summit, Springfield College.

our purpose, however, to discuss in detail the semantics or the many theories of emotions. It is rather our intention to present some thoughts relating to the feelings and emotional behavior of pupils, athletes, coaches and physical education teachers and indicate how these phenomena are involved in a great many of their thoughts and in their behavior.

3.4 PHYSIOLOGICAL MANIFESTATIONS

When unusual effort on the part of the human organism is required, when danger threatens, when emergencies arise, the adrenal gland is stimulated to secrete significant amounts of adrenalin and noradrenalin. This secretion reinforces the action of the sympathetic branch of the autonomic nervous system and brings about a number of physiological responses which prepare the organism for strenuous activity, be it attack or defense, flight or pursuit.

A summary of the occurrences within the organism as a result of the actions of the sympatho-adrenal system includes:

1. an increase in stroke-volume and total cardiac output (10 to 25 per cent);

2. an immediate increase in heart rate and blood pressure, which may be followed by a decrease as other mechanisms begin to operate;

3. a dilatation of the vessels of the skeletal muscles and the coronary arteries;

4. an increase in the discharge of red blood cells from the spleen and a gain in oxygen utilization;

5. a deepening of respiration and a relaxation of the bronchiolar muscle permitting increased oxygen to be supplied to the tissues;

6. improved muscle action and decreased fatigability due to increased blood supply and greater force of contraction;

7. raising of blood sugar levels by freeing the reserves in the liver;

8. diminishing of the blood coagulation time, thus lessening the danger from hemorrhage;

9. shunting of the blood from the abdominal region and the liver to the skeletal muscles and the heart;

10. dilatation of the pupils of the eyes and sometimes protrusion of eyeballs;

11. cutaneous vasoconstriction causing pallor;

12. contraction of smooth muscles in the skin causing "goose-pimples";

13. sweating in the palms of the hands, on the forehead, and under the nose;

14. inhibition of peristalsis and general gastric motility (nervousness and mild anxiety and very moderate exercise sometimes increase gastric activity);

15. onset of unpleasant gastric sensations, probably due to the inhibition of the normal descending waves and the setting up of reverse waves (heartburn and nervous dyspepsia are examples).

Recent research has indicated at least one possible explanation for the difference in responses to rage, anxiety, and fear. Man may be angry at something or someone outside himself or he may direct his anger inward. In the latter case, he exhibits symptoms of depression and anxiety, and the physiological responses are much the same as those produced by fear. It is hypothesized that the adrenal medulla may, depending on the precise stimulation from the hypothalamus, secrete either adrenalin or noradrenalin. These two substances differ markedly in their physiological effects, adrenalin producing responses similar to depression and anxiety and noradrenalin responses similar to anger directed outward.

Perhaps the significant conclusion is that the psychological factors involving emotions are intimately related to and intermingled with physiological processes and that it is impossible to understand emotional phenomena without some knowledge of the mechanisms operating to bring about the related behavior.

3.5 MIXED EMOTIONS

Very few feelings consist of a "pure" emotion. In fact, there may be no such thing in the life of man. Fear combined with sorrow might be described as despair, while acceptance and fear could be submission. Anger together with joy are probably pride, while acceptance and joy might constitute love. Fear and anticipation can be described as anxiety, while anger and fear may be guilt. In this way, emotions such as jealousy, hate, remorse, disappointment, delight, indignation, hope-fulness, adoration, and many others might be analyzed. But the complexity of emotions goes further than merely indicating possible mixtures. There are degrees of intensity of each emotion involved, and the number of "formulas" for the many mixtures of pure emotions which make up the feelings of human beings is therefore infinite. Physical education activities are by their very nature replete with emotionally charged situations. For the optimum development of students and participants some understanding of these emotions is not only desirable but necessary.

3.6 EMOTIONS, A SOURCE OF POWER

We have all heard of men and women performing nearly impossible feats under the influence of great emotions. A newspaper contained the story of a mother who lifted a car to release the body of her son pinned underneath. A magazine article reported the great difficulty with which several strong attendants subdued a frail but emotional patient. There was the Air Force officer who, while in flight, almost fell out of the bomb bay and pulled himself and his parachute up and in with one arm. During war men have run great distances and carried comrades to safety, feats which would have been impossible for them under normal circumstances. Reservoirs of power do exist and can be released under conditions of emotional excitement and in emergency situations.

Great speakers are convincing when they speak with conviction. Leaders are inspirational when their followers sense a strong feeling of mission. Action often is initiated by a person with a deep emotional involvement. Statesmen, generals, musicians, coaches, and industrial tycoons have become great because they felt intensely about their cause. Up to a given point intense excitation does influence people to move more quickly, act with greater force, maintain a strenuous pace for a longer time, and perform with a determination and zest not normally manifested. In sports, teams have risen to great heights, runners have broken world records, wrestlers have conquered stronger opponents, crews have overcome "favorites," and athletes have exceeded their own expectations when something occurred which caused all their skill, their speed, and their endurance to be called forth.

3.7 HAZARDS INHERENT IN EMOTIONAL INVOLVEMENT

There are also dangers that arise from too much or the wrong kind of emotional involvement. Emotions such as fear, hate, and anxiety can be detrimental to mental health, especially if they persist over a long period of time. Prolonged feelings of guilt, which some psychologists have called a mixture of pleasure and fear, can lead to conflict and undesirable consequences, such as withdrawal or regression. Many an athlete has regretted his actions and words brought on by uncontrolled anger. Too much emotional excitement can reduce the effectiveness of the mental processes and decrease the concentration on the immediate task. Prolonged anxiety or anger is usually manifested in increased muscular tension and inferior performance. Maintaining a high level of emotional involvement for any length of time is exhausting and eventually leads to a "flat" performance.

Guilt-prone athletes may blame themselves for defeats to the point where they withdraw completely. Athletes who lack adequate motor ability but who see membership on the varsity team as the only satisfactory goal may become so frustrated as to develop a fixation or apathy. Conflicting goals such as advancement in business on the one hand and participation in a lengthy physical fitness program on the other, each making heavy claim on available time, can result in nervous disorders and and eventually psychotic symptoms. The choice between spending hours practicing football and having that time free to be with a girl friend may pose a serious conflict for some.

Bruce Ogilvie and Thomas Tutko, in their recent book, *Problem Athletes and How to Handle Them*, have presented an interesting summary of certain emotional problems faced by those who have difficulty adjusting to participation in sports. Such matters as the following are discussed in this book: the "athlete who resists coaching", "the con man", the "hyperanxious athlete", the "injury-prone athlete", the "withdrawn athlete" and the "depression-prone athlete". Case studies are presented and methods of dealing with the various problems are suggested. The need for some knowledge on the part of coaches and physical education teachers as well as for qualified counselors is emphasized. The deeper relationships between the emotional phenomena with which athletes are involved are indicated[19].

Arnold Beisser has written an interesting volume entitled *The Madness in Sports.* He emphasizes the need for an awareness of the psychological significance of sports in the life of Americans and the importance of such psychological factors in each person's early life. In high school, college, and medical school most of Beisser's spare time was spent participating in sports. After completing his medical program and the day after reporting for duty as a Naval Reserve officer he was stricken with polio and for a while could not move at all. He writes in the preface:

As soon as I was able, I began to prepare myself for return to medical practice, now in the field of psychiatry. My study of the behavioral sciences led to a natural synthesis with my interest in sports and I became interested in understanding their psychological and sociological function and meaning. With my active participation in sports blocked and and transformed into thought, I began to try to understand my own sports interest and experiences, and that of athletes I knew and heard about, now within the framework of my growing knowledge of existing facts and theories in the behavioral sciences.

I became increasingly aware of how an athlete competes well or poorly under pressure, of how a coach or a crowd may influence his performance, and the symbolic meanings of each. I realized that the psychological condition of the athlete is of equal importance to his physical readiness in determining his performance. Based on psychodynamic theory I became aware of the influences of parents and siblings during the athlete's developmental years on his choice of sports, his style and his ability. I began to understand how losing could be more important than winning to some athletes and how others constructed elaborate rituals when winning to ward off magically retaliation from dim, nearly forgotten figures.

During my years of active competition I had very little interest as a spectator in the performances of others and was bored by sports statistics. Now I became a fan. As a passive observer I enjoyed a vicarious excitement in competition. The psychology of the fan, as one who could gain pleasure from identification with the players without the actual dangers of competition, became clear to me.

The most profoundly revealing insights, however, came after I became a practicing psychiatrist, when I had opportunities to study athletes who became psychiatric patients. The intimate relationship of psychotherapy was the major method of investigation. A segment of my psychiatric practice became specialized as former athletes whom I had known or who knew of me sought help. They felt that their problems could best be understood by someone knowledgeable in sports, but I was surprised that they sought an athlete whose career had come to a sudden and final conclusion due to illness. I learned that the action-oriented athlete tends to equate emotional disorder with physical disability. Moreover, their emotional difficulties began with such factors as graduation from college, retirement due to age, or new responsibilities, which precluded continuation of their customary roles in sports.

Participation in sports served as an integrating personality force and when deprived of this their psychiatric symptoms appeared. In the course of psychotherapy the psychological meanings of their sports activities became clear. For some the athletic field was a place where they could act out certain desires that were unacceptable elsewhere. For others sports were a way of relating to people in what was otherwise a forbidding world. Sports were a way of pleasing or identifying with parents for some, whereas for others they were a way of rebelling, in a socially acceptable way against parents or the culture in which they lived.[1]

In his *Sports and Mental Health*, Robert Moore, who is also a practicing psychiatrist, discusses the psychological values of sports, their utility in therapy, and the harm that may accrue from their use and abuse. He reviews the classical theories of play and indicates its importance in the development and life of the child; he traces the biological development of the human organism and the formation of the "ego protective mechanisms"; and he mentions the "maladaptive attempts to maintain equilibrium" which lead to mental illness. The "evolution of play and sports" are traced, "sports as a social institution of control" is discussed, and a chapter is devoted to "sports as a therapeutic technique". His final chapter, entitled "Misuse and abuse of sports," emphasizes his concern about the overemphasis on winning, the overorganized competitive sports at a young age which serve the parents more than the children, and the risk of injury on the part of certain persons with "deep psychological experiences." He concludes with the following remark:

However, no one should be misled to think that the misuses and abuses of sports outweigh the tremendous advantages of sports and recreation participation as discussed in earlier chapters.[16]

It is evident that the mental-health hazards in athletics may be as significant as the risks of physical injury. Those holding leadership roles and having responsibility for teaching and coaching athletes obviously cannot all be psychiatrists. They should, however, be conversant with the possibilities of emotional damage to participants as well as with recommended preventive measures.

3.8 FRUSTRATION AND AGGRESSION

Frustration, as used here, is any interference with a goal-response or the solution of a personal problem. Frustration exists in various degrees. It may be an abnormal condition or fixation which results from the persistent blocking of efforts to satisfy needs or from the inability to resolve problems. More commonly it refers to a state of feeling characterized by bafflement, discouragement, and persistent annoyance.

Anger and aggression are typical responses to frustration and their intensity tend to be proportionate to the severity of the frustration. The stronger the goal response and the greater the degree of interference, the more powerful will be the urge to aggression and the more serious the need for its expression.

Minor frustrations are not necessarily harmful. These may be in the form of challenges which can be inspirational and developmental if they are of the right kind and of appropriate magnitude. On the other hand, if individuals are challenged before they are ready or if they are asked to do the impossible, frustration and a sense of failure which will impede progress and hinder accomplishment will result.

L.L. Robbins has pointed out that complete gratification of needs is impossible and that gradual and continual frustration is a phenomenon of life itself. Appropriate hurdles, challenging but not impossible objectives, and problems which can be solved through real effort, are an important part of the development of the total organism[23].

Frustrations may arise from experiences in physical education and need the attention of the instructor. They may result from lack of achievement in sports, and the responses to frustration may be in the form of unacceptable social behavior or regressive individual action; they may be caused by repressive and authoritarian discipline at home or in school. In the latter case, individuals may find an outlet for aggressive tendencies in games such as football, soccer, handball, and the like. Aggressive action, frowned upon in other circles, may actually lead to success in athletics. Such success may lead to improved behavior and achievements in other areas. Many a boy who has had disciplinary problems in adolescence has been helped by the opportunities afforded him for the expression of aggression in sports.

In the inner city, where conditions are such that young people and adults feel thwarted and frustrated because of their inability to achieve normal goals, where their standards of living are below those in most other areas, and where their work is boring and lacking in challenge, sports can afford a partial answer. Hostilities which arise because of poverty, language difficulties, and repressed sexual desires need means of expression which are developmental and goal-oriented rather than antisocial and self-defeating. Sound recreational and athletic programs under good leadership may bring about a healthier mental attitude and a less hostile frame of mind.

Hostility and aggressive behavior are not always directed at the cause of the frustration. There may be reasons why it is unwise to attack the responsible individual or group. The angry person may not know who is the real cause and merely seek out the most available object upon which to vent his aggression. The author recalls a coaching experience where a tall but rather awkward player who had striven mightily to make the basketball team sat on the bench until near the end of his senior year when he was finally sent into the game early in the final period. After one or two miscues, and in a scramble for a loose ball, he tripped over the feet of an opponent and fell flat on his face, much to the amusement of the home crowd. He scrambled up and violently attacked the nearest opponent with his fist. This was quite contrary to his principles of sportsmanship and was not typical of his previous behavior. In a subsequent interview it was revealed that he had desperately wanted to make the team for many years but had been thwarted by his own awkwardness. Furthermore, he had been humiliated and had been the object of derision because of it. He was not certain that his opponent intentionally tripped him, but this opponent was the nearest target at the time of the young man's final humiliation and therefore made the object of his retaliatory attack. Here is an illustration of a person whose frustration changed to anger after having been thwarted in the achievement of his goal, and who reverted to aggressive behavior, acted to relieve his tension, and selected the most available target for aggressive response. This is also an example of behavior which was not goal-oriented and which resulted from the cumulative effect of years of frustration.

A coach may be so critical and demanding or he may lose enough games so that he is continually frustrated. If he emphasizes mistakes and shortcomings and expects too much of his players, they may become defensive and hostile. This may in turn cause the coach to respond in like manner, and then tension will mount to a degree that will be detrimental to all concerned. In most cases, unless a coach has superlative players, emphasis on excellence and continual improvement will be more effective than expecting and demanding the impossible.

John Dollard and his collaborators have expounded the "catharsis" theory of aggression. Essentially the theory says that when an individual attacks or blames the cause of his frustration (person or object), the impulse toward aggression is reduced. Similar reduction may be achieved if he "displaces" his agression on some other person or object (including himself). Such aggressive action will serve to drain off some of the urge for aggression. Participating in a soccer game, fighting with one's brother, or climbing a mountain might have such an effect. In the words of Dollard,

The expression of any form of aggression which is not dangerous to the society should have a cathartic effect and reduce the strength of the instigation to other more socially dangerous forms of aggression. It would be advantageous to any society, therefore, to permit the expression of certain forms of aggression.[3]

It is apparent that good judgment must used in the matter of setting goals and presenting challenges. Problems and frustrating situations which are of appropriate magnitude can be overcome and in the process stimulate growth and development. Problems which are too difficult or tasks assigned which are impossible lead to a feeling of overwhelming failure. This feeling may be followed in turn by apathy, withdrawal, introversion, dependency on antisocial behavior and aggression. Appropriate challenges, on the other hand, can lead to greater effort and more intense desire, and determination to achieve the goal, even if by a different route.

3.9 ANGER: ITS UTILITY AND HAZARDS

Anger is one of the classic emotions. The difficulty of defining it has caused many psychologists to substitute other terms for it such as aggression, hostility, hatred, and rage. These are all related as are the emotions of wrath, resentment, indignation, ire, and fury. In athletic circles, however, the term anger is perhaps understood better than most others and it is used here to identify the emotion which is aroused by a sense of injury or wrong, by unjust treatment, unfair play, or unprovoked attack. It is characterized by preparation of the organism for attack rather than flight. Anger is a reaction to an annoyance, and there can be various degrees of arousal.

Most normal and healthy people have a desire to be individuals in their own right and resent interference with their prerogatives. They have generally learned to play the game by certain rules and resent encroachment on their rights even more if these rules are violated. Interference by persons not in authority generally provokes more anger than by parents, teachers, and coaches. "Strict but fair" authority figures generally arouse less resentment than those who are lenient and partial.

Fatigue, hunger, illness, and anxiety increase the tendency toward anger, and teachers and coaches should take into consideration aggressive responses which come after an exhausting day, an impossible assignment, or after prolonged physical and mental effort. Anger is also often the response to inconsistent demands, real or imagined unfairness, the shattering of built-up hopes, or injury to a person's pride.

Coaches should be especially understanding with regard to this emotion. Frustrations which result on the part of athletes who fail to make the team, training rules imposed which interfere with the players' private life, humiliations which develop when one player exposes the weaknesses of another, personal fouls of the body-contact type, and long, hard, tiring practices and trips present situations where tempers are apt to flare and where aggressions need to be vented.

Anger is often displaced. Coaches and players have been known to make someone else the "whipping boy" when their own performance is challenged. Throwing the bat when a ball player is called out on the third strike, slamming a basketball down on the floor when a foul is called, sharply criticizing a younger brother after having been punished by parents, or kicking a dog when an annoying accident happens, are all instances of displaced aggression resulting from anger. Coaches have been known to kick the bench when a foul was called on their team in a critical situation, to become violently profane after losing a key game, and to blame the officials when the team played poorly. These are

Fears of others	Male	Female	Total
Being alone	2%	11%	13%
Separation from loved ones	4	4	8
Parental disapproval	4	4	8
New experience and change	2	22	4

EMOTIONS

Fears related to ability of self			
General (failure and insecurity)	46	29	75
School	30	20	50
Death	18	11	29
Finance and job	22	7	29
Marriage and parenthood	11	9	20
Wrong decisions	7	11	18
Future and philosophy	13	5	18
Fears related to material environment			
Heights and falling	13	9	22
Sickness	12	7	19
Pain (accidents, childbirth, etc.)	1	18	19
Darkness	0	14	14
War	7	5	12
Snakes	4	7	11
Deep water	3	7	10
Spiders, moths, and rodents	1	7	8
Lightning and electricity	0	5	5
Fire	1	2	3
Closed places	1	2	3

Perhaps the greatest lesson to be learned from this particular study is the realization that our fellow students are people just like ourselves—people with emotions like ours—people with worries like our own and with problems as bad as or worse than ours. If we can recognize in other individuals our own failings and good points, we will be able to achieve a balanced outlook on the world.[29]

Some highly respected and experienced coaches include fear as a factor which can contribute to preparations for a high-level performance; the functioning of the physiological mechanisms connected with fear prepares the organism for struggle. The fear of failure and humiliation can help in producing the right amount of anxiety. On the other hand, one athlete who was asked to comment on the emotion of fear indicated that one should never be afraid of opponents, the result of the game, or the possibility of injury. A baseball coach felt that fear of making a mistake was detrimental to performance and caused fielders to be too cautious in their efforts. It is obvious that there are many kinds of fear, and they may be detrimental or helpful.

In a little book, entitled *Psychology for the Fighting Man,* which was prepared for the soldiers in World War II, we find the following two paragraphs on fear which give additional insight that may have application to physical education and athletics.

The experienced soldier who has been through all this the first time and many other times has found out for certain that every man going into battle is scared. His hands tremble, his throat is dry, he must swallow constantly because his "heart is in his mouth." He does idiotic things like looking at his watch every few seconds or examining his rifle a hundred times to be sure it is loaded. The soldier green to battle may think he is the only one so disturbed, but it is true of the veteran as well. And it is true of the enemy.

The bad moments do not come during actual combat, however, but in the time of tense waiting just before. As soon as the frightened man is able to go into action—to do something effective against the enemy, especially if it involves violent physical action—his fright is apt to be dispelled or forgotten because he is too busy fighting to remember it.[18]

While there may be differences in innate tendencies to be apprehensive and afraid, most fears are specific and are grounded in some experience. A veteran coach and former Marine once remarked "There is no such thing as a 'yellow' person. I have seen individuals who were considered fearful in football but who performed rare feats of courage in combat." Fears tend to be specific.

Leaders in sports as in other enterprises where risk is involved should know how to deal with fear. The following suggestions, gleaned from many sources, may be helpful:

1. Try to discover and treat the cause of the fear.

2. Approach the fearful situation gradually (fear of water, fear of falling).

3. Prepare participants for the situation (a definite plan, specific tactics).

4. Examine and analyze the reasons for the fear. Help the players recognize why they are apprehensive (previous injuries, unfamiliarity with the problem).

5. Encourage group interaction and "camaraderie" (talk together, sing together, etc.).

6. Suggest that experienced veterans help "rookies."

7. Improve their strength and skills.

8. Do something—action dispels fear.

9. Most fears disappear at the start of contest.

3.11 ANXIETY, STRESS, AND TENSION

Anxiety is a complex emotional state characterized by a general fear or foreboding usually accompanied by tension. It is related to apprehension and fear (often unexplained) and is frequently associated with failure, either real or anticipated. It often has to do with interpersonal relations and social situations. Feelings of rejection and insecurity are usually a part of anxiety.

Stress is a state in which the natural homeostasis (equilibrium) of the body is disrupted. Stress is caused by any threat to the organism. Disease, trauma, heat, cold, thirst, fatigue can all be causes of stress. Emotional arousal can also bring about stress.

Tension reflects a state of readiness characterized by a partial continuous contraction of certain muscles of the body, a feeling of nervousness and bodily unrest, and preparation for action upon reception of a stimulus. Tension may be produced by pressures on the organism, by emotional stress, and by the assignment of a difficult task.

Anxiety, stress, tension, and emotional excitement are all descriptive of the state of the human organism as it prepares or is prepared for action. As they increase in quantity and intensity the physiological mechanisms described under the discussion of emotions begin to operate and the organism is prepared to flee, to retreat, to fight, or to attack. We may best describe it as a state of emotional excitement. In athletic parlance it might be termed "keying up" or "getting set." More recently the term "psyching up" has come into use. Mental and physical preparation for a game or contest might involve all of these, anxiety, stress, tension, and emotional excitement. These factors are of course, an integral part of the "motivation for peak performance" and they will be discussed in greater detail in Chapter 4.

3.12 EMOTIONAL AROUSAL AND MOTOR LEARNING

It is generally conceded that too much anxiety and tension, too much emotional stimulation tend to interfere with the early stages of motor learning. Whether it be in the learning of fundamentals in a game such as soccer or the learning of an element of the routine on the horizontal bar, the beginner cannot perform as well or learn as readily when the pressures are too great, when stress, anxiety, and tension levels are too high. As skill and confidence improve, anxiety and stress tolerances increase. Additional experience also tends to reduce the amount of stress. The high-level varsity performer in the advanced stages of motor learning can therefore, within limits, continue to learn, in most tense and stressful situations. Joseph Oxendine relates emotional excitement to motor learning and performance in these words:

Generally, the evidence relating to the role of motivation in motor learning and performance suggests that:

1. An above average level of excitement or motivation aids learning and performance in most motor tasks.
2. A high level of excitement is advantageous for performance in gross motor activities involving speed, strength and endurance, and for the learning of simple motor tasks.
3. A high level of excitement interferes with performances involving fine muscle movements, coordination, steadiness, and concentration, and with the learning of complex motor tasks.[20]

Duffy explains these facts in more detail and bases her hypothesis on the examination of cues for learning. She states that the learning of complex tasks may be handicapped by a high degree of anxiety, while the learning of simple tasks may be facilitated. In a complex task where there must be a high degree of selectivity of cues eliciting the response, emotional excitement hinders the process. However, in a simple task, irrelevant cues are often excluded under high emotional stimulation and learning may be expedited[4]. Easterbrook also indicated that where proficiency requires the use of a wide range of cues, a high anxiety level will tend to reduce the quality of the performance[5].

3.13 LOVE AND AFFECTION

We are referring here to the wholehearted acceptance of individuals as persons and recognition of their right to be their own individual selves. The concepts of love and affection include loyalty to members of the group, to the team, and to the teacher and coach. It is a "two-way proposition" where both parties involved can contribute and can accept. The human need for attention and love is a dominant one but very complex. It includes the need for security and for esteem on the part of both peers and authority figures. Self-confidence and self-acceptance usually engender feelings of affection.

Pupils and athletes who know they have the affection of their parents, teachers, and coaches are generally more relaxed and more daring than those who are insecure. They will risk more, explore more freely, and their actions will be more spontaneous. They are not as sensitive to criticism and generally manifest less aggression. Occasionally lack of love at home will cause extreme obedience, especially at an early age. It is important for coaches and teachers to realize that they must demonstrate their concern for the welfare of every member of the

The Victory Embrace

Fellowship and friendship, camaraderie, shared victories, affection ... *By permission*, Page Cotton and Jeff Muncell, Springfield College.

class or team. Each must feel that he is being helped to achieve, each must feel that he is being recognized and accepted as a person. There must be a real feeling of "all for one and one for all."

3.14 INSPIRATION AND ACHIEVEMENT

To attain "peak performances" in sports, to be inspired, many dimensions of the human organism must be stimulated. Many emotions and numerous different motivations have a role. In his book, *The Heart of a Champion*, Bob Richards wrote:

Secondly, if you're going to be great in sports you've got to have something else. You've got to have inspiration. You think I'm talking in the abstract? What is inspiration? How I wish I could tell you. How I wish I knew what inspiration is. If I did, I would be the greatest psychologist the world has ever known, because even those people who rely upon inspiration most can't tell you what it is. The poets, the artists, the musicians—they don't know what it is. But we can all see it. I've been amazed to see mediocre athletes, fellows drifting along with great potential but never really realizing their full abilities, suddenly inspired by a great coach, or by some great ideal or a sweetheart—something would lift them up and they would do the impossible. In a matter of a few months they would become sensational and people would wonder what had happened.

I can't describe it or define it, but I'd like to give you one facet of what I think it means when a person is inspired. *It's when they see themselves not as they are but as they can become.* It's when they see themselves, not in terms of their weaknesses and shortcomings, their failures and inadequacies, but in terms of what they can be, when they begin to believe they can be what their vision tells them—that's when they're inspired. When they no longer see their weaknesses, but their greatnesses, by emphasizing their strengths they go on to do things they never dreamed of.[22]

The right kind and the appropriate amount of emotional arousal can truly help a man to reach peaks of achievement which would not have been possible without it. Teachers and coaches should study individuals and try to inspire them. Emotions are not the whole answer, but they do have an important role.

Not all students are successful in their efforts in physical activities or in sports. Disappointment is the inevitable lot of some of those who engage in competitive activity, for whenever one person or group wins, another must lose. Measuring success and failure by the number of wins and losses can be harmful to the least able and skillful. Too many frustrations and too many failures can be debilitating and disorganizing. The true measure of success for an individual must therefore be his achievement in terms of his potential and the degree of self-fulfillment achieved through participation. To aim high and to strive mightily is commendable. To maintain a level of aspiration which is challenging but realistic is necessary for self-realization. Inspiration tempered with reason is necessary for a satisfying and productive life.

REFERENCES

1. Beisser, Arnold R., *The Madness in Sports.* New York: Appleton-Century-Crofts, 1967, pp. ix-x

2. Catell, Raymond B., "Some psychological correlates of physical fitness and physique," *Exercise and Fitness,* Athletic Institute, 1960

3. Dollard, John, Neal Miller, Leonard Doob, *et al., Frustration and Aggression.* New Haven, Conn.: Yale University Press, 1939, p. 183

4. Duffy, Elizabeth, *Activation and Behavior.* New York: Wiley, 1962

5. Easterbrook, J. A., "The effect of emotion on cue utilization and the organization of behavior," *Psychological Review,* Vol. 66, No. 3, 1959, pp. 183-201

6. Hilgard, Ernest R., *Introduction to Psychology.* New York: Harcourt, Brace and World, 1962

7. Jackson, C. O., "An experimental study of the effect of fear on muscular coordination," *Research Quarterly,* Vol. 4, No. 71, 1933

8. Johnson, Warren R., "Emotional upset—a coaching hazard," *Journal of Health, Physical Education and Recreation,* Vol. 25, No. 10, 1954

9. Johnson, Warren R., "The problems of aggression and guilt in sports," *Psicologia Dello Sport, Proceedings of First International Congress of Sport Psychology,* Ferrucio Antonelli, editor, Rome, 1965, pp. 187-189

10. Jokl, Ernst, *The Medical Aspect of Boxing.* Pretoria: Van Schaik, 1941

11. Laban, Rudolf, *Modern Educational Dance.* London: MacDonald and Evans, 1963

12. Lord, John C., "Anxiety and motor performance," *Canadian Association for Health, Physical Education, and Recreation Journal,* Vol. 35, No. 4, 1969, pp. 6-8

13. Maier, Norman R. F., *Frustration.* New York: McGraw-Hill, 1949

14. Martin, Lawrence A., "The effects of competition upon the agressive responses of basketball players and wrestlers," unpublished Doctoral Dissertation, Springfield College, June 1969

15. McGill, V. J., *Emotions and Reason.* Springfield, Ill.: Charles C. Thomas, 1954

16. Moore, Robert A., *Sports and Mental Health.* Springfield, Ill.: Charles C. Thomas, 1966, p. 108

17. Morehouse, Laurence E., and Augustus T. Miller, *Physiology of Exercise.* St. Louis: C. V. Mosby, 1959

18. National Research Council, *Psychology of the Fighting Man, The Infantry Journal,* Washington, 1943, p. 297

19. Ogilvie, Bruce C., and Thomas A. Tutko, *Problem Athletes and How to Handle Them.* London: Pelham Books, 1966

20. Oxendine, Joseph B., *Psychology of Motor Learning.* New York: Appleton - Century - Croft, 1968, p. 189

21. Plutchik, Robert, *The Emotions: Facts, Theories, and a New Model.* New York: Random House, 1962, p. 3

22. Richards, Bob, *The Heart of a Champion.* Westwood, N.J.: Fleming H. Revell, 1959, pp. 19-20

23. Robbins, L. L., "Emotional reactions to frustration and failure," *Stress Situations,* Samuel Liebman, editor. Philadelphia: J. B. Lippincott, 1954

24. Ruch, Theodore C., "Neurophysiology of emotion," *Physiology and Biophysics,* Rush and Patton, editors. Philadelphia: W. B. Saunders, 1965

25. Skinner, B. F., and W. K. Estes, "Some quantitative properties of anxiety," *Journal of Experimental Psychology,* Vol. 29, 1941, pp. 390-400

26. Skubic, Elvira, "Emotional responses of boys in little league and middle league competitive basketball," *Research Quarterly,* Vol. 26, 1955, p. 342

27. Stennett, Richard G., "The relationship of performance level to level of arousal," *Journal of Experimental Psychology,* Vol. 54, 1957, pp. 54-61

28. Turner C. Donnell, *General Endocrinology.* Philadelphia: W. B. Saunders, 1955

29. Tussing, Lyle, *Psychology for Better Living.* New York: Wiley, 1959, pp. 231, 240-241

30. Ulrich, Celeste, and Roger K. Burke, "Effect of motivational stress upon physical performance," *Research Quarterly,* Vol. 28, 1957, pp. 403-412

31. United States Department of Health, Education, and Welfare, *Hypertension, National Institutes of Health, No. 1714.* Washington: U. S. Government Printing Office

4 MOTIVATION AND AROUSAL

*There is a space between man's imagination
and man's attainment that can only be
traversed by his longing.*

Kahlil Gibran

4.1 THE NATURE OF MOTIVATION

Motivation is the key to accomplishment, whether it be in sport, in teaching, in medicine, in business, or in some other important and challenging endeavor. As used here, motivation has to do with the various factors which incite and control behavior. Motives arouse, sustain, and direct the actions of individuals. Often included in discussions of motivation are analyses of how behavior is initially stimulated, how it is energized and sustained, how it is controlled, and how it is stopped.

Volumes have been written on the various theories of motivation. It is not the purpose of the writer to elaborate on these at this time. Rather, an attempt will be made to summarize the basic concepts of motivation, regardless of specific theories, and apply them to participation in, and the teaching of, physical education and athletics in our society today.

Behavior is caused and directed by intricate combinations of motives and emotions, some of them internal and others external, some physiological in nature and others psychological, some genetic and others environmental, some conscious and others unconscious, some individual and others social. Terms such as drives, needs, urges, incentives, original tendencies, and instincts have been used to describe factors which motivate behavior. Anxiety, tension, stress, and the various emotional states discussed in the preceding chapter each has its own specific influence on the actions of man. Whatever the final result in terms of decisions and behavior may be, it is obvious that the motivational phenomena involved are exceedingly complex. Intricate patterns of internal and external stimuli impinge on the central nervous systems of countless individuals, each of whom responds in his own distinct and different way to even identical motivating factors.

4.2 DRIVES, NEEDS, AND SELFHOOD

Regardless of the exact semantics and classification, some mention must be made, before making specific application to physical education and sports, of the general kinds of motives which impel people to act and give direction to what they do.

The satisfying of hunger and thirst, the avoidance of pain, the seeking of pleasure, and the gratification of the various kinds of sexual impulses are the age-old hedonistic drives which are still operating today. The needs for security, affection, belonging, approval, acceptance, and achievement appear again and again as important motives. The urge to run and play when young, to excel when competing, to struggle when hindered, to prove something when challenged, to escape when confined, to be aggressive when angered, and to flee when frightened are typical of man as he matures and develops and moves through life's many dangerous and competitive situations.

Social incentives have a great deal of influence on man's behavior. To be liked and respected by one's peers, to be an accepted member of a team or group, to know that one looks well in the eyes of one's playmates and associates, to be invited to parties and social functions, to be an elected officer of a class or club, to be a captain of a squad or team, to be admitted into the "inner circle," these, and many other social needs are important determinants of behavior.

Motives pertaining to selfhood are perhaps the most important of all, but they are also the most subtle, intangible, and the hardest to measure. Regardless of what defense mechanism is used to conceal them, there are intense desires to think well of oneself, to succeed in life, and to discover a cause to which one can give himself completely. Self-respect, self-fulfillment, and self-realization are not only significant goals to most individuals, but they furnish powerful motivating forces to action. There continue to be large numbers of people of all ages who are idealistic, religious, altruistic, and self-actualizing. Many of the greatest achievements of men have come about through this kind of motivation. It is the lack of such motivation that makes for the feeling of emptiness and frustration which is at the root of many of the social problems of our times.

Citius, altius, fortius. Swifter, higher, stronger. These inspiring words continue to represent goals for which Olympic athletes strive. In a larger sense, they represent the aspirations of the whole human race, for within every person there exists at one time or another the desire to reach upward, to surpass, to become stronger, better, and more courageous.

4.3 MOTIVATION FOR PHYSICAL ACTIVITY

Why do children play? Why do some young people like physical education while others do not? Why do people engage in sports? Why do some students elect weight-lifting and others volleyball? What can teachers do to motivate their pupils in physical education? These and many other questions need to be .considered as we seek to make physical education and recreation more enjoyable, more interesting, more educational, and more worthwhile.

Das Spiel

The writer has been studying intently Liselott Diem's book, *Das Spiel*[15]. It is fascinating to review the one hundred and seventy pictures of children and adults at play and to search for the meanings which might be inferred from their expressions, their postures, and their movements.

Dark-skinned boys are pictured running for the sheer joy of it; a group of small girls from the Orient are racing with all their might; a young boy with a beautiful look of triumph and exhilaration has just

"For within every person there exists at one time or another the desire to reach upward, to surpass, to become stronger, better, and more courageous." *By permission*, Arthur Sandison, Washington State University.

The Culminating Effort

leaped from a cliff to land no one knows where; and elementary school girls are shown jumping in unison over a long rope being swung around and around by their companions. Children and adolescents are shown scaling old concrete walls, climbing on a tepee-like structure of branches and trees, circling on primitive "merry-go-rounds" made of logs, swinging and jumping on chain-like swings, gliding on roller skates between the cars, and romping aimlessly in the surf as the tide moves in and out.

There are pictures of soccer games with the cheering crowds and the fantastic contortions of the players; of young and aspiring football players charging and tackling, some with helmets and some without; of monks in their black gowns playing handball with white-suited opponents; of mature ebony-faced ladies with long dresses and improvised hockey sticks competing with fervor and intensity; of cricket players in full regalia trying to swat the ball; of beautiful white-clad young ladies chasing the badminton shuttlecock; and of masters of stave and staff, foil and sabre, advancing and retreating, defending and attacking.

There are the "rooster fight" between pairs of competitive young men, sailors and canoeists trying to conquer the rapids and the wind as they strive with all their strength and skill, and men on skis fighting to keep their balance as they zigzag through the powdery snow. There are pictures of pool and marbles and bowling and dice being played; of fishing and hopscotch and hammering and sewing; of printing and clamming and seining and building castles in the sand; of mud-pie baking and pasting and carving and derby racing; of men participating in music and drama and art and reading.

But more than activity, more than movement, is portrayed in Das Spiel. People, boys and girls, young and old, are doing other things, more intangible but in some ways more meaningful. They are laughing and exclaiming, cheering and exhorting, explaining and directing. Some are competing, some are imitating, and some are singing. There are those who look worried and anxious and those who look relaxed and happy. Many are concentrating and in deadly earnest; others are reckless and in a "devil-may-care" mood. Some are undoubtedly giving vent to aggressions, others are expressing their desire to achieve. There are budding artists, embryonic musicians, prospective athletes, all seeing themselves some time in the distant future, all with eyes on a distant star. They are exploring, experimenting, imagining, and daring. They are winning and losing, failing and suceeding. They are playing but, in truth, also doing much more.

Why do people play?

People play because it's fun. This is the most common answer received from participants, from leaders, from parents and from educators. Play resists, as Huizinga says, biological analysis and logical interpretation[23]. Those who have observed the frolicking of puppies and kittens, the scrambling of monkeys in a cage, the bounding and cavorting of calves let out to pasture, recognize the expression of sheer exuberance in many of their movements. Parents who have observed their children closely over a period of many years know that the most common answer to "Why do you like to play marbles, kick-the-can, hide-and-seek or tag?" is, "Because it's fun." And in a sense that should be enough. For the joy that is expressed spontaneously as any living thing moves gracefully, explosively, skillfully, and exuberantly is answer enough. When running, leaping, dodging, and throwing are combined with the shouting and laughter of children at play, no explanation is needed.

Yet, play is more than fun and joy. In play the child and the man find ways of exercising their powers, of discovering new abilities, of expressing their emotions. It is in play and through play that people first encounter and deal with problems of social life. A sense of camaraderie and fellowship is generally first experienced while engrossed in games. Interactions with teammates and opponents, with leaders and followers, with boys and girls take place in the realm of play.

There are many deeper and more complicated theories of play. Each has made its contribution to the understanding of the play phenomenon. Each has its appropriate application in specific instances. Some apply to therapy, some do not. Some express the values and objectives as seen by parents and teachers; other are proposed by psychiatrists and philosophers. All should be studied by those who wish to fully understand the psychology of physical education, recreation, and sport.

Energy accumulates in the healthy organism and, when not needed for survival, finds expression in spontaneous, joyous, and vigorous action. Such activity, however, is usually more than aimless running and moving. For, in play children plan, imitate, fight, flee, and chase. They express aggression, affection, and fear. They practice behavior which they have seen in the life of the adults.

Much confusion concerning theories of play would be eliminated if a careful distinction were maintained between the child's objectives of play and the purposes as seen by adults. Scholars seeking, in

retrospect, to explain behavior, physical education teachers trying to effectively motivate, parents trying to understand their offspring, and psychiatrists working in therapeutics are looking at play from a vantage point different from that of the children. To the adults the surplus-energy theory, the catharsis theory, the relaxation theory, the self-expression theory, the genetic theory, and the psychoanalytic theory are meaningful. To the child they are not. To the adult, observing the play of children, the play seems utilitarian, developmental, and adaptive. To the child, it is the satisfaction of his need to be active, the opportunity to have fun and express himself, the chance to explore, to try new experiences, and to be with his playmates.

4.4 INTERVIEWS WITH ATHLETES, COACHES, AND LEADERS IN PHYSICAL EDUCATION

In addition to reviewing the most recent literature on the topic of motivation in physical activity and sports, the author gathered and analyzed information as in other ways:

1. He interviewed approximately one hundred athletes, coaches, physical education teachers, and YMCA physical directors to discuss with them motivational phenomena.

2. He assigned each of twenty students, who were members of a Psychology of Physical Education class taught by the writer, to interview four athletes on the topic, "What Does Sport Mean to Me?"

3. He asked each of the twenty students to interview a coach regarding:

   (a) the best game ever played by his team and the motivating factors;

   (b) the worst game ever played by his team and the motivating factors.

Beauty and Rhythm

"The joy that is expressed spontaneously as any living thing moves gracefully, skillfully, and exuberantly." *By permission,* Judy Markell, Springfield College.

4. He sent a questionnaire to approximately fifty selected coaches throughout the United States asking the two questions above [3 (a) and (b)] and also asking for comments on "motivating for peak performance."

In 1, 3, and 4, the "critical-incident" technique was employed in both the questioning and the analyses. The results of the interviews and the responses to the questionnaires are included in the discussions of motivational phenomena which follow. The material is organized under three main headings as follows:

1. motivation for physical activity;

2. motivation for health and fitness;

3. motivation for peak performance.

Motivation for Physical Activity

How can a physical education teacher motivate his pupils, not only to participate in physical education, but to do so willingly, whole-heartedly, and enthusiastically? For a partial answer to this question let us review some of the replies received during the interviews conducted by the author. Interviewees were experienced physical education teachers and directors.

Joe Rossomando, a college teacher of squash and handball who had been exceptionally successful in obtaining wholehearted participation and enthusiastic response, emphasized the necessity of *personal involvement*. The instructor, he said, must give himself fully and unreservedly to his teaching and to his students. A complete dedication on the part of the teacher, close personal contact, a spirit of warmth between student and teacher, and a love for one's job and the students he is teaching, were points of emphasis in the interview. One sensed that in his classes each individual student had a feeling of identity and of individual worth. Each student sensed the enthusiasm, the dedication, and the interest of the teacher. There actually developed a kind of bond between the two as if they were partners in a common endeavor[58].

The need for *security* was cited as an important motivating factor by an experienced teacher and director of physical education. As a person achieves and contributes to the group, he begins to feel secure. If he is unable to make much contribution elsewhere, he may do so as games are played and stunts are tried. His contribution, however, is not necessarily just in terms of physical prowess but may be manifested in helpfulness, good sportsmanship, and team work. As his own feeling of worth is enhanced he becomes a more integrated and happier person.

Setting appropriate goals was described by one instructor as the key to highly motivated classes. This is, of course, closely related to the concept of *level of aspiration*. Goals should be high enough to be challenging and developmental but not so difficult as to be frustrating. As each rung on the ladder to self-realization is mounted, growth and satisfaction accrue.

The *sense of achieving* was emphasized by several interviewees. Everyone is interested in knowing what he is accomplishing and how he is progressing toward specific goals. Physical education teachers should therefore use various means to keep their students informed. Daily records, posture tests, anthropometric measurements, achievement tests, and knowledge tests were mentioned as important. Mirrors in activity rooms, charts showing skill progress, films of student performances and immediate replay on closed-circuit television were emphasized as meaningful motivating devices. *Knowledge of results* in every form was felt to be important.

Closely related is the matter of *success and failure.* "Success begets success and failure begets failure" was a principle often enunciated in one way or another. While there was some difference of opinion as to the exact proportion of criticism and praise thought to be the most effective, it was generally agreed that the approach should be positive and optimistic and that criticism should be constructive and generously sprinkled with encouragement.

A number of those interviewed spoke, in one way or another, of *self-image* and *self-concept.* As young men and women see themselves developing, gaining in strength and endurance, becoming more manly looking or beautiful, achieving or advancing in their understanding of themselves and others, they become enthusiastic about the activities or the persons they believe to be responsible. As their self-image improves and as they relate this to what they are doing, they become highly motivated.

To illustrate the concepts of achievement, success, and self-image, Erwin Blesh related the story of two students, both of whom were enrolled in physical education at his university. One was highly skilled and possessed wonderful physical endowments. The other was crippled and needed to be taken to the natatorium in a wheel chair and helped in and out of the pool. The former set as his goal the becoming of an all-American football player, while the latter set as his objective swimming across the pool. By dint of hard work, careful attention to instructions, and perseverance both achieved what they had set out to do. "Now I ask you," said Blesh, "which of these had the greater sense of accomplishment?"[46] His point was obvious and significant. Too often instructors feel that it is most important to give attention to and assist those who are blessed with great abilities and skills.

Peer approval was unanimously regarded as an important objective at all ages beginning in the upper elementary grades. To do what one's friends are doing, to be thought highly of by classmates, to achieve in activities in which the others also take part—this is one of the great joys of boys and girls as they move through childhood, adolescence, and young adulthood. Even college students are very concerned about doing things of which their friends approve.

Self-discovery and self-realization were discussed as outcomes rather than motives, and yet it was agreed that older students and those who were aware of what was occurring were intent upon "achieving their potential." This, too, is an individual matter, but it is a significant dimension of physical education, and students as well as teachers should be aware of the role of physical activity in the realization of this goal.

Reference was also made, in the discussions of motives and outcomes, to longevity, to health, to social interaction, to physiological benefits, to understanding and knowledge of today's world, and to the elimination of aggressions and tensions. These are also significant and are factors analyzed further in other sections of this book.

Fun and enjoyment were also stressed by several of the interviewees. Enjoyment is undoubtedly the reason that many elect to take physical education where it is not required and elect one activity rather than another. This appears to be a more valid and acceptable motive at some institutions than at others, and the degree to which this motive is operative may to some extent reflect the philosophy of the college and the culture of the community. Perhaps also it is because many activities in the physical education courses are so enjoyable that one physical education director stressed the point that physical education consisted of "natural" activities and therefore needed no special motivation.

Motivation for health and fitness

Fitness "is the capacity of the individual to live and function effectively, purposefully, and zestfully, here and now; and to meet confidently the problems and crises which are among life's expectations." Thus did the President's Council on Youth Fitness define it in 1959.

The fit person is free from those diseases, deformities, and handicaps which can be cured or corrected. This is sometimes termed "medical fitness." Beyond this he possesses adequate strength and endurance, agility and skill to live a productive and happy life. He is, in terms of his own capacities and attributes, zestful, vital, and energetic. He is reasonably serene, stable, and mature, and knows how to relax. He is integrated and rational and has the motivation to act as well as think. He is moving toward self-fulfillment and self-realization and has found a cause, something greater than himself.

It is recognized that the above description of the fit person is an ideal and that no human being achieves that state of perfection. It is, however, a goal toward which those who aspire to be "totally fit" may well strive.

While "total fitness" is the ultimate goal, it is now generally agreed that those who conduct "fitness programs" have as their special responsibility the development of cardiovascular efficiency and endurance, the increase in strength, coordination, agility, and skill, and the establishment of habits and activity patterns which will serve the individuals throughout life. Of these factors cardiovascular efficiency is considered the most important. Many of those working in fitness programs accept as its best measure the ability of the organism to deliver oxygen to the tissues. An increase in this kind of fitness is accomplished by exercise which places on the organism demands the satisfaction of which strengthens the cardiac muscle, increases the stroke volume and the number and size of the blood vessels, improves the oxygen-carrying capacity of the blood, develops greater strength and elasticity in the walls of the arteries and veins, and improves the efficiency of bodily movement.

Motives, incentives, and motivational techniques

To secure first-hand information regarding motivational procedures and devices employed in good fitness programs, the writer interviewed a number of successful YMCA physical education directors. Much of what they said can be related to the answers of the physical educators in schools and colleges, but there are also a number of differences. It should be kept in mind that those working with fitness programs in social agencies are dealing with noncaptive audiences and that, for the most part, they are working with adults of all ages. While there are, in the YMCA programs and those in similar agencies, many activities which aid in the development of health and fitness, "fitness programs" per se now consist mostly of calisthenics, jogging, bicycling (stationary or outdoors), walking, rhythmic and isometric exercises. These activities are often supplemented by aquatics, weight training, vigorous sports, hiking, mountain climbing, and membership in health clubs.

All of the YMCA physical directors indicated that there are two phases in a fitness program during which the individual needs special attention and extra motivation. These are:

1. the period in which he becomes aware of the need but has not yet started;

2. the period after he has been in the program for a short while, is feeling the "fatigue effects," but has not been participating long enough to sense the beneficial effects or to experience the "lift" that comes from being in good condition.

It was the general experience that, while it was often difficult to persuade people to register for the program even though they felt it would benefit them, it was often more difficult to keep them coming when they began to feel stiff, sore, tired, and bored, and when they had not yet reached the point where workouts were exhilarating and where the increase in zest, vitality, and endurance was noticeable.

The motives that bring people to the YMCA for physical activity are many and varied. Their effectiveness depends on the individual's age, his condition, and the particular circumstances surrounding his life at the time he first makes contact. Young people in their teens generally come for the following reasons:

1. They are bored and looking for something to do.

2. They want the opportunity to swim, take part in gymnastics, or participate in some specific activity offered by the "Y."

3. Their friends are going and have persuaded them to join.

4. They want to "build themselves up."

5. They can't make the team in high school or college, but they still want to play basketball, volleyball, handball, etc.

6. They are looking for fun and enjoyment and they like, or think they would like, the activities of the "Y."

7. Their parents feel that what the YMCA has to offer will be good for them and are encouraging them to join.

The motives listed and emphasized by the YMCA physical directors as those which cause people to enroll in the fitness programs may be summarized as follows:

1. The individuals are obese and want to reduce. They are concerned about their obesity both for health reasons and for the sake of appearance.

2. They have become frightened by symptoms which they believe indicate the imminence of a heart attack. Sometimes this is their

own diagnosis; sometimes they infer this from a medical examination; sometimes they are told to go by a physician.

3. They are concerned about their lack of energy and fatigability. This is accompanied by a desire to be more vigorous and productive.

4. They wish to retain or regain an attractive figure and a youthful appearance. This a more common motive for women than for men. Exercise for mothers after childbirth is generally prescribed by a physician but often taken at the "Y."

5. They are despondent, depressed, and generally unhappy. They are persuaded this is related to their poor physical condition, lack of exercise and recreation.

6. They have tried home fitness programs but are unable to sustain and maintain a level of exercise which produces fitness. They believe that joining a class at the "Y" will enable them to achieve this fitness.

7. They are seeking a chance to "unwind." Some feel the need to express pent-up tensions and aggressions. Surgeons and business executives report feeling less fatigue after workouts.

8. A few, mainly those who join health clubs, feel a real need for relaxation. Usually they are older people who carry heavy responsibilities and who feel benefited by steam or sauna treatments and massage.

9. Some men, especially those whose college days are not too far behind them, feel the need to express their competitive urge and to achieve the other satisfactions that come from vigorous and hard-fought contests.

10. Many are eager to make the most of their lives and believe that physical soundness and vigor are basic to achieving their potentials.

After individuals become a part of the fitness programs their motives for continuing with the programs usually change somewhat. The following observations were reported by those working with such programs:

1. The greatest stimulus is the warm, empathetic, personal, and helpful attitude on the part of the leader. Directors and instructors therefore must try to individualize their teaching and accept the role of personal counselor on physical fitness to these individuals.

2. Continual evaluation of progress and knowledge of results are among the most effective motivators. A good testing program, through which the individual can see portrayed graphically and in black and white his personal condition, is the key.

3. A sense of accomplishment and the overcoming of challenging hurdles will keep many participants enthusiastic. Seeing their weight reduced, witnessing their waist measurements decrease, and observing their time for a mile improve are examples.

4. A feeling of fellowship and of acceptance by the group is a strong motivating factor. When a person no longer feels odd or different, when he can relax with his own handicap, when he can share problems and goals with others, he is likely to continue.

5. A feeling of well-being, sensing that the body is functioning smoothly and efficiently, and perceiving the increased zest and enthusiasm become lasting motives.

6. The discovery that they are more productive, tire less easily, and that leisure is more enjoyable will keep people interested and involved.

7. Finally, when habits of beneficial exercise and healthful relaxation become a "way of life," the satisfactions and benefits are evident and become a constant motivation and guiding influence.

Douglas Boyea said, "Self-motivation in the YMCA, where you have a noncaptive audience, is a must"[47].

Motivation for peak performance

In Mexico City in 1968, Debbie Meyer performed almost impossible feats in the pool; Al Oerter proved that age can be overcome if one has the confidence and will; Bob Beamon exploded to an unbelievable distance in the long jump; and Kip Keino showed his heels to the field in running long distances. In 1968, the New York Jets, in an upset victory, demonstrated to the world that the Colts could be beaten; Bill Russell led the aging Celtics to another world championship; Yale convincingly upset Stanford in a dual swimming meet; and Denise Long not only scored sixty-four points in one game but led the Union-Whitten girls' basketball team to an unexpected victory and the Iowa state high school basketball championship. While these events were taking place, thousands of other athletes, young and old, boys and girls, were striving to win games, to defeat their opponents, and to become champions.

In such competition, athletes often ignore and endure pain, work long hours to perfect their skills, submit themselves to the guidance and direction of the coach, and tax their bodies and their spirits to the utmost. It is such endeavor on the part of many that leads to peak performances, to individual and collective accomplishments which were hitherto thought to be impossible; it is this kind of effort which makes the champion. Fred Russell describes it in these words:

So the time comes when an athlete gains that confidence, that emotional maturity, of being at his best when the going is roughest, when he experiences that tremendous satisfaction of keeping his presence of mind in the deepest difficulty, that genuine joy of being able to function in the disaster—and finish in style. That's the true champion.[35]

What motivates a man to do these things? What drives him through long and tedious practice, what makes him willing to punish himself, what causes him to be so eager to excel, what stimulates him to all-out effort? For answers to these and similar questions let us turn to the thoughts of great coaches and athletes at all levels of competition.

Personal pride in peak performance

No other psychological concept related to peak performance was as universally mentioned by athletes asked to analyze their motives as that of *pride in performance*. Tom Woodishiek, the great fullback for the Philadelphia Eagles, was asked to state the two most important motivating factors in professional football. Without any hesitation he mentioned as the first one "the pride the individual has in himself as a professional to go out and do his job in his field endeavor"[65]. Pete Retzlaff in a separate interview was analyzing motives and concluded: "I had to look for another source of motivation and that was basically pride in performance".[57] Professional athletes, college coaches, and athletes in both high schools and colleges mentioned this as an important motivating force. Closely related to this pride is the desire to be the best in one's particular sport and level of competition. Recognition, prestige, approval, and similar factors certainly have their place, but the deep, abiding motive is the desire to excel, to do one's job and do it well.

Self-image

Perceiving oneself as a successful person, feeling that one has the qualities of a great athlete, picturing oneself as a determined individual who refuses to be pushed around, and wanting others to think of him as

a great champion combine to form a powerful motivating force in athletics.

Self-image may be defined in two ways: (1) the way in which an individual perceives himself and (2) the way in which he thinks others perceive him. It is evident that the latter definition involves the concept of audience influence. The author asked athletes and coaches about the effects of parents, girlfriends, friends, and fans on the performance of individuals and teams. While a number of them insisted that they were unaware of who were in the audience, others agreed that they did receive inspiration from friends, parents, and loyal supporters. Some indicated that they felt an obligation not to let them down, others indicated that the presence of these people gave added stimulus to perform well, and a few reported being inspired to try harder. Some coaches stated that they did use, on occasion, the presence of parents, fans, alumni, and other supporters in their attempts to motivate teams to better performance. One coach reported that, like other people, all great athletes have a certain amount of showmanship within them and that the knowledge that they were playing before a great many people was an important stimulus to peak performance. Geoffrey Cardinali analyzed this factor as follows:

The very nature of gymnastics makes the concept of self-image important. It is almost entirely comprised of individual exhibitions on the various pieces of apparatus and their performances are evaluated by judges. They must be concerned about how they appear to others.[48]

The use of film and closed-circuit television for motivation is related to the notion of self-image. A person sees himself as he performs, as he misses or executes blocks, as he meets his responsibilities or fails to do so, and as he moves smoothly and efficiently or with extraneous movements and wasted effort. An individual who is concerned about his image and sees himself as others see him finds in such motion pictures very real motivation for improvement.

The Effort of a Champion

"The deep, abiding motive is the desire to excel, to do one's job, and do it well."
By permission, John Van Reenen, Washington State University.

"Self-image" is, of course, also an important concept as far as team motivation is concerned. When a team has over a number of years developed a "proud heritage" or a "winning complex," the consciousness of this image serves as a powerful motivating factor. Leaders and coaches over the years have tried to develop and have utilized such a tradition in preparing a team for contests.

Humiliation, revenge and atonement

Somewhat related to the concept of self-image is the idea of *humiliation and revenge.* When an individual is badly beaten and when he is made to "look bad" his self-image receives a severe setback and he remembers it for a long time. This feeling is augmented by unkind remarks by fans and unfavorable publicity in the news media. When humiliation generates anger, the end result is likely to be a desire for revenge. There is, however, a difference of opinion regarding revenge as a motivating factor. Some interviewees stated that revenge was a realistic, legitimate, and effective motive, while many felt that the idea of revenge has no place in the realm of sports. It appears to the author that this difference of opinion is partly a matter of semantics. By whatever name it is called, there seems to be general agreement that a humiliating defeat is not easily forgotten and that it will generate in those who are beaten an intense determination and a desire to atone for the poor performance in a return engagement. Generally speaking, the coaches and athletes interviewed did not look favorably upon revenge as a motive for peak performance. They did recognize, however, that a team that had been beaten and humiliated in a game could be easily aroused to maximum effort in a return engagement. Individuals who take great personal pride in the excellence of their performance feel the "sting" of a poor game deeply and for a long time.

Level of aspiration

"Hitch your wagon to a star" is an admonition which has been handed down from parent to child for generations. This tells us that to achieve greatness our goals must be high. It implies that the level of our accomplishments will be related to the greatness of our objectives. There is much truth to these statements, but there is also a dilemma connected with them: in sports, achievement is related to size, age, and innate ability, as well as to "desire."

The concept of "level of aspiration," while not simple, can be, and has been, one of the important and desirable considerations in developmental motivation. If we apply it realistically and intelligently,

Living Statuary

Aspiration: The level of our accomplishments will be related to the greatness of our objectives. *By permission*, Springfield College Gymnastic Team.

we can bring about growth in all dimensions of life and a high degree of self-fulfillment. If applied thoughtlessly and irrationally, we can easily cause frustration and apathy. John Fox said:

In all young men there is a built-in ambition to achieve—to mount that next rung on the ladder. One isn't content until he achieves the next step. If he doesn't achieve it, he loses confidence and sometimes quits.[49]

Most scholars who have studied this concept agree that repeated success tends to cause individuals and teams to raise the level of their aspirations and that repeated failures tend to bring about an inordinate lowering of goals. Most great athletes have an aspiration for high achievement and set challenging goals for themselves. Inferior athletes tend to be satisfied with mediocre achievements. Achievement must not, however, be measured in terms of absolute scores if we are to aim at maximum development of all the individuals involved. What is a challenging task for a fifteen-year-old boy of mediocre ability may be easily accomplished by another of the same age but with much greater experience or innate talent.

To motivate athletes most effectively, the level of aspiration should be related to the past achievement level and the potential of each person. Fred Holloway, who has coached soccer successfully for thirty-one years, sums it up this way[54]:

1. Every athlete needs a goal or goals.
2. The goals must be worthy.
3. The goals should be achievable.
4. The goals shall be high goals which require dedication and effort.
5. The achievement of the goals should result in a better self.
6. Reaching the goals should bring one as close as possible to the achievement of his potentialities.

It is evident that the "level of aspiration" is an important factor in motivation. If it is too low, it can serve as an escape or lead to self-satisfaction or lack of effort. If the aspirations are unrealistically high, frustration may develop with all its attendant problems. A rational application of the "level of aspiration" concept, therefore, would consist in aiming at a step-by-step development of the individual through striving toward higher and higher goals, beginning with reasonably unambitious ones.

Challenge, frustration, and self-discovery

"Challenge" was perhaps the idea most frequently mentioned in answers to questions regarding motivation. The challenge to guard a high scorer in soccer or basketball, to win a state high school basketball championship, to achieve victory as an "under-dog," to better one's previous mark when running or swimming, to vault higher than ever before, to defeat a favored opponent in wrestling or boxing, to better one's score in gymnastics or diving, to make an Olympic or All-American team—these and many other challenges are attested over and over again to be significant motivating factors in developing peak performances. Great athletes are invariably competitive individuals, eager to "pick up the gauntlet." To challenge a team or an individual athlete is, therefore, an effective means of eliciting an intense response and prodigious effort.

If, however, individuals are challenged before they are ready, if they are asked to do the impossible, then frustration and a sense of failure may result. Too many failures and too much frustration may not only slow down progress but hinder accomplishment. The persistent blocking of efforts to satisfy strong desires and needs, the psychological conflicts which come from "drives" toward incompatible goals, and repeated disappointments which result from being motivated to do the impossible may give rise to an overwhelming frustration, which in turn can lead to aggression, regression, fixation, dependency, apathy, or other disruptive behavior.

On the other hand, it is natural for the human organism to respond with varying degrees of aggressiveness to frustrating experiences and to seek an outlet for the accompanying tensions. Unless the frustrations are reduced through some form of expressive behavior, their effects will continue to accumulate and lead eventually to a more violent reaction. Depending on the strength of the drive, the degree of interference with that drive, and the individual's frustration tolerance, the experience of frustration may stimulate positive action in the form of problem-solving and purposeful behavior, or it may lead to other adjustive and defensive behavior.

Both the athlete and the coach are subject to many experiences of conflict and frustration. The athlete will usually benefit greatly from participation in sports, which will afford him many opportunities to express his natural aggression and to relieve tensions in a way that is positive and socially approved. On the other hand, a substitute who has a tremendous desire to play but who spends most of his time on the bench often finds too few opportunities for an activity outlet and thus may tend to want to prove himself by unwholesome aggressive action.

The coach is involved in many frustrating situations. Conflicts between his moral code and his need to win can pose problems with respect to recruiting practices, player subsidy and the achievement of educational goals. His deep emotional involvement in a game and his inability to release tension through participation in it may give rise to serious emotional problems. The frustration of a competitive coach with a high achievement need and a team with inadequate ability may eventually lead to fixation and apathy.

One of the responses to frustration is compensation. An individual who is too small for football may be an intensely aggressive and eager wrestler; a trackman who is too slow to run the dashes may be willing to push himself to an extreme degree in a distance race; a poor student may be a very ambitious athlete; lack of social acceptance may drive an athlete to seek status through achievement in sports; and being a member of a minority group may be one reason for the tremendous "desire" exhibited in competition. In such instances it is actually the response to frustration which produces such intense and continuous motivation.

Confidence and self-discovery

A few years ago the author observed the operation of the Outward Bound program for Peace Corps trainees in Puerto Rico. As these prospective volunteers climbed mountains, rappelled down the side of a high dam, participated in survival swimming, and were dropped off for isolation hikes, the words of Charles Froelicher came to mind. He tied together the concepts of challenge, *self-confidence*, and *self-discovery* in these inspiring words:

Without self-discovery, a person may still have self-confidence, but it is a self-confidence built on ignorance and it melts in the face of heavy burdens. Self-discovery is the end product of *a great challenge mastered*, when the mind commands the body to do the seemingly impossible, when strength and courage are summoned to extraordinary limits for the sake of something outside the self—a principle, an onerous task, another human life. This kind of self-discovery is the effective antidote for the indifference and insensitivity we have bred into modern youth.[19]

Coaches and athletes interviewed were asked to discuss the concepts of overconfidence, underconfidence, and "just-right-con-fidence." Roy Simmons summarized the thoughts of many of the coaches when he said, "I want my teams to have confidence that they can win, but I never want them to underestimate the ability of the opposition. Many of our poorer performances have occurred when a team has gone into the game believing it was won before the first whistle blew"[62].

There were some athletes who believed that no one could be overconfident. The absolute necessity of believing firmly that one could achieve the goal, be it winning or bettering a previous record, was emphasized again and again. A distinction between overconfidence and underestimating your opponent was made by some. All agreed that lack of respect for the opponent could be fatal.

There was also some confusion as to the merits and dangers of underconfidence. The physiological mechanisms which result from fear and which prepare the organism for combat were pointed out as absolutely necessary for peak performance. Again, however, there must be a distinction between uncontrolled, paralyzing, and debilitating fear and an anxiety which is necessary and which calls forth appropriate responses from the glands, the nervous system, and the other systems of the body which are responsible for action.

False confidence was distinguished from true confidence by some. The above-quoted words of Froelicher provide a clue. Pete Retzlaff spoke in a similar vein when he said:

False confidence is based on fear. Individuals who are fearful and actually lack confidence exude false confidence. They are trying to convince themselves to try something hazardous. They are often quite vocal and noisy about it. People with genuine confidence are usually rather quiet and subdued about what they can do. Genuine confidence is something that has been tested and is the result of a series or sequence of events in which the individual proves himself. Once I had been exposed to enough situations on the football field against world champions, I knew then that I had the ability to play professional football. I knew also that it had to be refined. Such confidence grows and is enhanced by every situation in which you are challenged and where you "come through".[57]

It is obvious as one analyzes the statements of Retzlaff and Froelicher that something else, *self-discovery*, is occurring as one meets challenges. The individual is finding out that there are hidden resources that can be called out in times of stress and that most human beings have the potential to accomplish things and perform feats which they had not previously believed possible.

Self-discovery and self-confidence are involved in overcoming *psychological barriers.* The four-minute mile, the sixteen-foot pole vault, the twenty-seven-foot long-jump were at one time said to be impossible. Once these barriers were overcome by single individuals, similar performances by others have followed almost immediately. To see a peer accomplish some feat of skill or strength not only challenges an individual but give him confidence. It is as if competitors say to themselves, "If he can do it, I can." The impossible feat is no longer impossible.

Self-discovery through sports, however, does not involve merely the discovery of one's ability to perform athletic feats. The satisfaction that comes from achieving something for which one has paid a great price, the knowledge that you can face up to an opponent as a man, the understanding that, when you are both mentally and physically prepared, you can do great things, the recognition of what it feels like to help a teammate succeed—these and many other features are discovered about the self. Bill Miller, a member of the Northeastern University crew, described it this way:

In crew you're fighting yourself, more than anything. You keep pushing yourself, you really get to know yourself, exactly when you break, how far you can go, what you can do—and you sit back and you really feel good—you feel you've accomplished something, you know.[56]

A coach should be sensitive and discerning as he assists the player progress step by step towards peak performance. He helps the athlete discover the latter's capabilities and weaknesses, his goals and ambitions, and through these endeavors discover some of the truths that go into the building of a philosophy of life.

A sense of responsibility and love of the game

Both athletes and coaches interviewed felt a deep sense of responsibility about their performance in their respective roles. Responsibility to the team, to themselves, to their parents, to the fans, respectively to the coaches or athletes, and especially responsibility to the game were mentioned spontaneously and sincerely by a large number of interviewees. One example is the following statement of Bob Rust, line-backer and wrestler for Syracuse University:

When I am out there wrestling and feeling as if I am losing I say to myself that people out there are expecting me to win. This has completely changed my attitude and I more or less "go berserk." I hate letting people down—and the worst thing is the week after the match after you have lost and knowing deep within yourself that you could have won. Because it takes sometimes a week, in a major contest like that, before you can forget it—actually you never forget it. So letting yourself down is one part of it—but there is also the matter of letting someone else down. And personally I find you can actually think about this on the mat.[60]

An interview with Bob Wanzer and Arne Johnson, both former basketball greats with the Rochester Royals, elicited from Wanzer this comment:

I believe that every athlete—and especially the professional athlete—has a tremendous amount of pride, and they go out there to do their best—and there is the love for the sport—and as long as a fellow is giving forth his best effort and he loves the game and he "gets the butterflies" beforehand, you know that he's going to be a good competitor.[64]

Practice is Fun: Coach Arlett and the Northeastern University Crew

The sensitive and discerning coach helps the athlete discover his capabilities and weaknesses, his goals and his ambitions, and through these, some of the truths that go into the building of a philosophy of life. *By permission*, John P. Grinold, Northeastern University.

Arne Johnson said:

Basketball meant a great deal to me. I wouldn't want to change the life I've had in sports. You make many fine friends and meet many wonderful people. Coming from a small town, it was a great education for me. I just wouldn't change a thing if I could do it all over again.[55]

There were other testimonials as to how the sense of responsibility and love of the game had motivated great athletes. The writer came away from many of the interviews with a feeling that sport was actually a form of self-realization for them. It was also obvious that a sense of dedication and commitment to the game and to the performance was, for those who had it, a stabilizing and continually motivating force.

The desire to win

The "winning mind," the "desire to prove that they are the best," the "unwillingness to lose," "an overpowering desire to excel" were only a few of the expressions used by coaches to describe the champion. Robert Giegengach, the coach of the 1964 United States Olympic Track Team, in describing the champion said:

The great champion over the years is the man who wants to win and must win all the time. There is nothing ungentlemanly about this. Some of the mildest people who walk the face of the earth are some of the most vicious when it comes to competition. A complete dissatisfaction with being in a subsidiary position—this must be the motivation of the great champion competitively. Others are satisfied with making the team, being the second man, with being on the squad, with having improved their condition and similar objectives. The great champion feels a tremendous need to be first.[51]

One must be careful to avoid oversimplifying the above statements. In the first place, one must realize that there are many who, regardless of their desire and motivation, simply do not have the physical endowments to become champions, and care must be used so as not to make them feel an overwhelming sense of failure when they don't become champions. Secondly, the desire to win is the resultant of an intricate pattern of motivating factors, some genetic, some environmental. The need for achievement may be compensatory, the personal pride in excellent performance may result from the need for esteem, aggressiveness may be increased by frustrating experiences, and so on.

What we are saying is that regardless of its origin, the "winning mind" is an important component of a great champion.

Dedication and Commitment

"A sense of dedication and commitment is, for those who have it, a stabilizing and a continually motivating force." *By permission,* "Brad" Kron, Springfield College.

4.5 MOMENTUM

All coaches and athletes agree that *momentum* is a very real phenomenon in competitive sport. Basketball teams take time-outs to stop the other team's momentum, and football coaches substitute defensive players for the same reason. Track coaches put strength in early races to establish their teams' own momentum, "underdog" teams try for extra emotional arousal to get a good start, and athletes live over and over again the experience of their team "catching fire."

The writer asked the British-born and very successful Northeastern University Crew Coach, Ernie Arlett, whether this concept of "momentum" applied also in rowing. Here is his revealing reply:

Absolutely. That is one of the beauties of sport—when suddenly something comes alive and the crew brings out the best in themselves—it's a great thing. It does happen and that's what we're always striving for. In crew this can sometimes be accomplished by the little fellow that sits on the stern of the boat and steers, the coxswain. He may say, "you're moving up," and providing it's true it spurs the crew to greater efforts—they come alive—they come afire—and it's beautiful to watch! This I think is part of what a coach is striving for. There is nothing finer than when a crew looks like they are losing—and then suddenly comes alive and goes ahead and wins. This is one of the beauties of sport.[44]

Once again we must remind ourselves that the real motivation may be a complex mixture of many things. Momentum may be the result of suddenly acquiring needed confidence, of the enthusiasm generated by shared success, of the exhilaration that comes when a cherished goal is within reach; it is a very real psychological phenomenon with which coaches and athletes must reckon.

4.6 MENTAL PREPARATION

Mental preparation cannot be separated from physical preparation. Fatigue and discouragement, lack of coordination and frustration, lack of practice and indecision are boon companions. Conversely, good condition leads to buoyancy, skill generates confidence, and physical preparation is a big step toward mental preparation. Nevertheless, successful coaches invariably indicate that, where teams are equal, it will be the "mental set" and the psychological preparedness that will make the difference. Willard Hammer states:

My personal view is that mental preparation is far more important than tactical preparation in achieving top performance. I have found that, if the psychology is right the physiological factors tend to fall into place and a team reaches its

A Test of Human Resources

"The coxswain may say, 'you're moving up, and providing it's true, it spurs the crew to greater efforts—they come alive—they come afire—and its beautiful to watch!' " Coach Ernie Arlett, Northeastern University. *By permission, The Sunday Bulletin,* Philadelphia.

maximum through planned motivation. No great accomplishment was ever achieved without motivation and emotion.[53]

For purposes of analysis we will deal with mental preparation in three phases:

1. long-term preparation;
2. preparation for a contest;
3. immediate psychological preparation.

Long-term preparation

The writer asked Vic Fusia, varsity football coach at the University of Massachusetts, about mental preparation. This, in essence, is what he said during the month of February:

Mental preparation is a "now situation." It goes on all the year around. It is chatting with them (the players) in the dormitory, the office, the fraternity. It consists of letters to them throughout the year and communicating with them in many ways. Spirit is not built in a day, it is a slow, long, steady process. Mental preparation is trying to develop each man totally and to make him realize that there is more to it than just the score.[50]

Orv Bies, track coach at St. Olaf College, put it this way:

I do not believe in "psyching up"; nor do I expect super-performances from an athlete. Great performances come from self-confidence built over a long period of time, from loyalty, team spirit, attention to fundamentals and sound preparation.[45]

There were many replies which repeated the same general idea. To summarize, mental preparation consists of the development of each squad member into the kind of individual who can become a great athlete. Such persons will be disciplined and have themselves under control at all times. They will take personal pride in every performance. They will be loyal, consistent, confident, and determined. They will believe in themselves as men and as athletes. They will think of their sport as something to which they can give themselves without reservation. They will be willing to pay the price for excellence. Most important of all, they will concentrate on what is best for the team and not just for themselves. When a coach is fortunate enough to have athletes with that attitude he will generally find them prepared for every contest.

Preparation for a contest

Different athletes and different coaches will use different methods to prepare for specific contests. A long-distance "walker" informed the writer that he needed a week to "psych himself up" for the Olympic trials. A swimmer said he had tried using music (marches, etc). Several athletes stated that they liked to be alone and think about the coming contest. A heavyweight wrestler said that all he had to do was watch one or two preliminary contests and he would be ready. A crew member stated that he liked to "think through" the race the night before. A miler said he wanted to walk around all by himself for awhile. A hammer-thrower wanted to "just sit down and put his head in his hands and think." An oarsman told one coach just before a contest that he was working up a terrific hatred for his opponent.

When asked about their reactions to "pep talks," to coaches' efforts to key up players, and to emotional appeals by coaches, athletes responded differently. Some thought they were ineffective, some said they worked some of the time and with certain individuals. All indicated that sincerity and honesty were the best approach and that emotionalism which was "an act" could be harmful to the effort.

Many athletes feel that their problem is to keep from becoming too "keyed up." They indicate the real possibility of emotional exhaustion; they are more disposed to visit with teammates and talk about other things besides the contest. A baseball player said he played best when he could sleep for awhile before the game. Several athletes said they were best prepared when they were deeply concerned about the outcome of the game but at the same time felt very relaxed.

Coaches use many tactics in their attempt to bring about the proper "mental set" on the part of their athletes. All agree that it is a process involving several days. Yet, there will be times when contests come too close together, when special effort is needed, when players are lackadaisical, and when there appears to be need for some special mental stimulation. It is also generally agreed that team mental preparation is taking place throughout the days when defenses and strategies are being practiced, when films are being shown, and during "skull sessions."

There is, however, need for work with individuals. Direct man-to-man conversations about the game and the responsibilities of each athlete, challenges issued subtly to players who are known to react favorably, words of optimism and confidence to the nervous and anxious athlete, newspaper clippings on the bulletin board, expressions of confidence and belief in the players are all effective. Nothing can do so much, however, as the attitude of the coaching staff. A hard-working, enthusiastic staff intent on the job of preparing for the contest, demonstrating by action and by word how they feel, cannot help but impress the athletes and, if the right spirit exists, be emulated by them. A word of caution is in order, however, because all great coaches have recognized the need for the light touch at the right time, the sense of humor that keeps the atmosphere from getting too heavy, and for the "break" that keeps the task from becoming too monotonous and onerous.

Two coaches felt that trying to instill the right degree of *fear* was important. Ralph Ginn, veteran South Dakota State University football coach, indicated that he felt that an important factor in the great performances of teams was fear—fear of getting beaten, fear of being humiliated, fear of letting one's teammates down, fear of failure, and in some instances fear of the coach[52]. Coach Charles Silvia of Springfield College explained this phenomenon in the following words:

All topflight athletes are fearful to begin with. The fear of failure is ever present in the swimmer. The fear that he cannot repeat a performance is dogging him all the time, as is the fear that he is letting someone down, his teammates, his parents, his coaches and so on.

The swimmer must be helped to understand that through fear the sympathetic division of the autonomic nervous system is stimulated. This is one of man's oldest systems and has an important role in preparing him for action. When he recognizes that because he is afraid he will be more efficient but that at the same time he must not let fear overwhelm him, he will be achieving the right degree of confidence and will be ready for a peak performance.[61]

Assuming that continual, year-round preparation is taking place, the crucial purpose in preparing for a contest must be to achieve the right degree of emotional arousal, the correct level of anxiety, the appropriate level of confidence, and the realization and acceptance of victory as a worthy and significant objective. There is no single answer, there is no way which is always right. Coaches must study players until they know as much as possible about them, they must plan far into the future, know psychology, physiology, and their sports. There are many who believe that the most effective mental preparation is simply to develop a philosophy which emphasizes the importance, in all endeavors and contests, of doing the very best that one can, and let the results take care of themselves.

Immediate psychological preparation

As one observes divers standing motionless on the board, gymnasts ready to jump for their rings, pole-vaulters leaning on their poles before take-off, basketball players preparing to shoot free throws, and pitchers just before they start their throw, he cannot but wonder what is occurring psychologically. This question was asked of both performers and coaches. Here is the reply of Jon Rose, champion pole-vaulter, at Springfield College:

Yes, I do this myself. I've never seen a pole-vaulter who doesn't. It's just a period where you stop and think through all the things you've spent hours practicing. I understand you are only in the air a period of one and one-half seconds and there's just not enough time to think about anything up there, and it's a period of mental preparation before actually getting up on the pole. You think through every movement and try to visualize it in your mind as being perfect. When you feel that you are ready, when you feel that you are keyed up enough, you just go down the runway.[59]

In answer to the same question, Bernard Wrightson, the Gold Medalist in diving at Mexico City, responded:

I am trying to shut out all extraneous stimuli. It's a period of mental concentration. Once the dive begins I rely completely on muscle memory. My best dives have been when I'm completely unconscious. The different combinations in a particular dive are all turned into one trained response. My job is to get the right position on the end of the board and initiate the dive. It then becomes a learned response reacting to momentum and to light and to angle.[66]

Jeff Cardinali, an Olympic gymnast in 1960, made the following statement:

There is a lot of "psyching up" in gymnastics—you are working both for the team and for yourself as an individual. A gymnast, as he prepares to perform, should think only of the exercise and nothing else. He should think only of how he is going to perform it as close to perfection as possible. Shut out everything else from your mind and then try to relax. A gymnast can be too "psyched up" and be stiff as a board.[48]

These three quotations indicate the general psychological preparation which occurs immediately before beginning an individual performance. Many others confirmed the idea that great competitors have tremendous powers of concentration, that they can shut out extraneous stimuli when they are ready to perform, and that they are in an almost unconscious or self-hypnotic state as they go through their routine. Apparently movement patterns are laid down in the central nervous system and, once called out, govern the particular performance.

4.7 PERSONAL INVOLVEMENT AND COMMUNICATION

If the coach is to be able to effectively motivate individuals or teams and if he is to influence their actions and reactions, thorough communication is absolutely essential. To obtain the trust and confidence necessary for breaking down all barriers to communication, the coach must involve himself personally in the lives and problems of the players. Charles Smith summarized one of his coaching experiences in this way:

The meet that comes to mind involved unbelievable performances where some of the swimmers dropped as much as ten to fifteen seconds in the 200 and 400 yard

events. This team was especially receptive to leadership, and the communication between the coach and the team members was unusually fine. I feel it was because we shared an honest experience, a truthful environment, and goals that brought out the very best that was in them.

We talked a great deal about "awareness," "sensitivity," "being prepared," and the whole thing became much more than the routine of swimming and diving. It became true involvement and for me one of my most rewarding experiences.[63]

4.8 SUMMARY

Motivation is a complex, important, and often incomprehensible phenomenon. The biological complexities of the human organism, the understanding of social determinants of behavior and the environmental influences of culture, parents, and climate are involved. In addition, there are the imponderables in the emotional world of sport. When we consider all these factors, we realize that motivation is a fascinating and significant aspect of our individual lives and the society of which we are a part. All who work with physical education and athletics will be better prepared for their roles if they make it a serious study.

REFERENCES

1. Andrews, Thomas G., and Lee J. Cronbach, "Transfer of Training," in W. S. Monroe (ed.), *Encyclopedia of Educational Research*, Revised Edition. New York: Macmillan, 1950, pp. 1483-1489

2. Appleton, Lloyd O., "The depth dimension of physical fitness," *Sixty-second Annual Proceedings*. Washington, D.C.: College Physical Education Association, 1958

3. Arnold, P. J., *Education, Physical Education, and Personality Development*. New York: Atherton Press, 1968

4. Atkinson, John W., *An Introduction to Motivation*. Princeton, New Jersey: Van Nostrand, 1964

Up and Over

"There's not enough time to think about anything up there." *By permission*, Jon Rose, Springfield College.

5. Berkowitz, Leonard, and Bernard I. Levy, "Pride in group performance and group-task motivation," *Journal of Abnormal and Social Psychology*, Vol. 53, 1956, pp. 300-306

6. Bindra, Dalbir, *Motivation*. New York: Ronald Press, 1959

7. Bishop of Portsmouth, "Beyond his grasp?" *Outward Bound*, David James, editor. London: Routledge and Kegan Paul, 1964, pp. 212-217

8. Bowen, Wilbur P., and Elmer D. Mitchell, *The Practice of Organized Play*. New York: A. S. Barnes, 1929

9. Brumbach, W. B., and J. A. Cross, "Attitudes toward physical education of males entering The University of Oregon," *Research Quarterly*, Vol. 36, 1965, pp. 10-16

10. Catell, Raymond B., "Some psychological correlates of physical fitness and physique," *Exercise and Fitness*, Athletic Institute, 1960, pp. 138-151

11. Cofer, C. N., and M. N. Appley, *Motivation: Theory and Research*. New York: Wiley, 1964

12. Cooper, Kenneth H., *Aerobics*. New York: Bantam Books, 1968

13. Cureton, Thomas K., Jr., "Anatomical, physiological and psychological changes induced by exercise programs (exercise, sports, games) in adults," *Exercise and Fitness*, The Athletic Institute, 1960, pp. 152-182

14. Davis, Elwood Craig, and Gene A. Logan, *Biophysical Values for Muscular Activity*. Dubuque, Iowa: William C. Brown, 1961

15. Diem, Lieselott, *Das Spiel*. Frankfurt am Main: Wilhelm Limpert-Verlog, 1960, pp. 12-145

16. Dollard, John, Neal Miller, Leonard Doob, *et al.*, *Frustration and Aggression*. New Haven, Conn.: Yale University Press, 1939

17. Fleishman, Edwin A., "A relationship between incentive motivation and ability level in psychomotor performance," *Journal of Experimental Psychology*, Vol. 56, 1958, pp. 78-81

18. Friermood, Harold T., and J. Wesley McVicar, *Basic Physical Education in the YMCA*. New York: Association Press, 1962

19. Froelicher, Charles, "Make use of us," Outward Bound, Inc., Reston, Virginia

20. Godfrey, Barbara B., and Newell C. Kephart, *Movement Patterns and Motor Education*. New York: Appleton-Century-Crofts, 1969

21. Hall, John F., *Psychology of Motivation*. New York: Lippincott, 1961

22. Hosek, Vaclav, and Miroslav Vanck, "The influence of success and failure on the resulting mental activity of sportsmen," *Psicologia Dello Sport, Proceedings of First International Congress of Sport Psychology*, Ferrucio Antonelli, editor, Rome, 1965

23. Huizinga, Johan, *Homo Ludens: A Study of the Play Element in Culture*. Boston: Beacon Press, 1950, p. 2

24. Keogh, Jack, "Extreme attitudes toward physical education," *Research Quarterly*, Vol. 34, 1962, pp. 27-33

25. Kretchmar, R. Scott, and William A. Harper, "Why does man play?" *Journal of Health, Physical Education, and Recreation*, Vol. 40, No. 3, 1969, pp. 57-58

26. Krumdick, V. F., and N. C. Lumian, "Motivating the athlete," *Scholastic Coach*, Vol. 34, 1964, pp. 50-51, 65-67

27. Kucharski, G. H., and R. F. Yeager, "Incentives for weight training," *Scholastic Coach*, Vol. 34, 1964, pp. 86-87

28. Laban, Rudolf, *Modern Educational Dance*. London: MacDonald and Evans, 1963

29. Lehman, Harvey C., and Paul A. Witty, *The Psychology of Play Activities*. New York: Barnes, 1927

30. Loader, W. R., *Sprinter*. New York: Macmillan, 1961

31. Madsen, Charles H., Jr., Wesley C. Becker, and Don R. Thomas, "Rules, praise and ignoring: elements of elementary classroom control," *Journal of Applied Behavior Analysis*, Vol. 1, No. 2, 1968, p. 139

32. Miller, Bernard T., "Soft music and hard training in high school wrestling," *Scholastic Coach*, Vol. 34, 1964, pp. 26-28, 40

33. Radler, D. H., and Newell C. Kephart, *Success Through Play*. New York: Harper and Row, 1960

34. Robbins, L. L., "Emotional reactions to frustration and failure," *Stress Situations*, Samuel Liebman, editor. Philadelphia: Lippincott, 1954

35. Russell, Fred, "What makes a champion," *Dimensions of Physical Education*, Charles A. Bucher and Myra Goldman, editors. St. Louis: C. V. Mosby, 1969, p. 70

36. Ryan, E. Dean, "Effects of differential motive-incentive conditions on physical performance," *Research Quarterly*, Vol. 32, 1961, pp. 83-87

37. Shlosberg, H., B. F. Skinner, N. E. Miller, and D. O. Webb, "Control of Behavior Through Motivation and Reward," APA Symposium, *American Psychologist*, Vol. 13, 1958, pp. 93-113

38. Slovenko, Ralph, and James A. Knight, editors, *Motivations in Play, Games and Sports*. Springfield, Ill.: Charles C. Thomas, 1967

39. Smith, Orville A., "Physiologic basis of motivation," *Physiology and Biophysics*, Theodore C. Rush and Harry D. Patton, editors. Philadelphia: W. B. Saunders, 1965

40. Ulrich, Celeste, and Roger K. Burke, "Effect of motivational stress upon physical performance," *Research Quarterly*, Vol. 28, 1957, pp. 403-412

41. Wessel, Janet A., and Harry Webb, "Body image, culture and females in sports," *Psicologia Dello Sport, Proceedings of First International Congress of Sport Psychology*, Ferrucio Antonelli, editor. Rome, 1965, pp. 692-701

42. Wilkinson, Robert E., "Effect of various motivational conditions upon boys of different age levels during muscular work," unpublished Doctoral Dissertation, Springfield College, 1965

43. Wilmore, Jock H., "Influence of motivation on physical work capacity and performance," *Journal of Applied Psychology*, Vol. 24, No. 4, 1968, pp. 459-463

Personal References

44. Arlett, G. Ernest, Crew Coach, Northeastern University, Boston, Massachusetts, personal interview, 1969

45. Bies, Orval, Track and Field Coach, St. Olaf College, Northfield, Minnesota, questionnaire response, 1969

46. Blesh, T. Erwin, Professor and Director of Physical Training, Yale University, New Haven, Connecticut, personal interview, 1969

47. Boyea, Douglas P., Director of Health and Physical Education, New Britain YMCA, personal interview, 1969

48. Cardinali, Geoffrey, Gymnastics Coach and Physical Education Instructor, United States Coast Guard Academy, personal interview, 1969

49. Fox, John W., Director of Men's Physical Education, Northeastern University, Boston, Massachusetts, personal interview, 1969

50. Fusia, Victor H., Football Coach, University of Massachusetts, Amherst, Massachusetts, personal interview, 1969

51. Giegengack, Robert, Track and Field Coach, Yale University and Coach of United States Track and Field Team, Olympic Games, Tokyo, 1964, personal interview, 1969

52. Ginn, Ralph, Football Coach, South Dakota State University, Brookings, South Dakota, questionnaire response, 1969

53. Hammer, Willard M., Professor of Physical Education and former coach, University of California at Santa Barbara, questionnaire response, 1969

54. Holloway, T. Fred, Soccer Coach, State University of New York at Cortland, personal interview, 1969

55. Johnson, Arnold, Director of Public Relations, Bausch and Lomb, Rochester, New York and former basketball player with Bemidji State Teachers College and The Rochester Royals, personal interview, 1969

56. Miller, William, Member of Crew Team, Northeastern University, personal interview, 1969

57. Retzlaff, Palmer, Former track and field performer at South Dakota State University and professional football player with the Philadelphia Eagles, personal interview, 1969

58. Rossomando, Joe, Instructor in Physical Education at Yale University and Professional Baseball Coach, personal interview, 1969

59. Rose, Jon, Outstanding pole-vaulter and a Physical Education Major at Springfield College, Springfield, Massachusetts, personal interview, 1969

60. Rust, Robert, Physical Education Major, Varsity Wrestler and outstanding linebacker, Syracuse University, Syracuse, New York, personal interview, 1969

61. Silvia, Charles E., Swimming Coach, Springfield College, Springfield, Massachusetts, personal interview, 1969

62. Simmons, Roy D., Lacrosse Coach and former Football Coach, Syracuse University, Syracuse, New York, personal interview, 1969

63. Smith, Charles J., Swimming Coach, Springfield College, Springfield, Massachusetts, personal interview, 1969

64. Wanzer, Robert, Basketball Coach, St. John Fisher College, Rochester, New York, personal interview, 1969

65. Woodishiek, Thomas, fullback with Philadelphia Eagles, personal interview, 1969

66. Wrightson, Bernard, Gold Medal Winner in Diving, United States Olympic Team, 1968, personal interview, 1969

5   THE NATURE OF LEARNING

*The process of learning, or of acquiring a skill,
if we have an eye to economy of time, is
subject to certain laws and principles . . . the
athletic field is no place for chance and we
must consider, therefore, a few of the most important principles that govern the process of
learning.*

Coleman R. Griffith[6]

5.1 WHAT IS MOTOR LEARNING?

It is fascinating to assist a young child learn to walk. After passing
through the stages of sitting, rolling, crawling, creeping, and standing,
he finally releases his hold on the playpen or chair and takes those first
few steps to the waiting hands of his father and mother, who have been
encouraging and coaxing him to come. This process of "learning to
walk" has included the building of confidence, the development of
perceptual ability, the response to motivation, the satisfaction of the
urge to explore, the approval of authority figures, and finally the
acquisition of the motor skill of walking.

The upper elementary and the junior high school years are those in
which truly dramatic changes occur. Running is intermingled with
sudden stops and changes of direction, as in basketball; with kicking
and dribbling, as in soccer; with leaps, twists, handsprings, and
cartwheels in gymnastics; and with an infinite number of other
movements in dance. Throwing is no longer simply projecting an object;
it is now the catcher's, pitcher's, infielder's, and outfielder's throw; it is
the underhand, overhead, chest, and bounce pass in basketball; it is
hurling the javelin, putting the shot, and throwing the discus. Striking
becomes the forehand, backhand, smash, volley, or serve in tennis; the
bunting, hitting, and slugging in baseball; the serve, the set-up, and the
spike in volleyball; the punt and drop-kick in soccer and football. The
intricate combinations of simple skills which make up swimming,
diving, wrestling, gymnastics, golf, surfing, rowing, and many other

sports are being learned at this time. Finally, all of the fundamental skills and movement patterns are combined with rules and strategies to make games. Motor learning takes place while all these developments are occurring.

The writer was, during the years he coached, very interested in the often astonishing improvement in the players' basketball ability during the period between the end of the freshman or sophomore year in high school and the beginning of the following season. Not only did the athletes grow in size and develop in strength, but they were found to have improved in their abilities to shoot, pass, and pivot, to have taken on a new confidence and an improved self-image, and in most instances to have learned some "new moves." There were also college athletes who were initially apprehensive, skinny, poorly coordinated freshmen and who entered their junior year two years later as confident, well-built, and smoothly moving members of the varsity team. In addition to maturation, much motor learning had occurred during the intervening periods.

At the top rung of performance we find the Olympians, the champions, and the professionals. In such individuals it is difficult to discern the improvement in performance from day to day, week to week, or even from one year to the next. The increase in skill is almost imperceptible, and the improvement in judgment can only be seen by the highly sophisticated observer or coach. Nevertheless, motor learning is occurring in them. Extraneous movements are being eliminated, perception is improving, accuracy is increasing, and motor patterns are being automated. In addition, different ways of performing the same skill are being discovered, and complex skills are being integrated into movement patterns.

In all such instances a multitude of processes take place. Neurophysiological development, sensory-perceptual modifications, attitudinal changes, muscular and cardiovascular adaptation, intellectual understanding, and a continuous reorganization of sensory input take place. We must again remind ourselves, however, that many modifications are due to maturation and growth and that learning, as we think of it, does not include changes that occur without the influence of instruction, practice, or other experience.

For purposes of this book, then, we shall define motor learning as *modifications in movement behavior resulting from experience*. It includes the acquisition of motor skills, the laying down of movement patterns, the gaining of knowledge and understanding pertaining to movement, and the development of good judgment and athletic "savvy." It is usually accompanied by an improvement in the ability to perform or an increase in knowledge and skill.

It must be recognized also that motor learning can occur unconsciously. As the learnings mentioned in the preceding paragraphs take place, organic changes are occurring, particularly in the nervous system. Nerve cells are growing and branching out, new connections are being made, various parts of the central nervous system are being modified, and messages brought in through the innumerable combinations of sensory stimuli are being interpreted and stored for later recall and use. Let us turn, then, to some basic principles of physiology as they apply to motor learning.

5.2 COORDINATION OF MOTION

Coordination of motion is under both nervous and chemical control. Metabolites and hormones are carried through the bloodstream and affect the quality and intensity of movement. The adrenal secretions are, in emotional situations, carried to the appropriate parts of the central nervous system, where they stimulate nerve centers in preparation for vigorous and sometimes violent action. Centers which coordinate and control the functions of respiration, circulation, and heat regulation, as well as those which regulate and adjust movement, are located in the brain and the spinal column. Some of these nerve centers are stimulated by the chemical substances carried in the bloodstream.

As we move from the lower to the higher levels of the central nervous system we find greater and greater integration, more complex nervous action and reaction, a larger amount of conscious thinking and reasoning, and less automatic and reflex action. Muscle tonus and the antigravity reflexes are controlled at the *spinal level*. At the *level of the medulla* are found the centers for the control of cardiovascular adjustments (heart rate, blood pressure, etc.), for the control of respiration, and for head and neck reflexes. The *cerebellum* has as its main function the adjustment of movement. It strengthens, steadies, and coordinates incoming stimuli, and adjusts and discharges efferent messages to the motor units.

The *reticular formation* or reticular activating system is receiving more and more attention from scholars working with motor learning. This system extends from the base of the medulla to the upper part of the brain stem and consists of interlacing neurons attached to, or connected with, the spinal tracts, which transmit messages from the periphery to the brain. It has as its principal function the interpretation of incoming stimuli, either reinforcing or deactivating them, or in some cases actually screening sensory impulses and determining which of them shall be referred to the cortex. This function of the reticular formation has significance for coaches in that it controls the degree of arousal and thus determines the extent to which an athlete may be able to reach his peak performance. Robert Singer adds these thoughts about the reticular formation:

Some writers have attributed great significance to this formation. In fact, it has been termed a program-selection mechanism that determines the nature of a response. As a response selector, the reticular system assigns priorities to messages, determines which are important, and selects the appropriate responses in order of importance. Nearly all incoming and outgoing impulses of the brain pass through the reticular formation.[15]

Two other bodies located in the midbrain are the *red nucleus* and the *corpus striatum.* In the former is located the seat of the body-righting reflexes, and in the latter an additional control center which can exert a suppressor effect on the muscular system and thus inhibit purposeless and disorganized movements.

The *cortex* consists of the "gray matter" found on the outer surface of the cerebrum. It is here that voluntary movements are initiated, proprioception occurs, and here, too, are located the sensory and motor areas. The cortex plays an important role in the learning of complex skills, the retention of movement patterns, and the selection of skills to be utilized for specific purposes. Activity in the cortex can also influence organic adjustments, especially under conditions of nervous excitement. Perspiration on the palms of the hands and on the forehead, increase in blood pressure, and increase of respiratory rate are examples.

5.3 KINESTHESIS, PROPRIOCEPTION, AND LABYRINTHINE RECEPTORS

Consider the blind piano player performing as only an artist can; recall the trombone player with his eyes glued on the notes; follow the expert hunter as he fires at a flying pheasant; watch the great dribbler as he maneuvers in critical situations without glancing at the ball. What guides these people's arms and joints and fingers in moving unerringly with the right speed and in the right direction?

The golfer with experience says, as he completes a beautiful drive, "That felt good." The great hitter in baseball says after he has hit a home run, "I knew it the moment I swung." Swimming coaches have been known to instruct their swimmers before a race to get into the water "and *feel* your stroke." And Ernest Sanangelo, a fine gymnast, said to the author:

I think of the routine before my event. I check up and think of what I'm going to do. Then they call me for my first event. I jump up to the apparatus and think of my first move—and that is all. The rest is taken care of by my kinesthetic sense. I go through what I have been practicing in my workouts—and that is all.[17]

Kinesthesis is the awareness or perception of the position and the movements of the body and its parts as derived from the feelings of muscles, tendons, joints, and other tissues. Sensory end organs assisting with position and space orientation can be either *proprioceptors*, which receive stimuli from within the organism, or *exteroceptors*, which receive stimuli from the external environment. Proprioception plays a role in guiding and coordinating all movements, but generally acts upon the stimuli fed into the central nervous system by the exteroceptors as well. Occasionally the term *somatic sensation* is used to describe muscle, tendon, and joint sense, including an awareness of the amount of tension, that is the stretching and contraction, of a muscle fiber.

Thus, included in the kinesthetic receptors are:

1. The *muscle spindles* which are fusiform bodies parallel to and between muscle fibers. They contain annulo-spiral nerve endings and flower-spray endings both of which furnish the central nervous system with information regarding the tension and condition of the muscle.

2. The *Golgi corpuscles* generally found in tendons and responding to tension. They consist of a bundle of tendinous fibers enclosed in a fibrous capsule and are sensitive to pressure and stretch.

3. *Pacinian corpuscles* composed of concentric laminae similar to the skins of a sectioned onion. They are located in tendons and joints and respond to firm pressure.

4. *Bare nerve endings* found between muscle fibers, in fascia and tendons, and in the joints. They mediate deep pain and respond to several types of stimuli.

The bony labyrinth of the inner ear consists of a series of cavities in the temporal bone. Within this bony labyrinth may be found the three *semicircular canals*, the *utricle*, and the *saccule*. These constitute the membranous labyrinth, which is filled with a fluid called *endo-lymph*. The space between the walls of the membranous labyrinth and the bony labyrinth contains another fluid called *perilymph*. A mound of sensory hair cells called the *crista* constitutes the receptor organ of the semicircular canals, while the *macula* is the sense organ of both the saccule and the utricle.

From the sensory receptors of the nonauditory labyrinth impulses may travel (a) to the ocular tract and stimulate reflex movements of the eye, (b) to the spinal motor neurons and thence to the skeletal muscles, and (c) to the cerebellum, where posture and balance are controlled and adjusted. The labyrinthine sense organs are responsible for compensatory movements of the eyes and limbs during position changes and they are actively involved in *"righting reflexes."* They also function in the perception of acceleration, deceleration, ascending and descending motions of the body, and vertigo. The vertical semicircular canals tend to maintain the normal orientation of the head in relation to the horizontal plane.

All of the kinesthetic, proprioceptive, and labyrinthine sensory impulses function cooperatively with the appropriate exteroceptors to maintain upright posture, provide proper orientation to the horizontal plane, assist in the maintenance of body balance, adjust and coordinate movements, and keep the organism informed as to the position of the head, trunk, and limbs.

5.4 REFLEX ACTION AND THE AUTOMATIZING OF MOTOR SKILLS

The simple reflex arc consists of a receptor organ, an afferent neuron, a connector or internuncial neuron, an efferent neuron, and an effector organ. The *stretch* or *myotatic reflex* is one in which a pull on a muscle tendon results in its reflex contraction. The "knee jerk" is a familiar example of such a reflex. A tap on the patellar tendon when the knee joint is semiflexed and the leg is hanging freely results in an involuntary contraction of the knee extensor. The physiological process is roughly as follows. The proprioceptor in the tendon is stimulated, the impulse travels via the afferent nerve to the center in the spinal column, the message to act passes along an efferent neuron to the quadriceps, the muscle twitches, and the leg jerks upward.

A reflex is a *consistent response to a specific stimulus and in which volition does not play a part.* Pulling one's hand away from a hot stove, curling the toes when tickled on the sole of the foot, the flexion of the leg when walking or running, the antigravity reflexes which keep the body extended and in the upright position, and the maintenance of muscle tone are examples of reflexes important in daily life.

Important to the study of motor learning is the fact that, while many reflexes are inborn and are not dependent upon previous learning experience, others may be acquired. Most learned reflexes are far more complex than the simple reflex arc. There may be more than one stimulus, in which case several internuncial neurons will carry messages to two or more components of the central nervous system, and a combination of impulses may be sent out through the efferent pathways, stimulating a number of effector muscles. Such reflexes may result from high-level motor learning or be a part of the acquisition of a simple skill by a novice. The question will also undoubtedly be raised as to whether the seemingly instantaneous reactions to various stimuli in sports situations should actually be considered as reflexes or as complex movement patterns which have become more or less automatic. Let us cite a few examples.

The baseball player facing a good pitcher must decide in a fraction of a second whether to swing or not. He knows that the ball should be over the plate, between the knees and the shoulders, and that the signal calls for him to hit the first good ball. The pitcher may throw a ball which is aimed directly at his shoulders and breaks sharply across the plate, he may throw it high, fast, and inside, or he may use a slow change of pace. If he is a good pitcher, he will not give away his pitch until he finishes his delivery. In the fleeting moment in which the ball travels to the plate, the batter must decide whether to dodge the ball, to swing faster or slower, to step slightly forward or backward as he moves into the ball, or to just stand there and let it go by. The batters who have faced this situation thousands of times will tell you that their reaction is automatic, that they do not have time to think, and many will say it is a reflex action. Regardless of what it is called, it is a complex motor response that had to be learned, that involves an intricate pattern of stimuli, not all of them coming at the same time; a semiautomatic decision had to be made, and a flood of messages must be sent to the effector muscles of the legs, trunk, arms, and neck.

Basketball players are faced frequently with a "three-on-two" situation. Assuming the middle man has the ball as he approaches the free-throw line, he must choose whether to drive on in for the lay-up, shoot a jump shot from where he is, pass off to the teammate on either side, or fake his pass and then drive. His decision is made on the basis of the action of the defensive men who should commit themselves before the player with the ball finally acts. Some players seem to "instinctively" do the right thing without the slightest hesitation and with a continuously smooth movement. Others hesitate, stop and think, and then often make the wrong choice. It is obvious, of course, that experience is an important factor and that beginners often do some very conscious thinking before they act, while the professionals act automatically if not by reflex.

A distinction must be made between the situations where an athlete must react to the thoughts and movements of an opponent and those in which he is merely trying to give his own best performance. A diver or a gymnast can learn simple motor skills and then gradually combine them into more and more complex movement patterns until the full routine of what he is attempting to learn is completed. What begins as a conscious intellectual as well as physical process is gradually simplified by making it an activity of the lower levels of the central nervous system and more and more reflexive in nature. Because of the complexity of the mechanisms involved and because movement patterns are thought to be stored in the cortex, it seems probable that, even though these movements become semiautomatic, the higher levels of the central nervous system are implicated. And as coach Silvia stated, "While the goal seems to be to make these high-level motor skills as unconscious as possible, we must remember that what we want to make unconscious must first be conscious"[18]. It must be remembered, also, that even though highly skilled performers can eventually reach the point where many of their motor skills are performed unconsciously and automatically, the highest centers in the central nervous system were involved in their learning.

5.5 FEEDBACK, SERVOMECHANISMS, AND KNOWLEDGE OF RESULTS

It has been found useful to compare the human organism to a computer which receives data of all kinds from the various sense organs, and then decodes, stores, and interprets them. The stored and interpreted information, together with additional incoming data, is then utilized to activate and discharge responses which influence and guide the actions of all kinds of effector organs. The incoming information, which is synthesized and interpreted in the light of stored and previously analyzed data, serves to correct and adjust the processes of both movement and thought. This process of receiving sensory input, interpreting it, and discharging impulses for the purpose of readjustment is known as *feedback*.

Feedback, can be internal or external. *External* feedback, much of which is also called *augmented* feedback, consists of sensory input which originates outside the body, while *internal* feedback refers to the information which comes through the proprioceptive and labyrinthine receptors and furnishes information regarding the movements of the body itself. The eyes, the ears, the taste buds, and the touch receptors bring in external feedback, while the Golgi corpuscles and the muscle spindles are examples of sense organs receiving internal feedback.

As previously indicated, feedback from the muscles, tendons, and joints can operate at either the conscious or the unconscious level. Many mechanisms function without involving the cortex and some without even reaching the elements of the midbrain. The human organism has its own *servomechanisms* which not only regulate and adjust but furnish cues for action and movement that has been learned and overlearned. Visual and conscious control may be operative during the early stages of learning motor skills and movement patterns, but when performance becomes habitual, internal cues, "muscle memory," and proprioceptive feedback take over.

Knowledge of results has been used for motivating and guiding the learner throughout the history of the human race. Cavemen throwing their spears and observing whether or not they hit the target, children being corrected by their parents as they learn to talk or eat, boys seeking to outdo each other in a primitive high jump, and dancers being taught the intricate steps of their culture—all knew whether they were succeeding or failing and what they should do to improve. More recently, the intense interest among athletes in testing and comparing results with previous performances of themselves and others serves the same purpose. Teachers explaining to pupils where they succeeded and where they failed, coaches pointing out the mistakes as they show films, and the instant replay as in closed-circuit television are all more or less sophisticated uses of "knowledge of results." In a sense, this knowledge is also a kind of "feedback."

"Success begets success and failure begets failure" is a slogan used by some teachers and coaches as they try to reinforce learning and motivate individuals for faster and better learning. When asked for his comments concerning this idea, Vernon Cox had this to say:

We've seen this happen. The fellow who is successful likes the feeling and will work that much harder to be more successful. The fellow who has experienced repeated failure, say in the shot put, doesn't enjoy it and may want to drop the event as not being worthwhile. But here is where your motivating factors come in. If you feel that the youngster has potential, you can point out to him that each little bit of improvement is a stepping stone along the way and that if he will stay with it he will soon achieve a new level of performance.[16]

Other coaches and athletes indicate that they feel that the most effective coaching includes careful analysis of performances, praising and criticizing at appropriate times. It is a unanimous opinion that praise serves to reinforce good performances and that encouragement should be used much more frequently than disparagement. Some feel that complete honesty is of paramount importance and that if criticism is to act as effective feedback, it must be both analytical and constructive.

Frequent testing can serve as an effective method of providing knowledge of results if comparisons are made primarily with the individual's own previous performances. Comparisons with other people's performance can often cause an athlete to set standards and goals which are either not challenging enough or so difficult as to be impossible of achievement.

The use of knowledge of results as a motivating and reinforcing factor is especially effective in physical education and coaching. Many activities are essentially self-testing, in which case knowledge of results is automatic. When a person shoots baskets, throws at a target, high jumps, runs against time, performs gymnastics for a score, plays a round of golf, serves a tennis ball, pitches horseshoe, hurls a javelin, or enters a skiing contest, he generally knows not only whether he fails or succeeds but also his score. What he often does not see, however, is the reason he failed or scored so poorly. It then becomes the responsibility of the teacher or coach to help him find out where the fault lay and how to remedy it.

There are also many activities where the knowledge of results is not so automatic and where augmented feedback is necessary to help the student progress. Dancers need to be assisted with their performances, baseball players need help to get out of a slump, soccer players can be shown where and how to improve, and swimmers often will benefit from good advise about their technique.

5.6 REINFORCEMENT AND READINESS

According to the law of effect, a learner tends to repeat responses which are satisfying and to fail to learn responses which are annoying. When behavior results in the satisfaction of needs, the responses become strengthened or *reinforced*. Reference has already been made to this principle in our discussion of feedback and knowledge of results. The concept of reinforcement is not quite so simple, however, and needs some amplification.

Reinforcement is related to both readiness and motivation. It is difficult to achieve satisfaction from something one does not want to do in the first place. A person who is highly motivated to become a good violin player will receive far more satisfaction from praise or recognition of progress than will one who thinks it is all a waste of time. A student who dislikes physical education and is taking a course only because he is required to do so will not receive as effective reinforcement from seeing himself perform well as will the one who is eagerly trying to improve. This points up the importance, in all teaching and coaching, of motivating the students and also providing activities which are appropriate to their state of readiness.

Readiness can be physiological, psychological, sociological, or a mixture of all three. A boy may be physiologically ready at a certain age to learn social dance but he and his peers may not be interested in girls. A teacher from another country may be trying to teach soccer to a group of boys who live in a community where it has never been played and where it is the goal of every youngster to play American football; before he can be successful he will need to spend some time convincing them that it is a great game and very worthwhile. A teacher may spend time trying to introduce advanced activities to elementary school children when they are not physiologically ready and are not prepared by experience to cope with such advanced skills.

A change in one dimension of readiness can alter both attitudes and behavior and affect other aspects of readiness. A junior high school boy who does not want to take tennis lessons with his sister may suddenly become eager to learn the game when two or three of his buddies decide to take it up. A high school girl who does not care to go to the pool for a swim with her parents feels quite differently about it when a girl or boy friend calls her. A person who says he does not like football because he had an unpleasant experience when he was young may suddenly become "ready" when he finds himself tough and strong enough to withstand it and when he achieves a little success. Physiological readiness can lead to psychological readiness, psychological readiness is influenced by sociological readiness, and all are related to maturation and learning.

When young people or adults are ready and are highly motivated it is easy to reinforce their responses and to make their learning experiences satisfying. Praise, rewards, recognition, winning, fame, the cheering of the crowd, the approval of teammates, the satisfaction of achieving, the knowledge that one is improving and growing, and the experience of self-actualization can all be important reinforcement factors.

There can be so much attempted reinforcement that it becomes ineffective. When praise comes too frequently, when success becomes commonplace, when one is so completely accepted that it is no longer a concern, or when children are showered with too much affection, the reinforcing factors become no longer as effective as when they are applied more judiciously. Some coaches interviewed by the author believe that when players know that praise must be earned they value it more, and it becomes a more effective incentive. Once success becomes too easy to achieve, when it is no longer a challenge, its reinforcing value is lost. Fortunately, in sports there is almost always a challenge. The golfer does not hit a good shot every time, the shortstop occasionally makes errors, the football end can miss a pass, and a rower can "foul up" the efforts of the whole crew.

It appears, then, that encouragement is more effective than discouragement, praise should be used judiciously, partial and occasional reinforcement is more effective than continuous and regular reinforcement, and that prompt reinforcement will accelerate learning more than delayed reinforcement. It is also evident that there are many different ways in which learners can obtain satisfaction from their behavior.

5.7 THE PHENOMENOLOGICAL APPROACH

The Gestalt psychologies of Kohler and Koffka, as well as the field theories of Wheeler, Tolman, and others, is giving way to what is now more commonly termed the *phenomenological approach*. Great stress is put on perception and on each person's seeing himself in his own total environment or his own private world. Facts are real to the individual only as they become relevant to him and to the circumstances in which he perceives himself. The whole situation, the entire pattern of experience of the child in his environment must be considered in connection with teaching and learning. The responsibility of the schools is to help the individuals learn, grow, and meet their own needs as they see them.

The student-centered problem-solving approach is suggested, with the emphasis on making learning meaningful to the learner in his own terms. It is *his* needs which must be satisfied and not those of the parent or coach or teacher. The emphasis should be on understanding the child or athlete, on establishing a sound base of communication, and on motivations and reinforcements which are meaningful to the person in his particular set of circumstances. The total situation must be conceived, not in terms of the sum of the parts, but in the Gestaltist manner of configuration or pattern. Similarly the behavior of the individual can be truly understood only in the light of the whole and not merely by an analysis of the action of the various parts.

The teacher must attend to the concepts of insight, trial-and-error learning, problem-solving, the whole method of teaching, meaningfulness, and mental practice. In terms of the phenomenological approach learning can occur without any new "input" but merely by a rearrangement of facts and perceptions already stored. A motor pattern can be changed, as it becomes necessary, simply by changing some of the motor skills already laid down in a movement designed for a similar situation.

5.8 SOME LEARNING CONCEPTS
APPLIED TO PHYSICAL EDUCATION AND SPORTS

While there is much to be gained by reviewing the various theories of motor learning, the crucial concern here is to discuss the application of the most commonly accepted psychological concepts to the teaching and coaching of sports. The following summary, drawn from many sources and the rich experiences of a large number of experienced physical education teachers and coaches, is an attempt to do just that:

1. A student or athlete who is highly motivated to learn will acquire new knowledge and skill more quickly than the one who is not so motivated. Part of this can be attributed to the effectiveness of reinforcement in the case of the motivated learner.

2. Learning takes place best where success rather than failure predominates. The teacher or coach should be generous with praise so that the learner does not regard himself as a failure. This is also related to the fact pointed out by almost all great coaches and athletes that one has to believe he can do something before he is able to accomplish it. Particularly in individual sports, underconfidence is more to be feared than overconfidence.

3. Repetitive practice and overlearning are important where motor skills and movement patterns have to be made automatic. Diving, gymnastics, pole-vaulting and the fundamentals of team games are examples.

4. Knowledge of one's performance and improvement, as well as one's goals and objectives are crucial to effective learning. Understanding of one's mistakes and what must be done to correct them is equally important. Care must be taken however that the underconfident, poor performer does not see himself in such a way that he gets an unfavorable self-image and regards himself as a failure.

5. There are important individual differences in the ability to learn and to perform. Some of these are innate and some are due to past experiences. All athletes cannot be expected to progress at the same speed. Chronological age should not be the only criterion on which to base expectations or method.

6. Emotional arousal is useful in motivating for peak performance and learning but too much excitement, anxiety, and stress can cause loss in the ability to think clearly, a decrease in muscular coordination, movements that are too forceful, and a lack of concentration on the task at hand. If the excitement is due to extraneous influences, the ability to recognize cues will be decreased and therefore both performance and learning will be hindered.

7. Kinesthetic feedback is a significant factor in motor learning and performance. Proprioceptive sensory input is combined with visual and auditory cues to keep the organism informed and to bring about proper movement adjustments. There should be effort on the part of the learner to develop an awareness or "feel" as he is practicing his motor skills and patterns.

8. The "whole-part-whole" or the "felt need" method of teaching should be given serious thought while plans are being made. The pattern, game, or movement must be perceived as a whole as the student or athlete strives to learn. The complexity of the skill or the movement pattern may be of such magnitude that it may later need to be broken down into its components for practice before being combined again into the whole. If this is done the learners should recognize the need for analysis and part practice so that motivation will be adequate and reinforcement can occur.

9. Intrinsic motivation in the form of a desire for excellence, personal pride in achievement, and a striving toward self-realization is the most effective form of sustained motivation. Emotional stimulation from extraneous sources, incentives, and rewards can only be secondary types of motivation and are only temporary in their effect.

10. Perceptual-motor learning includes the sensory input from proprioceptors, exteroceptors, and the inner ear; it includes the analysis, organization, and interpretation occurring in the central nervous system and particularly the cortex; it eventuates in movement resulting from efferent messages and the stimulation of appropriate muscles. It is the result of perception, interpretation

and action. It is affected by the individual's experience, his past history, his cultural background, and all the above-mentioned stimuli which are, in one way or another, brought to bear on the given situation or event.

11. Basic to motor learning are (1) the development of a clear perception of the task, (2) trial performances by the learner, (3) analysis of performances followed by additional trials attempting to correct mistakes, and (4) repetitive performance using the corrected technique. Proper understanding of the task may be achieved through demonstrations, films, pictures, directions by the instructor, written description of the desired performance, or a combination of these. The analysis of performance is best made through the cooperative efforts of the learner and teacher and could include a manually guided performance to utilize the kinesthetic sense and thus "get the feel" of the movement. The repetitions or drill on the correct performance should be accompanied by praise and approval to reinforce the learning and should result in enough overlearning to accomplish the "laying down" of the pattern in the central nervous system.

REFERENCES

1. Best, Charles Herbert, and Norman Burke Taylor, *The Physiological Basis of Medical Practice*. Baltimore: Williams and Wilkins, 1945

2. Bernard, Harold W., *Psychology of Learning and Teaching*. New York: McGraw-Hill, 1965

3. Burton, William H., *The Nature and Direction of Learning*. New York: Appleton-Century, 1929

4. Edwards, Linden F., *Anatomy for Physical Education*. Philadelphia: Blakiston, 1934

5. Gardner, Elizabeth B., "The neuromuscular base of human movement: feedback mechanisms," *Journal of Health, Physical Education and Recreation*, Vol. 36, No. 8, 1965, pp. 61-62

6. Griffith, Coleman, *Psychology and Athletics*. New York: Scribner, 1928, p. 85

7. Guilford, J. P., "A system of the psycho-motor abilities," *American Journal of Psychology*, Vol. 71, 1958, pp. 164-174

8. Hellebrant, F. A., "The physiology of motor learning," *Anthology of Contemporary Readings*. Dubuque, Iowa: William C. Brown Company, 1966

9. Kandel, E. R., and W. A. Spencer, "Cellular neurophysiological approaches in the study of learning," *Physiological Review*, Vol. 48, 1968, p. 65

10. Lawther, John D., "Directed motor skill learning," *Quest*, National Association of Physical Education for College Women and National College Physical Education Association for Men, Monograph VI, Spring Issue, 1966, pp. 68-76

11. Lockhart, Aileene, "Prerequisities to motor learning," *The Academy Papers*, No. 1, The American Academy of Physical Education, March 1968

12. Moore, Roy, "An analysis of modern theoretical approaches to learning with implications for teaching gross motor skills in physical education," unpublished Ph.D. Thesis, University of Iowa, 1949

13. Phillips, Marjorie, and Dean Summers, "Relation of kinesthetic perception to motor learning," *Research Quarterly*, Vol. 25, 1954, pp. 456-469

14. Robb, Margaret, "Feedback," *Quest*, National Association of Physical Education for College Women and National College Physical Education Association for Men, Monograph VI, Spring Issue, 1966, pp. 38-43

15. Singer, Robert N., *Motor Learning and Human Performance*. New York: Macmillan, 1968, p. 41

Personal references

16. Cox, Vernon, member of Physical Education Faculty and Coach of Track and Field, Springfield College, Springfield, Massachusetts, personal interview, 1969

17. Sanangelo, Ernest, Physical Education major and Captain of Gymnastics Team, Syracuse University, Syracuse, New York, personal interview, 1969

18. Silvia, Charles E., Swimming Coach, Springfield College, Springfield, Massachusetts, personal interview, 1969

6 FACTORS AND CONDITIONS AFFECTING MOTOR LEARNING

A boy who is a little slow in reaction time, or in speed of running, may compensate for this slowness. He may learn to recognize the situation so quickly that he has more time to field the ball, intercept the pass, return the serve, or deflect the puck.

John D. Lawther[15]

6.1 CUE-RECOGNITION AND SPEED OF PERCEPTION

The faster an athlete is able to perceive exactly what his opponent is going to do, the better are his chances of "beating" him. As an example, the game of basketball is replete with "one-on-one" situations, each of which constitutes a contest between a single offensive man and his guard. Fakes and feints, false cues, and deceptive moves are part of the repertoire of both men, and the person who has the quicker and more accurate perception and who follows up with action, will win.

The speed of perception can be improved by practice. While in the Air Corps the author had "aircraft identification" as part of his training. This consisted of practice in the recognition of planes whose silhouettes were flashed on a screen one after another. At each training session the length of time the silhouette appeared on the screen was shortened, and those being trained were soon able to identify each type of plane in an incredibly short time. While there were several cues in each picture which could be used in the identification, it soon became apparent that a certain nose shape suggested one type of plane, a particular tail signified another, and the number and shapes of the wings were enough to identify still others. The number of cues necessary for immediate identification was reduced sometimes to one. Thus it is in sports. Lawther expressed it this way:

The decrease with learning in the number of cues essential for recognition is due to the filling in of the rest of the stimulus pattern from a mental construct already established from previous experience. The term, "mental construct," is merely our

116

verbal symbolism to represent the phenomenon characteristic of highly trained perception, which produces the filling in of the whole stimulus situation from a greatly reduced number of cues. The very speed of these trained recognitions indicates their automaticity.[13]

As the level of motor performance and learning becomes higher and as the skills and movements become more automatic, the athlete learns faster cue-recognition and the number of cues needed to elicit the correct response is reduced. It is then that the player is freed from the necessity of carefully thinking out each move so that he can concentrate on strategy, leadership, and his relationship to the rest of the team. As his movements become more and more automatic, he can turn his attention to what must be done several moments ahead.

Cues play an important role in prolonged movement patterns, such as the floor exercises in gymnastics, the more intricate dives, the various dance routines, the pole vault, and the performances on the different pieces of gymnastic apparatus. These cues may be specific strains of music, the relationship of the body to the apparatus, the orientation of the body in space, or the immediately preceding movement in a pattern. Considerable "cue-recognition" operates below the level of consciousness; the performer is not even aware of what is transpiring as he moves smoothly from one motor skill to another. The human organism responds to each new situation by reference to the cues which have been developed from previous practice and all past experiences.

It becomes evident that a single explanation of cue recognition cannot be applied to all physical education and athletic situations. Team games differ from individualized contests, an activity such as gymnastics is not the same in method and philosophy as dance, and there is a difference between sports of an antagonistic or combative nature (e.g., wrestling) and those in which the performance of the opponent does not physically affect one's own (e.g., rowing).

Perception is the interpretation of all sensory input, past and present, in the light of the present environment and circumstances. Perception must be in terms of time, space, self, others, gravity, and figure-ground relationships. The athlete blessed with unusual perceptual ability will generally perform smoothly and without hesitation, exercise good judgment and do the right thing at the right time, learn motor skills quite readily, and react to proprioceptive, visual, auditory, and other stimuli with speed and efficiency. This is the reason that practice and experience are so important for the person who wishes to become a great athlete. For, according to the best evidence we now have, perception and cue-recognition can be improved with diligent attention and intelligent practice.

6.2 ATTENTION AND CONCENTRATION

During the past year the author observed physical education classes and athletic contests where the following occurred:

1. A high school boy "broke his dribble" in basketball and subsequently was obviously thinking about this instead of the ensuing play when he was caught flat-footed on defense.

2. A little league baseball player was so engrossed with his practice swing at the plate that he had the bat in the forward position when the pitched strike crossed the plate.

3. A defensive halfback in football was so concerned about covering the receiver in front of him that he did not see the player who caught the pass just behind him in his territory.

4. A baseball catcher became so involved in banter with the crowd that he failed to keep track of the number of outs and made the wrong play on the next ball.

5. A second-grade pupil failed to grasp an instruction from a teacher who had talked so long and so much as to far exceed the "attention span" of the child.

6. A fine college basketball player in an overtime period of a tense basketball game calmly stepped up and made two free throws while the crowd was screaming and the outcome was riding on his performance.

When the author interviewed professionals, Olympians, college and high school athletes, and coaches and asked them about the matter of attention, the message that came across over and over again was this:

The great athlete, the great champion, is the person who can exclude extraneous influences, who can shut out the rest of the world, and concentrate on the contest and the performance at hand.

The Skilled Performer
The great athlete can exclude extraneous influences and concentrate on the performance at hand. *By permission*, Steve Waterman, captain of the basketball team, Springfield College.

The crowd has often had an inspiring influence on an individual or a team. The anxiety level of the athletes may be affected by those who are in the stands. The atmosphere surrounding a contest is observed and sensed prior to the beginning of a game or an event. Momentum can be initiated, increased, or decreased by the cheering or lack of it on the part of a crowd. But an athlete, to perform at his best, must have such powers of concentration that, when the action starts, he can concentrate wholly on the task at hand, and can perform as if nothing else existed except himself, his spatial, and temporal environment, and the obstacles to be overcome, be they human or material in nature.

The more experienced and highly skilled an athlete becomes, the more he can control the "giving of attention." This is true in more ways than one. An experienced athlete can select the important cues and shut out the others. He can give focal or primary attention to one cue and peripheral or secondary attention to another. He can give unconscious attention to certain aspects of the game while concentrating on a specific phase or action. Let us cite two examples.

A college catcher in the late innings of a tie ball game is faced with a situation where a fast runner is on first base and there is one out. He knows that the opposing coach usually elects to signal the runner to steal in such situations but occasionally asks the batter to bunt. The batter is the opposing catcher and a consistent hitter but seldom gets more than a single. He is followed by the number-one pitcher who is performing well on the mound but is a poor batter. The catcher therefore feels that the runner will be asked to steal and the batter will not swing. On the other hand, his pitcher has been bothered by poor control and he does not want to waste a pitch. Yet he knows that to catch the runner trying to steal he must call for a fast ball and not too low. All these things pass through his mind as he gives the signal for a fast ball high and on the outside corner of the plate. As the ball comes toward him, he gives it just enough attention to be sure of catching it and at the same time looks for the runner by means of peripheral vision. If everything works as planned, he concentrates on a target about twelve inches above second base and he catches and throws the ball automatically as he recognizes the cue indicating that the runner is attempting the steal. All of these details of thought, of perception, and of his physical activity receive attention from the catcher. Many of these details are perceived automatically, some of them are registered semiautomatically, and others are the focus of his attention. Meanwhile, the crowd is cheering and screaming for a hit, the coaches on first and third are trying to distract the pitcher, the baserunner is dancing back and forth, the players on both sides are chattering and yelling encouragement. While the catcher is vaguely aware of the excitement, he shuts such distractions out of his mind and concentrates on the task at hand.

A football quarterback is faced with the situation of being three points behind with twelve seconds to go in an important game. He is both a good runner and a passer, but other backs have been gaining more ground carrying the ball. It is third down and eight yards to go on the opponent's thirty-five yard line. It takes a touchdown to win and a field goal to tie. One running play could consume the twelve seconds. A short pass down the middle might set up a field goal. Side-line passes where the receiver can move out of bounds seem the best choice, but the defenders are keeping their defense well back. Pandemonium reigns in the stands, and even the players on the bench show their excitement. The quarterback chooses to call for a roll-out pass with the option to run. As he receives the ball, he notes that the side-line receivers are well covered, that he is cornered and cannot make it out of bounds or gain any ground. He sees a partially open receiver in the middle and on the twenty yard line, but tacklers are behind him. He feels that there are about five seconds left. He fires the ball to the receiver, who catches it and is tackled. The quarterback meanwhile has rushed to the referee signaling time-out. The clock is stopped with two seconds to go and the opportunity for a field goal is set up. During the intervening ten seconds the quarterback handled the ball, dodged, ran, and passed without conscious thought, because these actions had been automatized. Cues of many kinds and from many sources were received and acted upon. Much of this was below the level of consciousness. Peripheral attention was given to the passage of time, the position of the defenders, the position on the field, and the potential receivers. Finally there was focal attention on the pass itself, which was the culmination of all the efforts going into that particular play. Again, no attention was given to the confusion and emotional excitement outside the boundary lines of the football field.

Much of athletic strategy is based on the concept of attention. If one can direct the attention of the opponent to false cues, to fake movements, to extraneous events, to decoys, or to anything else which will distract him from concentrating on the key players or the central movement, an important purpose is achieved. A moment's hesitation or a body lean in the wrong direction on the part of the opponent may be all that is needed. A pivot man in basketball may fool his defensive man by throwing a hand up or by a toss of the head; a football linebacker may be kept from coming up fast when he sees an end go down as if for a pass; a badminton player may be held in the back of the court by a fake smash; a runner on third may be sent scurrying back to his base by a "bluff throw"; a boxer by continuing to jab with his left is seeking to make his opponent attend to that act and thus leave himself open for the body punch.

The trained and competent performer has learned not only to direct his attention to some details and to shut out irrelevant cues, but also to concentrate specifically and primarily on the central and important cues and yet to keep in focus those things which, although not central, have meaning and significance for the occasion. Coleman Griffith distinguishes between the amateur and the veteran in this regard:

This is a kind of skill which makes the difference between the amateur athlete and the professional. We know it as a common fact that a professional team is not nearly so apt to "blow-up" as a young college team. The amateur has not yet developed those habits which will help him to collect the many threads of action on the baseball diamond or on the gridiron and act wisely toward the whole situation. The professional, like the skilled executive, has met complicated situations of this sort so many times that his habits will carry him through where his narrow span of attention would lead him into great trouble. The difference between the amateur and the professional is like the difference between the learner and the skilled automobile driver. The former has many things to "think about" as we say. There is the clutch, the accelerator, the spark, the choke, the wheel, the street, the passing cars, the pedestrians, too many objects of course to be clearly apprehended at one and the same time. His first attempt at driving is, therefore, a dangerous experiment. A similar situation on the baseball diamond or on the gridiron would be called a crucial moment of the game. But after a time the learner begins to commit some of the objects and the motions which at first were under the direct light of attention, to his nervous system. Finally he cheats his narrow span of attention by actually doing many things at once. His foot on the break, the clutch, or the accelerator, his hand on the wheel, his eyes on the road in front of him, and the light of memory and habit shifting rapidly from one thing to another. So with the professional in baseball. His motions of fielding a ball have been committed to his nervous system. He has learned the habits of base-runners, and he knows the strategy of the game. His memory and his habits then come to his aid when situations which we call crucial place the objects to be apprehended beyond the normal range of attention.[9]

6.3 THE LEARNING CURVE

There are usually three basic phases in the learning of motor skills, movement patterns, or entire games. First, one must perceive what is to be learned and gain insight into the task at hand and the performance required. For many people this first stage is not always very easy; it may take them some time to learn everything, and improvement in performance is relatively slow. This phase is followed by a rapid gain in skill and an improvement in both performance and understanding. As one becomes an accomplished performer, improvement becomes increasingly imperceptible, and the learning curve levels off (see figure).

Learning does not proceed in a steady, consistent fashion. There are periods when no improvement takes place; at times the learner seems almost to regress. And, yet, if we observe individuals closely over months and years, we will notice that they continue to learn and improve so long as they are motivated and within the limitations of their potential.

Coaches and teachers must be concerned about the plateaus in the learning curve, which may be caused by fatigue, poor physical condition, insufficient understanding of the next task, inability to recognize mistakes, or the absence of motivation. When a player appears to be in a slump, when a learner stops improving, when other interests replace the motivation for the sport, or when for any reason a plateau in learning is reached, it is time to take stock. This is the time for careful observation, for consultations between athlete and coach, for rest or additional practice, as circumstances indicate. It may also be that the plateaus are a natural part of the learning process and do not represent time wasted, for, in the words of Griffith,

The facts in the case probably are that the man has run into a period of apparent lack of progress which is being taken up by his nervous system in automatizing the fundamentals which were learned so easily. Automatization rests upon what we shall later describe as overlearning. It is only when the fundamentals have become absolutely automatic that we can begin to build upon them. The chances are that if the man who has fallen into a slump will hang on a few days and struggle to maintain his interest he will wake up some morning to find that he has the skill which has been denied him until that time.[9]

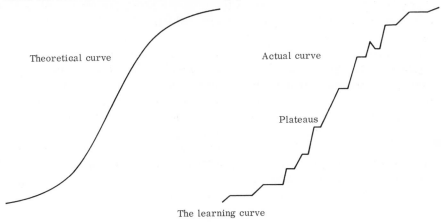

Theoretical curve   Actual curve

Plateaus

The learning curve

In the case of a complex movement pattern the learning curve will normally contain more plateaus than in the case of a simple movement. Robert Singer explains this phenomenon in these words:

A hypothesis set forth to explain the plateau in learning is that there is a hierarchy of habits to be mastered by the individual when he attempts to learn a complex task. After succeeding in the first order, he might be fixated at a level for some time before becoming able to integrate the patterns needed in the second order habits. Information is consolidated and reorganized. An example of this situation is found in tennis. First order habits might be the acquisition of basic strokes and skills underlying the sport, such as learning to stroke the ball when in a stationary position. Second order habits could include hitting the ball while on the move, and a third order category might include the integration of effective movement patterns in the game situation. Theoretically, depending on the manner in which the sport is taught and the performer involved, a plateau could occur at any one of these transitional periods.[17]

6.4 IMITATION AND LEARNING

Every teacher of physical education, every parent, every coach has observed countless instances of learning by imitation. The author observed his ten-year-old son playing basketball with the defensive stance and other mannerisms of his current college basketball hero. In another instance a junior high school youngster spent a good deal of his time walking and standing like the all-state basketball player in the local high school. Two prospective catchers, when asked about their stance behind the plate, said that they had seen a certain big league catcher do it that way. A gymnast, unable to learn a certain movement on the horizontal bar, suddenly gained "insight" and was able to do it after watching the performance of an Olympic gymnast. And a hammer-thrower who was having trouble with coordinating and timing the components of his movement pattern suddenly learned the trick when he saw a champion execute a throw in perfect form.

Experienced coaches and teachers would not continue to demonstrate and to show loop films of the great performers if they did not believe in learning by imitation. How many times do teachers stop a pupil and say, "No, not like that; like this," and then proceed to demonstrate? How many times do coaches tell one of their athletes, "You are not doing that just right; watch Joe a few times and see if you can do it that way." If imitation were not an effective technique, visual aids would not play the important role in coaching and physical education that they do today.

A word of caution, however, is in order. Teaching must not become merely the setting of an example by the teacher and then imitation by the pupil. Individuals differ anatomically, physiologically, and psychologically, and what is the most effective technique for one may not be so effective for another. Too much repression of individuality in learning can lead to "lackluster," stereotyped, and "robot-like" performance, which is neither enjoyable nor effective. The recent emancipation of basketball from being a game in which all fundamentals had to be executed in exactly the same way by everyone to one where "any shot is good so long as it goes in" is an example of the gains which can be made by allowing some freedom in the technique of execution of specific skills. There are, of course, some sound kinesiological principles which must be observed for best performance.

It is obvious that if imitation is to be used extensively as a method of learning, the model should be right. Imitating wrong and ineffective movements is generally wasteful of efforts, necessitating, as it does, relearning at a later time; this kind of imitation is to be distinguished from "trial-and-continuous-revision" learning, which involves learning from mistakes and is an inescapable part of the learning process. In general, it is also agreed that learning takes place more effectively when the learner concentrates on the result rather than on the movement itself. Nevertheless, it must be recognized that imitation continues to be an important method of learning motor skills and movement patterns. If recognition of the task is the first step in motor learning, then the next one is "learning by doing," which usually involves imitating a demonstrated performance, either live or in pictures.

6.5 SELF-ACTIVITY AND MENTAL PRACTICE

"Learning by doing" has long been an accepted, if not universally practiced, concept in education. This principle has been labeled the "doctrine of self-activity" by William Burton, who goes on to say:

A baby learns to walk by actually trying to walk. No amount of demonstration or discussion will enable him to do it. He must do it himself in order to learn. The principle of self-activity states that the learner learns by doing. This is a primary principle of learning. It is the opposite of what might be called the *doctrine of receptivity*. Education for long has been carried on as if the pupil passively absorbed what was put before him to be learned, as if he had education poured into him, as if he *received* his education. We cannot *give* any one an education; he must *get* it.[3]

If this notion of education is acceptable in traditional subjects such as English, the sciences, and history, how much more important must it be in physical education. There are numerous examples of physical education teachers who ask their pupils to sit down at the beginning of the class and then spend half of the period talking to them. Not only do these teachers violate sound motivational principles, but they also violate learning principles, for most learning occurs through activity and the sooner the pupils or athletes become totally involved in trying to perform the quicker will they learn the new movement. As we said before, there must first be a recognition of the task, but this should be followed as soon as possible by an opportunity for the pupils to try to execute the motor act. The teacher's responsibility is to stimulate and guide pupil activity.

Mental practice also involves self-activity. Considerable research has been completed with respect to the effect of mental practice on motor learning. While the evidence is far from conclusive, it points strongly to the proposition that improvement does take place as a result of "thinking through" movement patterns and motor skills. The skill level of the learner, the degree to which he is familiar with the task, and the integration of mental practice with physical practice, all have a bearing on the effectiveness of this method of learning. Evidence derived from interviews with top athletes and coaches certainly indicates that in the learning of high-level skills and in competitive situations, the performers are constantly rehearsing mentally each movement as well as the total motor patterns which will constitute their performances. Among the leading scholars of motor learning there is an increasing emphasis on the role of the cognitive processes.

Coaches and physical education teachers must try to determine the optimum combination of mental and physical practice. It seems reasonable to suppose that if the maximum beneficial physical practice can be determined, some additional intensive mental rehearsal will increase the rate of learning and the quality of performance. There may, of course, be factors of fatigue, stress, and tension, which would affect this relationship. Effective mental practice takes concentration, planning, and systematic thinking. There are of course times when an athlete will benefit more from rest, relaxation, or recreation, which takes his mind completely off the task at hand.

6.6 TRIAL-AND-CONTINUOUS-REVISION LEARNING

When an objective or goal involving physical movement is clearly perceived and wholeheartedly accepted, the individual is ready to move;

but the achievement of his goal is dependent on the repertoire of motor patterns which is available to him. If the required motor skill is a new one and must be learned, the individual will immediately set about trying various basic movements which are familiar to him, hoping that they may be combined into a new pattern that will accomplish his purpose. He will try one combination after another until suddenly he succeeds. And then, in response to the feedback and using his knowledge of the results, he will continue such *trial-and-error learning* until he is able more consistently and easily to repeat the successful performance.

—*Trial-and-continuous-revision learning* consists of repeatedly testing movement patterns and motor skills, improving them on the basis of feedback, and integrating them into new and more complex patterns, which may later contribute to the realization of a specific purpose. The nature of the feedback may not always be the same. Proprioceptive, visual, and vestibular feedbacks play an important role in the coordination of movements and the orientation of the individual throughout his performance. Teachers and coaches furnish feedbacks which enter by way of ears and eyes. Closed-circuit television and "instant replay" may be utilized to provide visual knowledge of results. Actual physical assistance by the instructor in correcting performance can also be effective.

Bryant Cratty emphasizes the importance of formal instruction during the initial phase of the learning process and of "trial-and-error learning" coming after the *learner has mastered the task* to some degree[5]. While this may not always be true, it is generally agreed that fundamental movements should be based on sound kinesiological principles and that exploring slightly different ways of accomplishing the purpose should come after a sound scientific foundation has been established.

Trial-and-error learning which relies entirely on random attempts to perform a motor act may well be wasteful of efforts. While some exploratory action is necessary during the learning of a motor skill, it is helpful if some guidance and feedback can be provided. Thus the basic movement which will accomplish the task can first be learned and then varied. As variations become more successful, they are reinforced and the original movement is slightly revised. This is what is meant by "trial-and-continuous-revision" learning. The emphasis, as the individual tries repeatedly to perform, is not on the errors but on the improvements which occur as slight variations of the original movement are attempted.

6.7 INDIVIDUATION IN MOTOR SKILLS AND PATTERNS

John Lawther's emphasis on *individuation* in learning motor behavior is closely related to the method of learning just discussed. He says:

Individuation of body-part movements is a major aspect in much of our motor-skill learning. In learning motor behavior, one has to reduce the gross acts to certain sequences of individuation. Individuation means a partial dissociation of the specific movements needed for a specific purpose from the gross total-body acts involving extraneous movements—movements not only unnecessary for the immediate purpose but also disturbing to its precision. Observation of a novice attempting almost any skill will reveal this excess movement and excess large-muscle activity, particularly if the skill is one requiring considerable precision of control. Drawing and handwriting by kindergarten and primary school children are good examples. At first, the child tenses much of his large musculature and gets much of his body into the act.[13]

Learning to control the movement of each specific body part is useful in learning new skills of a simple nature, refining complex skills, eliminating extraneous movements, and reeducating certain muscles in those who are handicapped. A child learning to write must be able to control his fingers; a polio victim with a tendon transplant must learn how to flex and extend the foot using this new arrangement of muscles; a swimmer trying to gain in speed must be able to control the angle of his foot in the flutter kick; a gymnast, after learning a complex movement, must be able to concentrate on pointing the toes; and a pitcher trying to master a curve must learn to throw by using the hands and fingers in a new way.

Lawther lists a few helpful procedures in learning to separate out a new movement and control it voluntarily:

1. moving associated body parts and trying to move the specific part with them;

2. focusing attention and strongly toned stimuli toward the specific part to be moved until a "spill-over of energy" into the musculature of the part is obtained;

3. not only producing a movement in the part, but also feeling and identifying it;

4. relaxing so that tension will leave the associated but extraneous musculature;

5. practicing moving the specific part in an attempt to improve both control and performance.[13]

Two examples of individuation witnessed by the author are quite illustrative. During a "fitness" program an individual demonstrated from the stage his ability to move specific muscles. He was an expert at contracting individually and specifically, one at a time or in combination, his pectoral muscles, his biceps, his triceps, each portion of his latissimus dorsi, his trapezius, his serratus anterior, his glutei, his deltoid, and his gastrocnemius. He could contract the muscles in various combinations, or individually, in different sequences. He could do this while describing each movement, or he could perform rhythmically with many muscle parts taking part sequentially. It was an interesting demonstration and one that illustrated "individuation" to a high degree.

The other example was in an electrotherapy laboratory where we, as students, assisted with physical therapy of patients. An appropriate electric current was employed to stimulate muscular contractions where a degree of paralysis and atrophy had occurred. The electrode was applied externally to various motor points, and contraction of muscle units followed. The contraction caused by the electrical stimulation was alternated with efforts of the patient to contract the same muscle voluntarily. It was hoped that proprioceptive and exteroceptive stimuli would help the individual get "the feel" of contracting this particular muscle and result in the reeducation of that body part.

Individuation, where attention is focused on the action of a specific body part or specific combination of motor units, must be distinguished from the learning of a motor pattern, in which case best results can be achieved by attending to the goal to be achieved rather than the movement of the individual parts. A pole-vaulter concentrates on clearing the bar, with only peripheral attention, in the initial stages at least, to the individual movements of the hands and feet. As he perfects his technique, however, he may increasingly give his attention to portions of bodily movement, for example on one occasion to a hand that knocked off the crossbar on the way down, or on another occasion to the forceful thrust that pushes his body up and over.

6.8 EFFECTIVENESS OF PRACTICE

Time spent on intelligent planning of sports practice sessions and physical education classes may be the most productive of all the hours spent by coaches and teachers. Class periods and athletic practices are partially wasted if: practices are poorly organized, there is no logical or psychological sequence of activities, too much or too little time is spent on a certain drill, the methods are not appropriate for the activity taught, there is too much or too little verbal instruction, no attention is given to appropriate rest periods, or practices are too long, too short, or incorrectly spaced.

Many experiments have been conducted to determine how much practice is necessary for the learning of a motor skill or movement pattern. The arrangement and scheduling of practice periods have also been the subject of a good deal of research. In this area again we find some disagreement in the results; nevertheless, the following generalizations seem warranted:

1. The optimum length of a practice period is dependent on many factors. Some of these are:

    (a) the age of the learners (mature adults can learn effectively in longer periods than children or adolescents);

    (b) the strenuousness of the activity (fatigue and staleness will set in faster in some activities than others; when this happens learning is impeded);

    (c) the nature of the activity and the time necessary for dressing and preparation (skiing, golf, bowling, archery and certain other activities seem to benefit from longer periods);

    (d) the competence of the learners (highly skilled individuals can usually benefit from longer practice periods than beginners);

    (e) the size of a class or group (in a small group, where the number of trials per individual is high, the periods should be shorter);

    (f) the amount of exploration involved (if the problem-solving method is used, enough times to explore possibilities should be allotted);

    (g) the degree of motivation (where the interest and desire to learn are high, longer practices are warranted and profitable).

2. The massing of practices will bring mastery of a specific motor act sooner than widely distributed practices. On the other hand, this method of practice may eventually involve more total time spent on learning the skill in its entirety. The urgency of completing the learning in a short time may dictate longer and more intense practices. There is, however, a point beyond which further practicing of a specific skill or sport will bring no return, and good judgment must be used with regard to rest periods and reasonable spacing of practices. Too much time elapsing between practice

periods, especially in the early stages of learning a motor skill, may cause forgetting and the necessity of more relearning.

3. Opinion appears to favor longer and more closely spaced practice periods at the beginning of a specific skill unit and shorter periods with more spacing as proficiency increases. Coaches tend to decrease the length of the practices as contests approach and as the season progresses.

It becomes obvious that empirical evidence does not furnish all the answers. Good judgment based on experience coupled with knowledge of available research findings must determine the course of action in practical situations. There will be many different factors guiding decisions in this regard. Teams may be "bored" or "stale" and need a change of routine. There may be bruises or other injuries which cause athletes to withdraw from hard practice. It may become obvious that individuals are no longer motivated and some changes in practice procedures must be instituted. In a sport like gymnastics, too much hard work can cause blisters and sore hands, necessitating rest and a change in the routine. The development of endurance may be combined with the overlearning and automatization of a skill, as in swimming, and additional time may be needed to accomplish both these objectives. In some cases, the learning of tactics and strategy are superimposed on the learning of motor patterns, which again will prolong the time needed for learning.

It is evident as we discuss this topic that learning and performance are difficult to separate. Learning in sports is usually measured in terms of improvement in performance. Planning practices includes both consideration of learning principles and motivation for coming contests. Coaches are responsible not only for teaching motor skills and patterns, but also the optimum mental and physical preparation of each athlete for the performances hoped for in the next game, meet, or contest. The massing and the distribution of practice periods are often not within the power of the coach to control. In organizing the time allotted to him he should, however, consider the psychological principles of learning, the purposes to which practice sessions are dedicated, the capacities and frailties of the human organism, and the physiological principles governing training and conditioning. In so doing, he must take into account the individual differences in human beings, the wide disparity in the nature of the various sports, the climatic factors which govern the hours of day and night, the staff assigned to deal with the number of individuals practicing, the facilities available, and many other practical variables.

6.9 WHOLE AND PART LEARNING APPLIED

Learning by parts and by wholes has been the subject of research and discussion in physical education for a half-century or more. This subject has real significance for those who teach and coach sports. Oxendine's words provide a good point of departure for our discussion:

The whole method seems best when the amount of learning does not exceed what the learner can comprehend. This method is also better when learners are older, brighter, more highly motivated, and have a background in the task. The whole technique is also favored in late stages of the learning process and when practices are distributed. When the opposite conditions exist, then part methods seem best. A combination of the two methods is sometimes most successful. It seems desirable, therefore, that all teachers be able to make effective use of each technique and a combination of the two. An essential of good teaching seems to be flexibility, which is also important in the use of whole and part organization of learning tasks.[16]

The writer recalls attending coaching schools in the early thirties and being convinced by the great coaches of the day that the secret of success was teaching fundamentals. The emphasis on "fundamentals" became so overwhelming that it was, in some instances at least, excessive. It was not unusual to see carefully planned basketball warm-up drills where the players exhibited, in that context, beautiful form in passing, pivoting, and shooting. Strangely enough, the teams which looked the best during warm-up were not always the most effective when it came to playing the game. They were not able to react quickly enough to the various situations, and their form and accuracy suffered under the pressures of game conditions. Perhaps there had been too much emphasis on the teaching of parts.

In another case, soccer was being played for the first time, and a physical education teacher organized the group into squads for drill on heading, passing, and trapping. After a relatively short time interest lagged and one pupil was heard to say disgustedly to another, "Why do we have to do this? It will never do us any good!" It was obvious that the pupils did not know why they were required to know how to execute these particular skills.

There was the high school baseball team which in game after game, looked wonderful in their infield workout but which failed to score. An analysis of their practices revealed that they had spent almost no time on hitting practice. They were ineffective at the plate even against relatively weak pitchers. However, they ran bases well, looked good in the field, and seemingly knew what to do. The following year the coach discussed practice sessions with an experienced coach, analyzed the weaknesses of his team, and organized batting practices in the gymnasium beginning as early as January. The improvement in hitting was startling, and for years this team was a leader in the sport of baseball, essentially because they practiced hitting for hours before they were able to go outside for even a practice game. And the enthusiasm of the players for hitting practice never lagged.

A young boy who had grown up by a lake, but had never had formal instruction in swimming, was described by his father as being able to "swim like a fish." He tried out for the competitive swimming team in his school and found that he had difficulty keeping up with the other candidates for the team. The coach spotted one or two flaws in his strokes immediately, and they began working together on correcting the errors and improving his form. He soon became a valuable member of the team.

An indefinite number of such instances can be added to our list to indicate the fallacy of taking a position as to which is better, the "whole method" or the "part method." It is obvious that in most instances a combination is needed, and judgment must be used as to when each is the most effective.

Some guidelines, however, can be offered:

1. When any "part" is taught, the pupils should know the context in which it is to be used. By demonstration, by film, or through previous experience, they should gain an understanding of the "whole" of which this is a "part."

2. In teaching or performing, when it becomes evident that the "whole" is not being well done because of a weakness in the part, the point of weakness should be determined and there should be special drill and teaching of that "part."

3. When a motor skill or movement pattern is so complex that the learner cannot comprehend it in its entirety, it should be broken down and each part learned separately. Later the parts can again be combined into a single pattern.

4. The more intelligent and the more mature the student, the more likelihood there is that the whole method will be superior. Griffith states, however, that "the greatest weakness of the whole method as compared to the part method lies in the difficulty of keeping our attention directed upon an entire series of movements, especially when learning is still in its earliest stages"[9].

5. There are motor skills whose performance demands a continuous movement or rhythm, and it is difficult to learn to execute these by breaking them down into parts.

6. For the most efficient learning, pupils should be started at the highest level of their achievement.

These principles should be applied intelligently and not mechanically. Where good progress is being made in learning the whole, it may not be necessary to analyze and practice parts. Some parts may need no individual drill. The entire performance will be only as good as the weakest part, however, and the individual fundamental units and parts should be practiced as the need is discerned. Sometimes it is obvious; sometimes it takes study and attention of coaches and teachers to see what is needed. When the needed improvements are discovered, practice of these will be highly motivated, especially for learners and performers who are committed to excellence.

6.10 TRANSFER IN PHYSICAL EDUCATION AND SPORTS

Few people would quarrel with the belief that an expert baseball player is apt to have the ability, even without special practice, to swat a cricket ball. We have seen good soccer players move into football and become the team's specialist at place-kicking. Good squash players pick up badminton with little practice. Trampoline experts who can swim well usually learn intricate dives with ease. And individuals who have learned to accept the decisions of the officials in basketball are generally amenable to living by the rules in another type of community.

Nevertheless, there has been considerable controversy for many years as to whether something which is learned in one situation will carry over into another situation. Thomas Andrews and Lee Cronbach summarized their review of this topic by stating:

Transfer of a previously acquired behavior-pattern to a new situation will occur whenever an individual recognizes the new situation as similar to the situation for which the behavior was learned. We have therefore swung through a cycle, from blind assumption that transfer is widespread, through a period of skepticism when transfer was expected only in the narrowest specific knowledge and habits, to a theory which looks on transfer as common and to be expected, provided certain conditions are met.[1]

Transfer is basic to learning in physical education and sport. Fundamental movements are learned which become the nucleus for the performance of motor skills. Simple motor skills are combined to form motor patterns, some of which are quite complex. Parts of these motor patterns are individuated and used by themselves or combined to form new skills and different movement patterns. These parts or the whole patterns are laid down in the central nervous system and are called out in response to a combination of cues provided by the current set of circumstances. In motor learning, there is thus a continual transfer of what has been learned in one situation from that situation to another with similar needs.

The phenomenon of transfer also has other implications for sports teaching. If desirable values are to be fostered, if character is to be influenced, if better men and women are to be developed through physical education and athletics, there must be some transfer from the laboratory of sports to the realities of life. Care must be taken lest those who emphasize the values that can be derived from sports become too presumptuous and claim too much, for chauvinism is an ever-present pitfall and claims for the character-building values of sports must be supported by the best evidence available.

It must be emphasized, therefore, that the transfer involved in character-building is not automatic but must be carefully planned and nurtured. It does occur under favorable circumstances however. The following principles, which are now quite generally accepted, bring out some of the important factors affecting this kind of transfer:

1. The more similar two situations are, the more likelihood there is that transfer will occur. Identical or similar elements found in sports and nonsports situations increase the probability of transfer.

2. The common elements in the two situations must be recognized by the individual. If an athlete sees no similarity between the game and the life situation, the probability of transfer will be slight.

3. The more generalization and intellectualization that takes place, the greater will be the education for life. When a participant in sports recognizes that incidents occurring in athletic contests have meaning for later life, character development is taking place.

4. The more intelligent the individual and the greater the effort he makes to effect transfer and to generalize, the greater is the likelihood that transfer will happen.

5. Transfer cannot be guaranteed. There is a strong element of individuality in all learning.

6. The occurrence of transfer is related to the effort on the part of the coach and teacher, who should assist their players to recognize common elements in like situations and to generalize.

Cratty, in his summary on "transfer," writes:

Transfer will not always occur by chance, but must be taught. Insight into the nature of the task as well as continued practice on a preparatory task will facilitate transfer.

From an inspection of the available literature, it is difficult to generalize as to whether transfer is more pronounced from the simple to the complex or vice versa. At the same time, it is clear that attempting to learn a new response within a familiar situation will impede transfer, particularly during the initial stages of learning the second task. Many times, during the later stages of learning, error will occur which indicates that a latent response from a previous task is interfering with performance of the present one.[5]

The entire phenomenon of education is really based on the principle that what is learned under one set of circumstances can be applied in another situation. Nowhere is this more true than in physical education and athletics. Fundamental drills are a part of almost every athletic practice period. "Blindfold dribble drills" in basketball, passing drills in football, situation practice in baseball, land drills in teaching swimming, trampoline practice for divers, and hundreds of similar methods are based on the idea that players can practice something in one situation and apply what has been learned in another.

Negative transfer can also take place. The baseball player may have trouble adjusting his swing to golf, the badminton player has too much wrist action for tennis, the basketball player tends to "carry" the volleyball, the fullback plants his feet too far apart for sprinting, and the weight-lifter is not relaxed enough for swimming. Where situations are somewhat similar but different techniques are required, negative transfer can occur and will then impede learning.

Lawther's statement on generalization shows that adaptations and adjustments are an inseparable part of motor learning. Hence they are intimately related to the principle of transfer:

A highly developed skill is a skill so generalized that the performer makes the movement adjustments to varying conditions automatically, for the most part, as he attends to the cues for action. High skill level means generalization. Think of the relative impossibility of frequent success in kicking for the goal in a soccer game or shooting for a basket in a basketball game without this generalization. Distances, angles, body positions, one's postural base, physiological efficiency in function, all vary but the highly skilled athlete usually adjusts to these factors automatically in terms of the situation cues. His attention is on the precise cues to guide his action, but not on the action itself.[13]

6.11 RETENTION OF MOTOR SKILLS AND PATTERNS

It is fairly common for people to learn a motor skill or movement pattern quite thoroughly, then suddenly stop using that skill, and finally years later, to try to perform in a similar fashion often with surprising success. Many good golfers quit playing for a number of years and then renew their interest and participation in the game. Skaters, bicycle riders, swimmers, handball players, bowlers, and many other sportsmen have reported similar experiences. Very frequently it is found that the initial performance after the layoff is fairly good and that the skills which were originally thoroughly learned or even overlearned have been retained to a fair degree. Many motor skills learned in childhood, and not practiced for years, can be successfully recovered so long as the individual has retained a reasonable degree of agility and physical fitness.

Current thought with regard to the retention of the ability to perform motor skills includes the following:

1. The greater the amount of overlearning and the longer an individual uses or practices the particular skill, the greater is the degree of retention. A baseball player who coaches baseball for twenty years or plays professionally for that length of time retains some of his skill until old age produces deterioration of the cardiovascular, muscular, and nervous systems. He does not, however, *forget* how to bat or throw.

2. Some forgetting does occur and most of it almost immediately after cessation of that skill use. It may be, however, at least to a certain extent, that it is inability to perform, rather than actual forgetting, that is responsible.

3. While there is some controversy with regard to the comparison between the retention of motor and verbal abilities, the majority of those whose opinions the author sought believe that motor skills are retained longer and to a greater extent than knowledge and verbal abilities.

4. There is greater retention when an individual knows, before practice, that he will be expected to retain the material. Knowledge that he will be called upon to demonstrate what he has learned increases retention. Perhaps this is merely an illustration of the principle that one tends to learn and remember things learned in situations of high emotional excitement. It also illustrates the importance of motivation in both learning and retention.

5. When investigating "retention," consideration should be given to such variables as massed or distributed practices, "early-age" or later learning, and teaching methods. The large number of variables affecting learning and retention and the difficulty of their control make research in this area tedious and problematical.

6. Relearning takes place more rapidly than original learning. This seems rather obvious and reinforces the thought that a skill, once learned, is not entirely forgotten.

7. The immersion and involvement of the self in a conflicting activity and the complete neglect of a motor skill immediately after learning it appear to foster forgetting. This may well result from the elimination of normal mental rehearsals of a learned skill in the period following the initial learning of the movement or motor act.

8. It is important to remember that the strictness of a coach's conception of what constitutes learning affects the athletes' retention of skills insofar as it determines how much learning is regarded as sufficient. A player who is judged to "have learned" to shoot free throws when he can go through the motions with reasonably good form but can make only three out of ten shots, will forget quite easily and quickly. If he is judged to "have learned" only after he can consistently make an average of eight out of ten under game conditions, he will have had so much practice that he will never really forget.

Hypotheses concerning the mechanisms involved in remembering and forgetting are still quite tentative. Much more needs to be learned. For the present, therefore, it behooves the teacher and coach to use the best methods of teaching, the best organizational plans, and the best practice schedules he can devise. If personal involvement and sound motivational practices are added, and if the best available principles of motor learning are used as guides, motor skills will continue to be retained to a high degree by the athletes involved. The purposes for which learning is required and the deadlines which must be met also have an influence on scheduling and methodology.

REFERENCES

1. Andrews, Thomas G., and Lee J. Cronbach, "Transfer of Training" in W. S. Monroe (ed.), *Encyclopedia of Educational Research*, Revised Edition. New York: Macmillan, 1950, pp. 1483-1489

2. Arnold, P. J., *Education, Physical Education and Personality Development.* New York: Atherton Press, 1968

3. Burton, William H., *The Nature and Direction of Learning.* New York: Appleton-Century 1929, p. 70

4. Clark, L. V., "The effect of mental practice on the development of a certain motor skill," *Research Quarterly*, Vol. 31, No. 4, 1960, pp. 560-569

5. Cratty, Bryant J., *Psychology and Physical Activity.* Englewood Cliffs, N.J.: Prentice-Hall, 1968, pp. 118, 155

6. Cratty, Bryant J., *Movement Behavior and Motor Learning.* Philadelphia: Lea and Febiger, 1967

7. Dinkmeyer, Don C., "Psychology in athletics and physical activities," *Journal of Health, Physical Education, and Recreation*, Vol. 17, No. 7, p. 407

8. Garrison, Karl C., Albert J. Kingston, Arthur S. MacDonald, *Educational Psychology*. New York: Appleton-Century-Crofts, 1964

9. Griffith, Coleman, *Psychology and Athletics*. New York: Scribner, 1928, pp. 89, 90, 96, 130-131

10. Hartshorne, H., and M. May, *Studies in The Nature of Character*. New York: Macmillan, 1928

11. Jokl, Ernst, "The acquisition of skill," *Psicologia Dello Sport, Proceedings of the First International Congress of Sport Psychology*, Ferrucio Antonelli, editor, Rome, 1965, pp. 95-96

12. Jokl, Ernst, "The acquisition of skill," *Quest*, National Association of Physical Education for College Women, and National College Physical Education Association for Men, Monograph VI, May 1966, pp. 11-26

13. Lawther, John D., *The Learning of Physical Skills*. Englewood Cliffs, N.J.: Prentice-Hall, 1968, pp. 7-8, 9, 44-45, 68

14. Lawther, John D., "Motor learning at the high skill level," *Psicologia Dello Sport, Proceedings of the First International Congress on Sport Psychology*, Ferrucio Antonelli, editor, Rome, 1965, p. 98

15. Lawther, John D., *Psychology of Coaching*. New York: Prentice-Hall, 1951, p. 218

16. Oxendine, Joseph B., *Psychology of Motor Learning*. New York: Appleton-Century-Crofts, 1968, p. 259

17. Singer, Robert N., *Motor Learning and Human Performance*. New York: Macmillan, 1968, p. 12

18. Stone, Roselyn E., "Relationship between the perception and reproduction of body postures," *Research Quarterly*, Vol. 39 No. 3, 1968

19. Young, Olive, "A study of kinesthesis in relation to selected movements," *Research Quarterly*, Vol. 16, 1945, pp. 277-287

7 PSYCHO-PHYSIOLOGICAL PHENOMENA

*In order to demonstrate learning in the form
of successful performance, the development,
implementation, and control of a wide range
of physical, motor, cognitive, perceptual, and
emotional mechanisms are a necessity.*

Robert N. Singer[25]

7.1 VISUAL, AUDITORY, AND TACTUAL CUES

The success or failure of a batter in baseball is to a large extent dependent on his reception and perception of visual cues. He must know whether the ball is coming fast or slow, straight or in a curve, high or low, and inside or outside the strike zone. The basketball player must not only be able to focus on the ball and the player manipulating it, but also have within the range of his peripheral vision all or most of both teammates and opponents and as much of the playing floor as possible. The handball player not only must follow with the eyes the flight of the ball as it moves in many directions at an incredible speed but must also keep in view the location of his opponents and his partner. The boxer must be able to see every movement of each component of his opponent's body and at the same time be aware of his own position in the ring. The safety man in football must focus on the punted ball as it comes toward him but at the same time see the position of the opponents racing down to tackle him.

We have read about basketball players who were great because they could see "out of the corner of their eye" or who "had eyes in the back of their heads." Great ball carriers in football have been credited with phenomenal success because they always knew exactly the location of every potential tackler. This ability to focus on an essential and central action in a game and at the same time be aware of what is going on in a much broader arena is an important asset to any athlete and a common characteristic of most good ones, depending, of course, on the particular sport involved.

Visual perception is dependent on the type of stimulus, the intensity of illumination, the length of time of the exposure, and the brightness of contrast. Visual acuity is greatest in the foveal area of the retina where the cones are closely packed and diminishes toward the peripheral area where there are many more rods than cones. Light rays which come in from the side will strike the peripheral area of the retina and those which enter from the front will strike the foveal area. The important point is that people can through practice increase their peripheral vision and that drills for this purpose can be devised and should be used.

Good vision is more important in some sports than in others. When an athlete is handicapped by visual defects which cannot be corrected, he should be advised of this fact and perhaps be guided into sports where this defect is not so important. Swimming, wrestling, running, and dancing are examples.

Since colors are not equally well perceived in the peripheral areas, some attention should be given to the colors of uniforms, especially in sports such as football, soccer, and basketball. White and black retain their quality of visibility the best over the whole field of vision. Thus these are often the most desirable colors, although blue and yellow are also generally very satisfactory. The effect of bright lights and the contrast with the background are also factors which significantly affect vision.

The ability to hear well is very important in some sports but much less so in others. Basketball players use verbal signals in both defense and offense; baseball fielders are aided in their judgment of a hit ball by the sound of the bat; football players must hear defensive and offensive signals; hunters attribute significance to the smallest sounds; and track men must hear the starter's pistol. In some cases substitution of one sense for another is possible. And there are instances where poor hearing may assist an athlete in his attempt to shut out extraneous stimuli and concentrate on the task at hand.

Tactile sensitivity is often overlooked in analyzing movement and motor learning and yet it has an important role. The wrestler often reacts in terms of where he is touched and the degree of pressure exerted on a given spot by the opponent. The skilled dribbler controls the ball by his sense of touch and not by seeing it with his eyes. The great pass receiver develops his tactile sense by handling the ball hour after hour until it feels as if it were a part of him. The fine skill needed by the golfer is in part developed through his tactile sense. Gymnasts develop a "feel" for the horizontal bar, the parallel bar, and the sidehorse. Perception attained through the tactile sense is achieved through long hours of practice, constant handling of an object, and thousands of repetitions of touching and feeling. This is why coaches have told football players to "go to bed with the ball," baseball players to swing bats until they develop the right "feel," and basketball players to practice dribbling blindfolded.

7.2 REACTION TIME AND PERFORMANCE TIME

Fast reactions are characteristic of great athletes in most sports. To judge and hit a baseball thrown by a good pitcher who has a curve ball requires extremely fast reactions and most outstanding hitters who have been tested for this quality are found to react very quickly in comparison with ordinary players. The smoothness and effectiveness of a great infielder is dependent to a large extent on how quickly he can make the right choice and execute a play. Many double plays in baseball are dependent for their success on the saving of a fraction of a second.

Great basketball players seem to instinctively do the right thing and yet they must make judgments, change their minds, and execute several intricate movements all in a fraction of a second. Most basketball coaches and fans have seen, for example, a good player drive for the basket, start a lay-up shot with one hand, shift the ball to the opposite hand to avoid the defensive player's block, continue to carry the ball higher, sense that it would be stopped by a tall center guarding the basket, and at the last possible moment flip the ball to a teammate who is uncovered. In recent years it has become fairly common to see a player leap after a ball which has been passed by a teammate and is going out of bounds, grab the ball while in the air, and flick it against the legs of the opponent who is inbounds so that it bounces out and creates the opportunity for a planned play by his own team.

Champion sprinters win races and set world records by small fractions of seconds. Automatic timing devices and sophisticated equipment for photographing finishes have reduced the differences which can be measured and made it possible to record the time to within less than one hundredth of a second. The sprinter who can react to the sound of the starter's pistol slightly faster than his opponent has a considerable advantage. In a contest which may last less than ten seconds and where a yard is traversed in one-tenth of a second, reaction time becomes very significant.

Ball carriers in football are "running for daylight," "taking advantage of their blocks," reacting to the speed and number of tacklers bearing down on them, and zigzagging through a maze of teammates and tacklers, where choosing the right turn in a small fraction of a second may make the difference between victory and

The Power of a Sprinter

"In a contest where a yard is traversed in one-tenth of a second, reaction time becomes very significant." *By permission*, Richard Olson, Washington State University.

defeat. Similarly defensive men covering pass receivers must make the decision to react or not react to the many individual moves and false cues of their opponents in situations where half a step advantage may mean a touchdown or at least a completed pass.

Great badminton players must react and move with incredible rapidity as the shuttlecock flashes back and forth, up and down in close plays at the net. The volleying of a good doubles tennis team requires the same kind of quickness. The most successful volleyball teams seem unbelievably fast in their reactions as they field hard driven "spikes" and well placed returns. Handball, squash, and paddle-ball players have the same need for quick reactions and speedy movement.

It becomes clear that reaction time, movement time, and performance time are all involved in high-level sports performances. *Reaction time* is the time between the presentation of the stimulus and the initiation of the movement, *movement time* is what is required for the actual movement itself, and *performance time* is the sum of the two. "Response time" is an equivalent expression for performance time.

While there is some disagreement in the findings of investigators, it is apparent that there are many athletes who have very fast reactions but ordinary movement speed. There are also athletes with the opposite combination. And then there are those who have both very fast reaction time and great movement speed. Bresnahan, Tuttle, and Cretzmeyer claim that "a physiological analysis leads one to believe that both reflex time and reaction time are determining factors in running as well as in getting off the mark"[3].

Practically speaking, a coach in a sport where this is important would be fortunate to have a few athletes who could both react fast and move fast. Physical educators should be aware, however, that tests of reaction time do not always furnish the final answer, for there are many fine athletes who compensate for their ordinary reaction speed by great speed of movement.

The concern of most coaches and athletes is generally with "performance time" or "response time." They want to know how "to get the jump" on their opponent, how to change from offense to defense and defense to offense the most quickly, how to move to the left or right as fast as possible in order to field a ball, or how to react the most quickly to the movement of the opponent. The following are some generally accepted principles:

1. The stronger the stimulus is, the quicker will be the reaction. Other things being equal, brighter light, louder sounds, more painful pricks, stronger electric shocks (up to a point), sharper

commands, and more sudden and decisive movements, will cause faster reactions on the part of a responding human organism.

2. Both reaction time and movement time can be improved by practice, though only up to a given point. One cannot make a great sprinter or boxer out of a person who is not physically endowed to move that fast or explode that violently. Each individual, however, can improve his own reaction, movement, and performance times by diligent practice.

3. The more complex the movement is, the more numerous will be the choices which must be made in the selection of the reaction, the more components of the nervous system will be involved, and the longer the reaction time will be, but also the greater the possibilities of improvement will be. Such improvement will depend on reducing the number of cues necessary for eliciting the proper response, and automatizing the movements in response to specific combinations of stimuli.

4. The greater the readiness of the organism for response is, the faster will be the reaction time. Readiness in this instance is specific to the situation, the sport, and the particular performance required, and is related to attention and concentration. If the stimulus comes too early or too late, the response will not be so effective. Proper emotional arousal, the appropriate amount of anxiety, and the "peak of attention" will lead to the fastest reaction, movement, and performance.

7.3 SPEED AND ACCURACY

Speed is a magic word in sports. The person who can run faster, throw harder and more quickly, change direction more suddenly, stop more abruptly, and accelerate more rapidly than his opponent is likely to be a better athlete and win more contests. Coaches are constantly looking for speed and more speed. Professional scouts in most sports are especially concerned about this factor.

Accuracy is another important quality in high-level motor performance. To put the ball through the basket, to kick a soccer goal, to shoot an arrow into a bull's eye, to drive a tennis ball to an open corner, to consistently throw a baseball to within a few inches of the target—these and many other athletic feats all require a high degree of accuracy and the possession of accuracy of performance is characteristic of great athletes.

There has been, for a long time, considerable discussion about the relative importance of speed and accuracy when both are involved in the same skill. Questions are also asked as to which should be developed first and which should receive the greater emphasis as motor learning proceeds. Once again the individual circumstances need to be considered. In most sports the skilled athlete is able to move more quickly and precisely. The good shortstop must field and throw quickly, but his efforts are wasted unless he throws accurately. The speedy basketball player may move up and down the floor very rapidly, but if his passes are inaccurate and his shots miss the hoop, he is only a mediocre player. The tennis player who hits his serve with power and speed will lose more than he gains if he serves too many "doubles." In hockey the fast skater who has eluded the defense because of his speed does not achieve his objective if he cannot shoot the puck into the small unguarded part of the goal. Even the gymnast, who controls no ball or puck, is ineffective in his routines if he does not place his hands exactly where they need to be and move his entire body with precision and control.

With respect to the order of development, most good coaches today will work on both speed and accuracy simultaneously or as the level of performance is gradually raised. Much of what was said about the whole-part-whole and the "felt-need" methods of teaching is applicable here. When an athlete is performing with adequate or too much speed, emphasis must be placed on accuracy, at least temporarily. When performances are accurate but too slow, the effort must be toward faster movement. The speed at which an individual can move and accomplish the task with maximum effectiveness is the goal.

The author recalls experiences in coaching basketball when players would pass and shoot very accurately during fundamental drills but pass wildly and shoot poorly when scrimmages began. However, as more and more scrimmage became the order of the day and as the team embarked on its heavy schedule of games, the players gradually developed the ability to handle the ball under the pressures of competitive situations and shoot as well as or better than when they were in casual practice without opposition. Several fine basketball coaches have emphasized the importance of practicing under "game-like" conditions in order that accuracy might be attained when moving at appropriate speeds.

Speed and accuracy cannot be separated from other fundamentals when teaching sports. The correct stance of infielders and outfielders as the pitched ball crosses the plate enables them to start fast after the ball is hit. Proper balance and placement of weight makes possible the efficient, fast, smooth pivot in basketball or tennis. Practice on reacting to given situations increases the speed of perception. Passes to the exact spot where the ball may be easily handled will increase the speed of response on the part of a teammate in games such as soccer, water polo, and basketball. Increased experience reduces the reaction time in

wrestling and boxing. The development of power and coordination speeds up the movements of the shot-putter and hammer-thrower. Long hours spent diagnosing plays speed up the reactions and movements of the line backer in football. Correct placement of the center of gravity will provide a faster start for the sprinter. There are many kinds of speed and there are many kinds of accuracy. As a boy develops, as the beginner becomes the veteran, he perceives more accurately and readily, he makes fewer errors in both judgment and performance, he moves more precisely and swiftly, he accomplishes his objectives more efficiently and consistently, and thus he becomes a better and better athlete. Speed, accuracy, skill, and form have all been improved.

7.4 WARMING UP FOR ACTION

It is traditional to warm up before participating competitively in vigorous sports. Traditionally also three types of benefits have been attributed to the warm-up:

1. General preparation of the physiological organism for action. This includes the stretching of muscles and ligaments, increasing the heart rate and blood pressure, a mild rise in body temperature, and the facilitation of biochemical reactions. The reduction of muscle viscosity, the dilatation of vessels in the skeletal muscles, and the mobilization of the body's resources for action are also frequently mentioned.

2. Specific preparation of the body for the performance of a certain motor pattern. The pitching of a baseball, the clearing of hurdles, the punting of a football, the practice of a dive, going through the routine on a sidehorse, and the execution of intricate dance steps are examples. Peter Karpovich calls this *formal* warming up and indicates that it primarily affects the nervous system[13].

3. Mental preparation for a contest. As an individual punches a bag, takes a few practice starts, participates in infield practice, goes through a practice routine in gymnastics, or warms up by taking a few practice jumps, he is thinking about the coming competition, he is mentally rehearsing his movement patterns, and concentrating on the task before him. Not only is the nervous system affected, but also the endocrine glands and indirectly the many biological functions stimulated and controlled by the sympathetic nervous system.

Research evidence is not at all conclusive with regard to the beneficial effects of warm-up. Athletes and coaches, however, generally

feel that proper and appropriate warm-up is beneficial and necessary for peak performance. Participants feel more ready, tend to be more confident, and are more eager for the contest to begin when they are properly warmed up.

Warming up, however, is an individual matter. Some athletes become ready both mentally and physiologically with very little activity, while others feel the need to "break a sweat" before the contest begins. As a catcher, the author warmed up hundreds of pitchers in preparation for games. Some would start slowly and very gradually work up to game tempo. Others would declare their readiness after only a few pitches. The experience in professional baseball supports the idea of a thorough warm-up if the pitcher is to be at his best when he enters the game.

Whether it be merely a matter of tradition, or the admonitions of coaches and trainers, or something psychological, the vast majority of those with long and intense experiences in competitive sports agree that appropriate warm-up is desirable. Athletes who feel they are ready have more confidence, fewer apprehensions, and will tackle the task at hand with less hesitation and doubt than will those who fail to warm up as they have been instructed or as they feel is right for them. There is also considerable support from a scientific standpoint for proper warm-up before strenuous activity.

7.5 FATIGUE, LEARNING, AND PERFORMANCE

Fatigue may affect both learning and performance. The living organism is unique in that it can become tired and then has the ability to restore itself. Fatigue affects the total human organism, although the site of exhaustion from fatigue may be quite localized. A single finger can be "tired out" by exercising on the ergograph; the eyes can become fatigued from night driving in heavy traffic; the *quadriceps femoris* may tire from running the quarter mile; the pitcher's arm may become erratic and difficult to control from throwing too many balls. In a general way, the whole organism cries for sleep after a long day of labor; and athletic teams have been known to *go stale* after many games under taxing and unrewarding conditions.

Fatigue is generally accompanied by certain physiological mani-festations. Fatigue products accumulate in exercised muscles, and energy stores of the body tend to become depleted. Homeostasis is upset by a loss of water and salt. Glucose stores are reduced, and a lack of oxygen prevents the lactic acid formed from being reconverted into glycogen. An excess of metabolites including carbon dioxide and

phosphates accumulates, and changes in the physiochemical state of blood and lymph also accompany and contribute to fatigue.

Fatigue may be both physiological and psychological in nature. A decrease in the capacity for work, pain in the overworked muscles, a sensation of tiredness, sensitivity to criticism, impairment of judgment and reason, the loss of zest and eagerness, the lowering of powers of concentration, and the loss of energy, explosiveness, and drive are all symptoms and results of fatigue.

Staleness is one of the problems which often faces both athletes and coaches. It is inimical to both learning and performance. It usually comes after continued exertion under pressure and often is the result of intense and incessant efforts to excel and to win. The stale athlete has lost his vitality, is not refreshed by sleep, shows signs of irritability, and ceases to improve. This condition is akin to "combat fatigue" as experienced by many soldiers. Loss of appetite, worry, insomnia, and loss of weight can be both symptoms of and contributing factors to staleness. The entire routine of athletics becomes distasteful to a person who is stale.

The remedy for staleness is seldom more work. One must seek the causes and try to remove them. Complete rest, sound counsel, and understanding treatment may help. Laurence Morehouse and Philip Rasch have this to say:

Prevention of staleness is best accomplished, as mentioned before, by a balanced schedule of winning and losing. There are several means by which the coach combats staleness: planning team practice sessions to keep the season interesting; occasional unannounced layoffs or special events, or a team trip to a winter resort or the beach for a holiday weekend. Ingenuity in devising anti-staleness measures pays great dividends in releasing strain and pressure. The coach and the trainer devote constant attention to the development of the behavioral qualities which produce a spirited, hard-working team.[20]

The concepts of fatigue and staleness must be understood by coaches, trainers, teachers, and athletes. In some ways, principles of training and the phenomenon of staleness present a paradox. Hard and demanding work develops endurance and good condition. Good condition prevents fatigue and staleness. The human organism develops in response to the demands made upon it. And yet if these demands are too incessant, if the work is in response to a feeling of compulsion, if motivation is so high that it leads to a sense of failure if the top is not reached, the result may be staleness or, what is worse, a complete sense of frustration.

Practices must be demanding, yet rewarding. An athlete must work hard as he trains and conditions himself, and yet there must be some fun and joy in the effort. Ultimate rewards often come from long, arduous, and tedious practices. And yet if such workouts lead to staleness, they eliminate the reward itself, the feeling of achievement, the experience of victory.

The answer lies in the use of good judgment and common sense and in sound and moderate health habits. Overfatigue can be the result of excessive effort and an unrealistic appraisal of one's own ability. Rest and sleep have great restorative powers, but lose their value when apprehension and worry counteract their effects. Rest cannot be stored, at least beyond a point. Too much rest, when not needed, is debilitating. Rest to recuperate from work is developmental. The person who wishes to become the best athlete possible, within the limits of his potentiality, must balance exercise and practice with rest, must eat nourishing food in moderate amounts and must follow the precepts which lead to optimum health. He must also face realistically his own limitations and strive for excellence within those limitations.

7.6 PHYSIOLOGICAL AND PSYCHOLOGICAL LIMITS

It was not too long ago that the four-minute mile, the sixteen-foot pole-vault, and other marks and records in track and field were discussed as being beyond the capabilities of man. No miler seemed to be able to run the mile in less than four minutes, although a number of good runners came very close. This was termed by many a "psychological barrier." In other words, no one believed he could run the mile under four minutes. And then came Bannister, and Landy, and Bailey. They were soon followed by a number of others, and the four-minute barrier became a thing of the past. Dr. Roger Bannister said later, "The urge to struggle lies latent in everyone . . . no one can say, 'you must not run faster than this or jump higher than that.' The human spirit is undomitable."[30]

There may be real barriers or limitations to human performance, although records have continued to be broken over the years at a rather steady pace. If there are real limitations, however, they must be physical rather than psychological. It can be expected nevertheless that better athletes will be born as more great athletes intermarry. It is probable that a greater number of good performers will be discovered and developed as improved physical education and sports programs become available to more and more people throughout the world. Better equipment and better facilities will contribute to the breaking of current records. More effective techniques of performance are continually being found. Coaches are learning more about scientific teaching. Better food and more knowledge about nutrition are

The Loneliness of a Long-Distance Runner

"Ultimate rewards often come from long, arduous, and tedious practice." *By permission*, "Gerry" Lindgren, Washington State University.

contributing to the development of finer physical specimens. More and more is being learned about effectively motivating individuals for peak performance.

The 1968 Time-Life book, *The Olympic Games* contains performance charts (pp. 86-128) of the Olympic track and field, swimming, speed skating, and weight-lifting events beginning with the year 1896. The graphs portray a series of "ever-ascending performances, marked by one broken record after another."* Truly, the Olympic motto, *Citius, Altius, Fortius*, is being fulfilled year after year by athletes throughout the world.

Ernst and Peter Jokl, in their book, *The Physiological Basis of Athletic Records*, explain the patterns of evolution and the predictability of performance records:

We can, in fact, extrapolate human performance growth curves of various kinds, relate them to nutritional, epidemiological and other determinants, and thus arrive at reliable predictive forecasts of the effects of social and economic changes currently in progress in a given population. On the other hand, the capacity of man's brain to engender new motor patterns is unlimited. The motor act of man reflects his infinite creative potentialities.[12]

Bob Beaman's fabulous long jump in the 1968 Olympic Games illustrates how predicted marks are on rare occasions reached long before the anticipated time. An unusual coincidence of favorable circumstances, a fortuitous response, or the sudden emergence of a superathlete can account for this.

7.7 INTELLIGENCE, MOTOR ABILITY, AND ACHIEVEMENT

Acceptance of the concepts of biological integration and the interrelationships of all anatomical and physiological systems of the human organism would tend to support the conclusion that, other things being equal, intellectual processes will proceed more efficiently and effectively in an individual whose total body is healthy and when all parts are functioning normally. It seems especially logical that cortical functioning is dependent on all kinds of sensory input and that perception is dependent on accurate information provided by nervous impulses coming from the periphery. Intellectual processes, therefore, cannot proceed normally without an efficiently functioning perceptual apparatus.

The Olympic Games, Charles Osborne, editor. Time Life Books, Time Incorporated, 1968.

Research, however, is not very conclusive. A. H. Ismail and J. J. Gruber, in their book, *Integrated Development, Motor Aptitude and Intellectual Performance*, present a rather thorough review of pertinent literature and conclude that "relationships between intellectual performance and items measuring physical growth, strength, speed, and power were low"[11] as were the correlations between physical growth rate and mental growth rate. They did, however, conclude from their investigation that, while an organized physical education program has no effect on I.Q. scores, "it has a favorable effect on academic achievement scores"[11].

The United States Military Academy has continued to study the relationship of physical ability and physical fitness to academic success and the likelihood that cadets will graduate. A summary of results over a period of fifteen years reveals that those who score in the lower seven percent of the class on the physical aptitude test are less likely to graduate, more prone to academic failure, show fewer leadership qualities, and are generally poorer students than those who score higher[28]. Consideration must be given, however, to the strenuousness of the regimen at West Point and the exhausting nature of their programs.

Oxendine reviewed pertinent studies favoring a positive relationship between intelligence and motor proficiency and those showing no relationship, and then concluded:

Evidence concerning the relationship of general intelligence to motor learning is not consistent and, therefore, not entirely conclusive. Several studies report a low positive correlation, while others show no significant relationship. Almost no studies report a negative correlation between intelligence and the ability to learn skills. It seems reasonable to assume that, within the I Q ranges in most regular school situations, there is no more than a slight relationship between intelligence and the ability to learn the types of tasks reported in the literature.[21]

Marcia Hart and Clayton Shay, using partial correlational techniques, obtained a statistically significant but relatively low, correlation of 0.496 between the scores on the Physical Fitness Index and the cumulative grade point average of sixty sophomore women at Springfield College[9].

Robert Weber, in his study of 264 freshmen at the University of Iowa, reported a correlation of 0.41 between physical fitness scores and grade point averages[29].

It seems reasonable to conclude that a certain level of motor and organic functioning favors academic achievement and success in intellectual pursuits. It is questionable as to whether physical aptitude and conditioning beyond a certain level is of any value in the pursuit of intellectual excellence. It takes a degree of energy, vitality, determination, and drive to achieve in the competitive intellectual world as in the area of sports. The person who fatigues easily will, to a certain degree, be handicapped in his attempt to achieve his potential in all aspects of his life.

Perceptual development and organic health are necessary, especially during the first few years of life, if a child is to develop and grow and mature. The perceptually handicapped, the mentally retarded, and the subnormal are usually so in both their mental and their physical development. The energetic, active, adventurous, and healthy child will generally come closer to his potential in all aspects of his growth and maturation.

It seems probable, also, that the ability to balance and achieve fine coordinations may be more closely related to intellectual processes than the attributes of strength, height, and weight. A highly developed and sensitive nervous system, a fully functioning perceptual apparatus, and a cortex in which associations and motor patterns are laid down at a fairly early age are necessary to thinking, reasoning, balancing, and to finely coordinated movement patterns.

It should also be noted that, while research is not conclusive in supporting relationships between the mental and the physical, there are some positive correlations and some corelations that are very low or even insignificant. There are few, however which report a negative correlation. It appears, therefore, that there is an urgent need for extended research efforts in this area so that education can proceed on a more defensible scientific basis.

REFERENCES

1. Arnold, P. J., *Education, Physical Education, and Personality Development.* New York: Atherton Press, 1968

2. Asmussen, Erling, and K. Heeboll Nielsen, "Physical performance and growth," *Journal of Applied Physiology*, Vol. 8, 1956, pp. 371-380

3. Bresnahan, George T., W. T. Tuttle, and Francis X. Cretzmeyer, *Track and Field Athletics.* St. Louis: C. V. Mosby, 1968, p. 472

4. Clarke, H. Harrison, "Relation of physical structure to motor performance of males," *American Academy of Physical Education, Professional Contributions No. 6*, American Association for Health, Physical Education, and Recreation, National Education Association, 1958

5. Cratty, Bryant J., *Psychology and Physical Activity*. Englewood Cliffs, N.J.: Prentice-Hall, 1968

6. Cratty, Bryant J., *Movement Behavior and Motor Learning*. Philadelphia: Lea and Febiger, 1967

7. Grandjean, E., "Fatigue: its physiological and psychological significance," *Ergonomics*, Ergonomics Research Society, Vol. 11, No. 5, 1968, pp. 427-436

8. Griffith, Coleman, *Psychology and Athletics*. New York: Scribner, 1928

9. Hart, Marcia, and Clayton T. Shay, "Relationship between physical fitness and academic success," *Research Quarterly*, Vol. 35, 1964, pp. 444-445

10. Henry, Franklin M., "Independence of reaction and movement times and equivalence of sensory motivations of faster response," *Research Quarterly*, Vol. 23, 1952, pp. 43-53

11. Ismail, A. H., and J. J. Gruber, *Motor Aptitude and Intellectual Performance*. Columbus, Ohio: Merrill Books, 1967, pp. 33, 190

12. Jokl, Ernst, and Peter Jokl, *The Physiological Basis of Athletic Records*. Springfield, Ill.: Charles C. Thomas, 1968, p. 118

13. Karpovich, Peter V., *Physiology of Muscular Activity*. Philadelphia: W. B. Saunders, 1965, p. 12

14. Klafs, Carl E., and Daniel D. Arnheim, *Modern Principles of Athletic Training*. St. Louis: C. V. Mosby, 1963

15. Lawther, John D., *The Learning of Physical Skills*. Englewood Cliffs, N.J.: Prentice-Hall, 1968

16. Lawther, John D., "Motor learning at the high skill level," *Psicologia Dello Sport, Proceedings of the First International Congress on Sport Psychology*, Ferrucio Antonelli, editor, Rome, 1965

17. Leathers, Roger K., "A study of the relationships between physical performance and academic achievement of Springfield College Students," unpublished Doctoral Dissertation, Springfield College, 1967

18. Michael, Ernest D., Jr., and Steven M. Horvath, "Psychological limits in athletic training," *Psicologia Dello Sport, Proceedings of the First International Congress of Sport Psychology*, Ferrucio Antonelli, editor, Rome, 1965, pp. 77-78

19. Morehouse, Laurence E., and Augustus T. Miller, *Physiology of Exercise*. St. Louis: C. V. Mosby, 1959

20. Morehouse, Laurence E., and Philip J. Rasch, *Scientific Basis of Athletic Training*. Philadelphia: W. B. Saunders, 1958, p. 47

21. Oxendine, Joseph B., *Psychology of Motor Learning*. New York: Appleton-Century-Crofts, 1968, pp. 275-276

22. Prokop, Ludwig, "Adrenals and sport," *Journal of Sports Medicine and Physical Fitness*, Minerva Medica, Torino, Italy, No. 2-3, 1963, p. 121

23. Riedman, Sarah R., *The Physiology of Work and Play*. New York: Dryden Press, 1950

24. Seils, Leroy G., "The relationship between measures of physical growth and gross motor performance of primary-grade school children," *Research Quarterly*, Vol. 22, 1951, pp. 244-260

25. Singer, Robert N., *Motor Learning and Human Performance*. New York: Macmillan, 1968, p. 52

26. Slusher, Howard S., "Personality and intelligence characteristics of selected high school athletes and non-athletes," *Research Quarterly*, Vol. 35, No. 4, 1964, pp. 539-545

27. Tanner, J. M., *The Physique of the Olympic Athlete*. London: Allen and Unwin, 1964

28. "A fifteen year summary of the application of physical aptitude examinations for selection of West Point cadets," unpublished study, United States Military Academy, 1968

29. Weber, Robert, "Relationship of physical fitness to success in college and to personality," *Research Quarterly*, Vol. 24, 1953, p. 473

30. Bannister, Roger, *Sports Illustrated*, Vol. 5, No. 14, October 1, 1956

8 SOCIO-PSYCHOLOGICAL PHENOMENA

*A panorama of the ever changing, and yet
recurringly familiar pattern of man's participation in sports presents a fascinating field for
cultural research.*

Florence Stumpf Frederickson[32]

8.1 SOCIO-CULTURAL FORCES AND SPORTS

There are those who will argue that socio-economic status is an
important factor in sports success. Much has been written about the
"values" accruing from participation in physical education and particularly sports. Comparisons between men and women with regard to
their interest in athletics and their sports prowess fill many pages. The
relative benefits derived from competitive and cooperative endeavors
have been studied by psychologists and sociologists alike. Many
investigators have dealt with social interaction through sport, behavioral
characteristics of great athletes, and the influence of cultural environment and family background on participants. Amateurism and professionalism, affluence and leisure, social and philosophical foundations,
politics and internationalism have all been studied, in one way or
another, by those who have striven to understand the socio-psychologi-
cal phenomena involved in the fascinating and complex world of sports.
Crime and greed have not gone unmentioned, since contestants,
coaches, and administrators have occasionally fallen prey to the lust for
glory and an insatiable need to win.

Sport is an important ingredient in a democratic society. Sports
serve as a focal point for common loyalties and enthusiasms. The
sharing of victories and defeats, successes and failures, is a democ-
ratizing influence and fosters better understanding between both
individual participants and supporting groups.

Sport and culture are very much interrelated. A study of a nation's
physical education programs usually reveals something of its philosophy

157

and its political and international policies. It also tells much about the modes of life, the thoughts and value systems of its people. The cultural heritage, ethnic background, and the customs which are part of the early life of every person affect his choice of physical activity and his attitude toward it. Geographical and climatic conditions play a major role in determining the sports interests of a given community.

Peter McIntosh, in his *Sport in Society*, discusses this topic in historical perspective. The influence of the "Olympic ideal" on people both in ancient and modern times, the lessening of emphasis on sports during the Dark Ages, and the growth of certain forms of physical education and sports during the age of chivalry are pointed out and related to the culture and the politics of the times. Puritanism and its effect on sport, the emancipation of women and the subsequent increase in their sports participation, the philosophy of play as described by Huizinga, and the relationship of poverty and affluence to the development of sport are all included in his treatment. Amateurism and professionalism, urban life and leisure, politics and internationalism are related to the rise and fall, the growth and expansion, the organization and influence of sport [35]. One cannot read this book without becoming very much aware of the intertwining relationships of sport and the culture of man.

While it is not possible in this volume to deal in depth with the sociological phenomena, it is important that those studying the psychological concepts as they apply to the area of physical education and coaching be at least aware that cultural and social forces are operating constantly and that a minimal understanding of these is necessary in any attempt to unravel the many factors causing and revealing behavior and its changes.

8.2 COMPETITION AND
COOPERATION IN PHYSICAL ACTIVITIES

There is considerable disagreement in educational circles with respect to the appropriate roles of cooperation and competition. Certain individuals feel that all experiences should be of a nature that would lead to the development of more cooperative persons and a saner and happier society. They frown upon activities which are competitive in nature, for such activities, they say, may lead to tensions and various kinds of conflict. Others feel that competition in life is inevitable and that the educative process should assist with the preparation of individuals for the "battle of life." These people are usually enthusiastic about the use of competitive techniques as motivational devices which can serve as a stimulus to hard work and study. They are frequently strong supporters of highly competitive athletic programs.

The relative value of cooperation and competition as motivating factors and their effects on the physical and emotional health of the participants have been investigated by many people. The effectiveness of workers in team situations and the relationship of culture to both cooperation and competition also appear to be worthy of more detailed analysis.

Leslie Malpass, speaking a few years ago at the National Conference on Values in Sports, indicated a strong relationship between competition and cooperation:

Competition and cooperation are sometimes treated as antithetical. Although they do represent different forms of behavior, competition is dependent on cooperation. Competition in team sports requires in-group cooperation for maximum team effort. It also requires cooperation in setting rules and thus prescribing ways to permit equal means to victory for opponents. Obviously, rules can be read differently: some coaches read rules so they can beat their rivals; some are more interested in beating their opponents by beating the rules.

Inter-group competition usually encourages within-group cooperation. Few teams function optimally against an equitable opponent if there is dissension among team members. The ability to discourage within-group dissension is a mark of successful coaches. In sports, it is not enough to have individuals with great talent; the talent must be organized so that cooperation can serve competition. It is better that energies be expended against others in competition than in conflict within the group.[33]

There is no doubt that both competition and cooperation are very much a part of our culture and our national life. They are also important factors in the schools of today. The degree to which competition is emphasized and cooperation is encouraged has much to do with the climate in which learning takes place and development proceeds. It is generally agreed that when group or team achievement is the goal, in-group competitiveness can act as a hindrance, whereas when individual excellence is the aim, competition is often the spur that is needed for peak performance. Care, however, must be exercised so that "self-elevation" does not become the only goal of individuals trying to achieve success in our competitive society. There are many manifestations, from birth onward, of the competitive urge. It is essentially a self-centered need and it often develops disproportionately as compared to the desire to cooperate. Good judgment is necessary on the part of teachers, parents, and coaches to see that the encouragement to compete is balanced by an emphasis on cooperation and the subjugation of self for the good of the group. Focusing on the goals and the objectives rather than on individual performance will usually lead to a better working climate and the greatest productivity.

Individuals can compete against their opponents, against established norms, against nature, against their previous record, or against a group. While any kind of a challenge tends to stimulate a person who is competitive by nature, the greatest achievements have usually come about when members of a highly motivated group are united in a common cause. Heights of emotional stimulation are usually reached when teammates realize that they share a common goal and that victory is more readily attainable when individual objectives are sublimated to the aims of the total group.

Because athletes are by nature competitive, coaches often employ the tactic of challenging individual players, especially when they are in one way or another paired against an opponent. A basketball player is challenged to "hold" a high scorer to a given number of points, a football player is told to "outcharge" a good opposing lineman, a wrestler is enjoined to "dominate" his opponent, a quarter-miler is instructed to concentrate on beating a favored runner, and a batter is told that he is "doing battle" with the pitcher. It is held by many that this kind of prodding, too, is preparation for life, for executives must compete with each other across the conference table, statesmen are vying with diplomats from other countries, labor and management are in competition in many of their meetings, and people in all walks of life are often forced to struggle with other people, with nature, and with circumstances. Competition is, and will be for many years to come, an essential element in our culture.

The Swedish writer, Erik Westergren, summarizes some of his thoughts on this matter in the following words:

The cohesiveness of a group is a function of the ability of the group to satisfy the need of the individual members. There will be a close cooperation in groups where

Triple Balance
"The greatest achievements have usually come about when members of a highly motivated group are united in a common cause." *By permission*, Ron Grant, Bob Fletcher, and Stan Zalenski, Springfield College.

there are friendly relations between the members. These friendly relations and this cohesiveness of the group are perceived as pleasant and act (sic) as a motivation to join the group and stay there. In this fact we have to look for some of the motivation for taking part in recreative as well as competitive P. T. When it is the question of competitive P. T.-groups, the motivation of the members will of course—at least partly—be different, as I have already stated. Membership in some competitive groups, especially those which have very few members and high requirements for membership, gives to the individual member high prestige. This desire for prestige and status functions as a very strong motive for taking part in groups, which work with P. T.[52]

Competition and cooperation are both important ingredients of sports just as they are in most societies today. They operate together in great achievements and in athletic victories. They can both exist at the same time and within the same group. They are not necessarily antithetical, although they may often appear that way. A single individual may be both cooperative and competitive by nature. The circumstances, the nature of the groups, and the goals to be achieved will determine the right "mix" for success.

8.3 SOCIO-ECONOMIC STATUS AND ATHLETICS

An individual's socio-economic status may influence his opportunity for participation, his desire to excel, his choice of activity, and his success. A student's athletic prowess may enhance his social prestige and acceptance by his peers. The home environment often influences his motivation to succeed in sports and the degree to which success in this endeavor leads to inner satisfaction.

Young people growing up in poverty-ridden communities will have fewer available tennis courts, backyard swimming pools, and golf courses. They will have more difficulty finding means of travel to beaches, ski areas, and lake regions. They will usually be able to afford fewer fishing trips, mountain vacations, and bowling nights. Horseback riding, water-skiing, and golf will be too expensive in both time and money for most of them.

On the other hand, many of the greatest football and basketball players, boxers, and track and field athletes have come from the ghettos. When large numbers of children of all ages live in crowded quarters they are forced out of doors to play with each other. They compete and interact in both organized and unorganized play. They wrestle and fight and romp and chase. They learn to stand up for their rights and to accept hurts without whimpering. They often find in sports both an outlet for aggression and a way of satisfying their desires to achieve.

Children who grow up in middle-class homes in the United States are usually fortunate enough to have good facilities for physical education, an adequate number of qualified coaches, and considerable assistance and encouragement from their parents. Community recreation programs and school physical education and athletic programs usually complement each other. Opportunities for the early development of sports skills are normally present and motivation is reasonably high.

Children from wealthy homes often have tennis courts and swimming pools in their backyard and travel to ocean beaches or island retreats for vacations. They also have money, equipment, and transportation to go to ski lodges, golf courses, and expensive summer camps.

While young people are growing up and associating with their peers in many kinds of endeavors, they soon are able to recognize those who are especially able and those who have difficulty achieving. Outstanding ability to perform has been found to be the single factor that correlates most highly with peer esteem and with popularity. Jokl and Jokl, in reviewing the work of Ferenc Bakonyi, summarize it in these words:

The best athletes and the best scholars had the most personal friends, were most frequently chosen as members of a team, and most often considered worthy of sharing secrets.

Bakonyi pointed out that the conspicuous popularity of the best athletes and of the best scholars suggests that these two groups possess a common feature which renders them attractive to the group. This common feature, he says, is *excellence of performance*, irrespective of its nature. Children of the age range under study desire to establish their prestige in order to give expression to their emerging personality. They evaluate their classmates in accordance with the same criteria.

As focal point of sociometric validation, *athletic* excellence exerts a somewhat greater attraction than scholastic achievement; while the athletically least competent children are the loneliest of all. The results of Bakonyi's analyses were identical for boys and for girls.[24]

Social status and economic status are not synonymous, and yet those who come from poor families generally feel a greater need for status and for acceptance by their peers. When those who have money have already achieved these objectives to a satisfactory degree, they may not attach the same degree of importance to becoming a great athlete that their poorer schoolmates do. There are, of course, many ways of achieving both peer-esteem and the ego-satisfaction that is necessary for a well adjusted and balanced life. Some young people become honor students; others may be elected to important offices; and a number will participate successfully in dramatics, music, art, debate, or journalism. Each person will, in his own way satisfy his need to achieve and be recognized.

It seems reasonable, therefore, to give some credence to the theory that children from homes in the lower socio-economic brackets tend to participate more often and more successfully in football, soccer, basketball, and other combative sports, while those from wealthy homes are more apt to be found in tennis, golf, riding, swimming, skiiing, and similar sports.

Cratty believes that the middle-class individual will generally be the most competitive in the widest variety of situations. The lower-class persons will tend to feel that the odds are stacked against them, while the upper-class individual will feel that his position is secure regardless of performance. It is therefore not realistic to expect the same level of competitive behavior from different segments of society [15].

We must conclude, therefore, that family environment and socio-economic status do influence both the opportunities for, and the psychological attitudes toward, sports as individuals move through childhood, adolescence, and young adulthood. Not everyone who has great innate athletic potential is motivated to the same degree or in the same direction. Not everyone comes equally close to reaching his maximum capabilities.

8.4 RACE AND ATHLETIC ACHIEVEMENT

From time to time a given sport has appeared to be dominated by individuals of a specific race. This fact has given rise to claims that the Finns are great distance-runners, the Japanese are outstanding javelin throwers, the Norwegians excel in skiing, the negroes are tremendous jumpers, and many similar contentions. Anatomical and physiological evaluations have been made, and various theories to explain these phenomena have been propounded.

It is obvious that in the United States during the past decade or two the black athletes have been unusually successful in the world of sport. Basketball, baseball, boxing, football, and track and field are sports in which negroes regularly perform the greatest athletic feats and play starring roles. The number of black athletes participating and excelling in these sports far exceeds what would normally be expected in terms of their numbers in the total population.

Several years ago Carl Rowan, himself a black and a fine newspaper columnist, wrote a series of syndicated articles entitled "The Negro Athlete." He cited many instances of the phenomenal success they had achieved in basketball, baseball, football, boxing, and track and field. He discussed the performances of Jesse Owens in the 1936 Olympic Games and pointed out his anthropometric measurements; he also told of the exploits of Chubei Nambu, a short-limbed Japanese who leaped 26 feet, 2 1/8 inches; he reviewed studies which sought to account for the differences in performance of the various races; and he reported interviews with great black athletes. Opinions of anthropologists, physiologists, and psychologists were sought and summarized.

Rowan concluded that physical characteristics could not and did not account for the disproportionate number of black athletes who were successful. The desire to succeed in the white world, the tendency to follow successful examples, the expression of pent-up aggression, the pressure to make good, desire and more desire, the thing called "soul-force"—these were the factors mentioned by great black athletes. These were the items emphasized by Rowan [41].

Various theories with regard to the relationship between success in sports and ethnic background have been suggested. The earlier maturation of certain racial groups is frequently mentioned. Greater permissiveness and the encouragement of free expression in homes and schools have been said to account in part for the acceleration in skill learning. Encouragement by knowledgeable and enthusiastic parents and the stimulation of dedicated and determined coaches have been cited by many great athletes as the secret of their success. Hereditary characteristics and native abilities may be the most important of all. It seems that the safest conclusion is that there may well be genetic traits which give certain ethnic groups an advantage. It is also reasonable to assume that an individual's environment, at home, in school, in the community, and while traveling will also affect his final development and achievement. Much research needs to be done before definite conclusions can be reached concerning the exact effect of the many variables involved.

8.5 WOMEN IN PHYSICAL EDUCATION AND SPORTS

The role which women are expected to play in society differs greatly from country to country and, in the United States, even from one community to another. The traditional image of the tender, loving woman who bears children, tends home, and nurtures life rather than destroying it has changed considerably in the United States during the past quarter century. Women have in may ways been emancipated. Many women now share the responsibilites for making a living and for community involvement. They teach in schools, work in offices, hold jobs in factories, carry on welfare duties, and assist in many other capacities.

Research and study do not bear out long-held fears with regard to the anatomical and physiological weaknesses in women. There are obviously some biological differences between the female and the male, but these indicate a need for a slightly different selection of activities for the two sexes, and not the deletion of exercise for women.

Biological characteristics which distinguish women from men include a greater femoral angle, a relatively broader pelvic girdle, a wider knee joint, less bony mass, shorter legs relative to the trunk, a smaller breathing capacity, a lower metabolic rate, and a faster pulse rate. Men in general are taller, more muscular, rougher, and are able to achieve slightly more than women in most sports. All of these differences are relative, however, and cannot be applied indiscriminately to all individuals. Obviously menstruation and pregnancy will affect the ability of women to perform at given periods in their lives.

Clayton Thomas, in his paper entitled "Effect of Vigorous Activity on Women," summarizes more than a dozen studies dealing with exercise and sports as they affect health and as they relate to performance. He concludes that, on the basis of present evidence, healthy women will not be damaged by participation in strenuous sports. The internal organs of the female are quite well protected and will not be harmed by jumping and running. Thomas further believes that we should actively concern ourselves with fitness for all women and that intensive research is needed to provide more definite answers. He does include this significant statement:

Biologically, women experience a cycle which greatly influences their total lives. These hormonal phenomena cause menstruation and permit the potential for child bearing. It is generally conceded that hormones in the male have no similar cyclic activity.[50]

Most of the values we attribute to a program of physical education are as important to women as to men: the need to move gracefully, effectively, and efficiently; the necessity to develop a reasonable amount of strength and endurance; the desirability of being able to participate in lifetime sports; the opportunity to play and interact with others. Women also need good health, mental relaxation, fun and joy, and the opportunity to express themselves.

It seems reasonable, however, that, in view of the slightly different objectives that women may have in life, the activities they are likely to choose may be somewhat different from those of men. A few sports such as boxing, wrestling, football, and weight-lifting traditionally are not considered appropriate for women. Others such as dancing, free movement, and synchronized swimming are generally thought of as being particularly fitting for women's programs. Movement experiences which are expressive and creative are popular as are suppling, stretching, and balancing exercises.

One need only apply the motivational principles described in an earlier chapter to determine which activities should be included in the programs for women. Those which make a contribution to the survival of the race, the security of the individual, the need for belonging, the esteem of superiors, and the desire for self-fulfillment should be selected. In many instances they will be the same for both men and women.

8.6 COMPETITION FOR THE YOUNG

The kinds and amount of competitive activity to which children and adolescents should be exposed have been, and will no doubt continue to be, the subject of considerable controversy for generations to come. That competitive activities are a psycho-social phenomenon of considerable consequence there is no doubt. In most primitive cultures all males were taught to wrestle and joust and fight as part of their early education. Today we do not think it appropriate to plan physical education programs in terms of preparation for war. Instead, we think of education as preparation for life and self-realization.

There is general agreement that children need vigorous activity for optimum development and growth and that competition stimulates participation. There is considerable disagreement as to whether the values and benefits are great enough and important enough to outweigh the hazards of injury and emotional damage. Most authoritative statements by individuals and groups have concluded that there are real social, psychological, and physical benefits to be derived from, and moral and spiritual values to be developed through, competitive activity, but there must also be rules, regulations, and administrative policies to govern such activity. Careful matching of players, the observing of safety practices, regular medical examinations, good officiating, and sound parental involvement are prerequisites to a good program.

It is with the social and psychological concomitants that we are particularly concerned in this volume. During the growing years of a child the need for belonging, adventure, the expression of emotional impulses, the approval of peers, and identification with a man or woman other than parents is very evident. The child of elementary school age also often feels the need for someone who can sympathize with him, answer questions, and assist in the solution of his problems. The younger player must be treated with greater care than his older counterpart. In this connection, the words of Henry Coppolillo are worthy of note:

The grade school child is much more vulnerable to derision than his older high school brothers. Frequently with older boys derision is used to incite desire and drive. I would strongly recommend against this with grade school youngsters. Lowered self-esteem is corrosive for them. If discipline is necessary, a swat on his posterior parts is tolerated better, by far, by the youngster than derision.[12]

Fred L. Allman calls attention to the matter of "self-image" and relates this to success and failure. He says:

Some people have failure images while others have successful images. Those with failure images see failure as being final, while those with winning images see failure only as another step which has gained them experience that will help to achieve ultimate success. Too many failures, especially at a young age, tend to lower an athlete's level of aspiration. Reward usually has a greater motivation effect in improving performance than punishment, although in some cases punishment produces the greater effect.[1]

It is important, while we seek to identify benefits and values which may accrue through participation in sports, that we also remain alert to both the physical and emotional damage which may result from such experiences. When the amateur coach who knows little or nothing about growth and development imposes too rigid a regimen on young children, when inappropriate penalties are applied for mistakes, when small failures are enlarged to undue proportions, when coaches treat pre-adolescents as adults in every respect, the boy or girl may suffer damages to both mental health and physical health. There should not be too frequent or excessively deep disappointments, and children must not be made to feel frustrated. It is evident, as one observes youngsters at play, that many of them have the same drives, urges, and needs as their peers, and yet, on account of insufficient size, skill, strength, and experience, some of them cannot succeed either in the competition to "make a team" or in the highly competitive games and contests which ensue when leagues are organized and records kept. For these young-sters sound counseling and a sympathetic ear are absolutely necessary.

Athletic competition at an early age can be beneficial when parents are knowledgeable, understanding, and reasonable, when coaches are men of integrity and place the welfare of the individual participant higher than victory or fame, when sound educational and health practices are observed, and when programs are administered with the children's welfare foremost in the minds of all concerned. Such competition can be developmental, educational, enjoyable, and lead to self-fulfillment. It should be the goal of all who work with young people in competitive sports programs to make the competitions bear these fruits.

8.7 PERSONALITY TRAITS AND ATHLETIC PARTICIPATION

Are great athletes born or are they made? Is it possible to identify personality traits which characterize the outstanding performer in sports? Can individuals with mediocre natural talent become champions? What are the psychological characteristics for which a coach should be alert in the selection of a squad or team? Can attributes such as determination, courage, unselfishness, perseverance, and poise be developed or are they genetically acquired? These and similar questions are being asked by coaches, counselors, teachers, parents, sports writers, and fans. The answers are complex and often elusive.

There is considerable evidence that athletes tend to be dominant, energetic, and tough. Especially during adolescence and in their "teens", they are usually popular and often selected as leaders. Physical prowess is less of a factor in the popularity and prestige of girls and women and tends to diminish in importance at an earlier age for them than for men. Great athletes tend to have a tremendous need to achieve, are willing to work hard to excel, and in most cases enjoy competition.

Perhaps the most extensive research into the personality of athletes is that which was done by Bruce Ogilvie, Thomas Tutko, and their assistants at San Jose State College. Several thousand athletes were tested and studied in their investigations. In their paper, presented before the meetings of the North American Society for Psychology of Sports and Physical Activity in 1967, they tentatively identified the need for achievement, a high degree of dominance, endurance, ability to maintain poise, a willingness to learn, self-assertiveness, the ability to bear pain, and leadership qualities as being related to a high degree of success in sport[38].

J. E. Kane's studies have also contributed much to our understanding of the personality of athletes. In a paper presented in Rome a few years ago, he said,

There is now available an increasing amount of accurate evidence to relate general athletic ability with dimensions of personality. This relationship may be recognized among those of school age as well as among the more mature outstanding athletes. Personality ratings or traits of "aggression," "dominance," "persistence," "drive," "confidence" and general extroversion have been found to go most often with success in athletics skills. Some suggestions have been made recently however, that the outstanding athlete does not subscribe to the stereotyped description of him as an "easy-going" sociable individual without anxieties or inner urgencies.[25]

Kane concludes that both men and women athletes are highly surgent and extroverted. The men also tend to be tough-minded. Men and women have, he says, similar personality profiles, but the men tend to be more dominant, confident, and composed[25].

Arthur Steinhaus, in his summary of the conference on Exercise and Fitness in 1959, writes:

Whether fitness induces change in the psyche or the psyche change in the fitness, or whether both are due to a common force behind both will no doubt also become clear with time. Presently it appears that athletic ability is found in association with greater ego strength, dominance, relative freedom from anxiety, outgoingness, below average guilt proneness, extroversion, self-sufficiency, and little of that which is ascribable to an overprotective home environment.[48]

Charles Cowell and A. H. Ismail indicate that boys who do well on physical ability tests are "likely to have leadership potentialities, be accepted at close personal distance by their associates, and to be well adjusted socially"[14]. Jack Schendel's comments[43] substantiate these findings for ninth-grade athletes, but he finds that college students are somewhat different. College nonathletes tended to have greater tolerance for, and interest in, the needs of others, greater intellectual efficiency, more feminine interests and more status.

F. J. Ryan compares the "good competitor" with the "poor competitor" in track and field. Reviewing responses from fifty-seven coaches, he finds that the athlete who tends to perform better in competition than in practice is a hard worker, is constantly shooting for the next meet, blames himself rather than conditions for poor performances, and is generally friendly, happy, and rational. This athlete follows coaching instructions, learns easily, and is consistent in his performances[42]. Although Ryan's findings are statistically significant, there are nevertheless numerous exceptions to characteristic behavior on the part of both good and poor competitors.

The author inquired of most of his interviewees whether or not they could characterize the great athlete, the champion, the Olympian. The general opinion seemed to be that the behavioral traits of athletes, as of other human beings, tend to distribute themselves quite normally and that athletes cannot be stereotyped on that basis. Most coaches did agree, however, that the truly great athletes exhibit certain traits quite consistently. Coaches tended to feel that great performers possess a greater need to achieve, a greater dissatisfaction with mediocrity, a greater desire for excellence, and a willingness to pay the price for success. The ability to endure pain was mentioned by several, the love of competition by a few, and the ability to give that "something extra" in both practice and competition by still others. Almost all of the interviewees indicated that Olympians and other great champions must (1) have great natural ability, (2) be willing to work long and hard, and (3) possess most of the psychological traits just mentioned. Reference was also frequently made to the classical traits of courage, poise, endurance, and determination.

Care must of course be taken not to infer "cause and effect" relationships between participation in sport and specific personality traits. It is both possible and probable that individuals who have early success experiences through sports tend to participate more frequently and thereby become more skillful than some of their peers. The confidence gained by such accomplishments will often manifest itself in courage and poise. It is also possible that the determined, persevering individual will be more successful in sports than his peer who is born with less of these characteristics. On the other hand, games which challenge and situations which include risks and hazards may well bring out and develop innate character traits such as daring, cooperativeness, competitiveness, and coolness in the face of danger. In any event, the opportunity to test oneself and to call upon hidden resources can produce behavioral changes which are part of education. In that sense, the traits mentioned above may well be developed through participation in athletics.

The study of personality traits and their relationship to sports can assist the coach and teacher in the selection of players, in the guidance of those who seek help in choosing a sport, in teaching effectively, and in understanding the behavior of those who come under their leadership. The importance of these matters warrants an increasing emphasis on research and informal observation on the part of all concerned.

8.8 LEADERSHIP AND SUCCESS IN SPORT

Henri Peyre, in his treatise on "Excellence and Leadership," said:

There are at least three subjects . . . on which no wise man should ever attempt to write: love, genius, and leadership. Of the three, the last is the most mysterious and the most unpredictably and capriciously feminine.[20]

Daring, Strength, and Symmetry

"The opportunity to test oneself . . . can produce behavioral changes which are part of education." *By permission*, Ronald Grant, Springfield College.

Perhaps he said what he did because there are so many kinds of people who have become successful leaders or because there is such a great variety of tasks to be accomplished, or because there are so many divergent views of the methods by which it is believed people should lead. It may well be that a given task, a specific group of people, a certain set of circumstances each requires a special brand of leadership if the mission is to be successful.

While we are discussing leadership as it pertains to physical education and coaching, we may be thinking of a great coach of football, a dedicated teacher of swimming, a meticulous director of a research project, or an inspiring teacher of philosophy. Each of these may be a unique personality, with peculiar individual characteristics, methods, and philosophy of leadership. Nevertheless, they also share a number of common qualities. Let us see if we can delineate a few:

1. A great leader must have vision. He must be able to see a little farther ahead, a little more clearly than those who follow. He must chart the course, point the direction, and usually lead the way.

2. The leader must have energy, strength, and endurance. He who tires easily is seldom able to direct groups to a successful conclusion of a difficult project.

3. He must be courageous physically, intellectually, and spiritually. The final responsibility for difficult decisions will usually be his to make. The right decision may not be the popular one. Any semblance of hesitation due to fear, any cringing from physical or mental discomfort, any sign of domination by another will be noted by those who follow and will affect both the outcome of the effort and his acceptance by the group as the leader.

4. He must be determined and persevering. The final outcome of any contest, the result of a conference, the achievement of a goal are often determined by the degree to which the leader is willing to stop the argument, to accept the inevitability of defeat, to give serious consideration to retreat.

5. The effective leader must be able to communicate. Communication may occur through the spoken word, the touch of a hand, the pat on the back, the facial expression and physical gesture, or the unspoken message that flashes from one to another. The leader will be followed only where such communication exists.

6. Good leaders are sensitive to the thoughts and feelings of the members of the group. This does not always imply the expression of inordinate sympathy or basing decisions on group consensus. It

does imply careful consideration of the thoughts, the sentiments, and the concerns of those being led. Decisions must be made in the light of available information, the mission to be performed, and the circumstances of the moment.

7. The leader must be just. Unfavorable decisions and penalties will usually be accepted with good grace where the leader is known to be impartial and fair. Playing favorites is a sure road to unpopularity and defeat.

8. The great leader is a good teacher. Sometimes the teaching is subtle and indirect. In other instances it is direct and forceful. The objectives and the goals as well as the means by which they are to be achieved must be taught clearly and incisively, leaving no doubt in the minds of the learner as to what is expected.

9. A leader, to be successful, must be able to instill confidence. This ability may come as a result of experience, it may be related to a deep knowledge of what is being taught, it may be related to courage, it may be a demeanor, a quality of voice, or a combination of all of these. Very probably it will be related to successful experiences previously shared by those involved.

10. The leader can remain a leader only if he is concerned about each member of the group as an individual. He must not only be sensitive to their physical welfare and needs but he must assist each one to develop a sense of his own worth and a realization of the importance of his contribution to the group effort.

Perhaps as important to effective leadership as any personal characteristic is the willingness to accept responsibility and to carry out the requirements of that responsibility. Evaluating class members and giving them grades, selecting team members and making substitutions, rating subordinate faculty members and recommending them for promotion, releasing unsatisfactory performers—these are all part of a leader's responsibility. Some of these tasks are unpleasant, and for this reason there are many potential leaders who are unwilling to assume the role. Some form of evaluative activity, decision-making, and forceful action is an inescapable part of any leadership post.

Traditionally adult leadership is classified into authoritarian, democratic, and laissez-faire leaderships. We now discuss such matters as the group process, participatory democracy, student-centered classes, and informal methods of leadership. In some situations the teacher or leader serves only as a guide, a consultant, or an advisor. Circumstances will often require some degree of formality of procedure and some measure of authoritarian leadership. Many good leaders can adjust their procedures and attitudes to the situation. In emergency situations where speed of action is at a premium, group discussion and indecision obviously cannot be tolerated for too long. In small, closely knit groups, and in situations where time is not of the essence, informality which engenders a feeling of camaraderie may be the most effective. Also, teaching can often be most effectively done by the problem-solving method. Personal problems and morale problems are sometimes best solved in an informal atmosphere and through frank and open discussions. On the other hand, a coach who would hold a conference each time he needs to make a substitution or make a tactical decision would soon lose both the respect of the players and his effectiveness as a coach. Immediate decisions and prompt action are necessary.

As important as anything may be the leader's philosophy of life and his attitude toward the task at hand. If he is to convince others that what he expects them to do is important enough to deserve their time, their energies, and in many instances their entire lives, he himself must manifest a conviction that the goals are both worthy of their best effort and possible of achievement. Dedication and commitment to one's work and a willingness to make personal sacrifices to achieve the objectives are essential to great accomplishments. Leaders who demonstrate these qualities, regardless of their methods, usually have little trouble in obtaining followers.

The need for recognition is one of the most common and insistent of all human needs. Ignoring individuals on the team, in a class, or on the staff is a sure way to defeat. Readiness to involve oneself with a player's personal problems, his efforts and his projects, and with his expressions of individuality is generally an effective way of developing allegiance. Shared aspirations, successes, joys, and defeats enable a leader to exercise his influence in securing cooperation, in achieving group goals, and assuring one hundred percent effort in the projects of the team, the class, or the staff. Deep personal involvement in the affairs of the group is certain to engender affection and loyalty.

8.9 SPECTATOR INFLUENCE AND CROWD BEHAVIOR

The author asked many of the interviewees what effect, if any, spectators had on their performance. The answers were almost as many and varied as the number of respondents. Some indicated that a large crowd increased their anxiety to the point where they performed better. Others stated that the crowd had no influence whatsoever on them. A few indicated that they played better when parents or girl

The Coach's Reward

"Shared aspirations, successes, joys, . . . enable a leader to exercise his influence."
By permission, Coach Archie Allen and the Springfield College baseball team.

friends were in attendance; others said that their performances deteriorated. The roar of the crowd served to "key up" certain athletes; others claimed they were not aware of it.

It seems reasonable to suppose, and this is corroborated by the opinions of experienced coaches, that athletes of the "anxious" type can be easily overstimulated by spectators and their enthusiasm, particularly if there are close friends, sweethearts, parents, and classmates in the stands. It is also true that athletes who tend to be phlegmatic and have a high anxiety threshold will usually perform better when the noise and enthusiasm of the crowd is above normal and when individuals are present whom the performer hopes to impress.

A number of the interviewees insist that to perform at their best, it is necessary for them to concentrate completely on the game or contest and shut out the stimuli from the crowd or individual spectators. The more intricate the game, the more it is necessary to do this.

John M. Cooper, when asked about what produced great performances, said:

The higher your level of concentration, the more apt you are to perform well. Concentrate as deeply and firmly as you possibly can on just playing the best game you can. Forget all about yourself and just concentrate on the game. Shut out everything else, try to make sure that nothing escapes you, be alert to make use of every opportunity, and just concentrate on playing the best game possible. The rest will take care of itself.[53]

Yet, we talked about momentum and related the performance of teams or individuals to the cheering and enthusiasm of the crowd. It is often difficult to know what initiates the momentum and what keeps it going or causes it to be lost. Perhaps the safest guess is that a brilliant play, a surge by a runner or a team, or an incident which causes a discouraged crowd to come to life is the factor which triggers the momentum. This feeling of exuberance infects the crowd, and from then on there is a reciprocal emotional exchange between audience and players.

There are times, during an exciting game for example, when the audience seems to revert to primitive emotions and behavior. Cries of "kill the Ump," "get the Ref," "fight, fight, fight," "hit 'em hard," and many others are indicative of emotions which are violently aroused. Violence occasionally erupts among partisan fans, and there are instances reported where highly emotional fans actually attacked officials in soccer, in football, in basketball, in wrestling, and in boxing. Spectators participate vicariously in the sport and can become exceedingly emotional. Not being able to express their aggressions, frustrations, and emotions through direct participation in the game, they seek an outlet by violently opposing another spectator, an official, or even a player. Gambling and betting on games frequently make defeat harder to bear and add to the frustrations and resulting aggression on the part of the losers. Because of the deep involvement in an exciting game, a "mob spirit" may make itself felt, and even well-meaning persons may become caught up in what they otherwise would consider an unfair or brutal reaction. The victims of such excitement may be the coaches, players, game officials, or other fans. The more partisan the spectators, the less they are able to look at actions and decisions objectively and impartially. Parents of athletes often have the greatest difficulty restraining themselves. Occasionally the action gets out of control.

Many of the psycho-social phenomena associated with well-attended competitive contests are beneficial and healthful. People find a needed opportunity in such contests to vent pent-up emotions; there is a sharing of fun and joy on the part of spectators; and common interests and loyalties assist in the integration of our culture. Class lines and economic status disappear when people from many walks of life sit side by side and cheer for their team. People need opportunities to obtain some release from the drab and monotonous lives common to many, to find relief from the tensions of daily life by participating in sport as spectators. They also find competitive contests interesting subjects of conversation at barber shops, luncheon meetings, and social gatherings.

Games and contests can be and sometimes are conducted without spectators. The values of sports to the participant are of primary importance, and any opportunity for athletic activities is beneficial. Nevertheless, the presence of spectators, the noise and the cheering of partisan crowds, the vicarious participation of many people in the stands, the music and the marching, the food vendors and the ceremonies, these and many other things produce color and excitement and a special atmosphere. Highly publicized games have become a unique institution, with their own customs, value systems, benefits, problems, and their own contributions to the culture of the times.

8.10 VALUES AND MEANING IN SPORTS

Character development through sports activities continues to be a controversial topic. The evidence is not very conclusive as to the beneficial effect of sports on the character of its participants. Neither is

Through sports a person gets involved in many situations in which he must stand alone and experience intense emotions. This type of situation abounds in life and one must learn to face it. Lessons learned in sports can assist a person in making right decisions and ethical judgments later in life. Participants in athletics are influenced by the ideals, principles, and actions of outstanding leaders whom they admire and respect. Self-discipline, acceptance of rules, control of emotions, subjugation of the self for the good of the group, are examples of habits and principles which may be learned in sports and which can later be applied.

A. W. Kay, in discussing moral education, states:

There are probably two propositions with which most teachers would agree. Firstly, that the moral education of children comes high in the list of educational priorities ... and secondly, that moral education may be conducted as an integral part of almost every school lesson.[27]

Kay goes on to point out that the principles of readiness and maturation can be appropriately applied to moral development, that the acquisition of a mature moral system to guide our conduct is a culminating developmental task, and that methods which are effective in attitude formation and change are the techniques which should be employed in moral education[27].

Carolyn and Muzafer Sherif and Nebergall, in their discussions of attitude change, emphasize the importance of the fact that "the first and most crucial phase of most communication situations" is that "the communicator must secure and hold an audience for his message"[45]. Once again, the opportunities that coaches and physical education teachers have to assist their players in the development of sound value systems become apparent. In the vast majority of instances they are dealing with audiences who are "tuned in" and who are in a state of "readiness" to receive the message.

The Bishop of Portsmouth, writing for "Outward Bound," singles out for emphasis the young person's intense desire to learn the truth, his expectation that his teachers and leaders will help him find it, the importance of shared goals and challenges, the need to overcome resistance, and the psychological effect of having overcome fear and performed a courageous act[9].

Many athletes have attributed to their coaches a positive influence on them both as to their philosophy of life and their behavior. It is true that the good coach is usually able to establish that rapport with his athletes which is so necessary if he is to influence them. The length of time a coach spends with the athletes and the experiences they share enhance the chances of his influencing them.

the evidence concerning the inculcation of values by other mea
Moral education is an extremely difficult subject to investigate. T
individual human spirit, emotions, and behavior are complicat
enough. When one must consider also the emotion-packed athle
situations, the implications of hero-worship, the adulation of fans, t
effects of newspaper publicity, and the many other intangibles, it
almost impossible to determine by experimental procedures exac
what role athletics play in the development of personal and soc
values.

When other evidence fails, one usually relies on opinions
experienced people who have thought deeply about a problem. T
kind of evidence abounds. Athletes, coaches, sports writers, a
physical education teachers attest to the lessons learned from spoi
Authors have written reams pointing out examples of how this learn
comes about. P. J. Arnold, in his discussion of "character and physi
education," states:

In physical education, because of the social and live decision provoking situation
engenders, education has a distinctive character-forming force which, with car
handling, can be for the good.[4]

Seth Arsenian, speaking at the National Conference on Values
Sports a few years ago, uttered these words:

Physical education, including health and recreation, as part of education in gene
and of college education in particular, shares in the responsibility for
development of student values. In many respects physical education, if it centers
play as a basic characteristic of human behavior, is better situated than any ot
course in the school curriculum in influencing the development of values.[5]

The problems of transfer and generalization are not yet solved
the satisfaction of all. Nevertheless, it is generally agreed that the wh
process of education is dependent on these principles. If an individua
to learn from previous experience, if education consists of behavio
changes resulting from experience, then it must be possible to trans
what is learned in one situation to a subsequent situation. The cumulat
effect of many experiences, which may be thought of as one form
generalization, is certainly evident in many aspects of human devel
ment.

Coaches and physical educators can only make a contribution
the development of values in an individual. There are many otl
influences which assist in molding a person's character. The poi
however, is that leaders in the field of sports do have a role to play—a
it can be an important one—in moral education.

There is one point, however, which needs special emphasis. If the habits of an athlete are to carry over into later life, if the lessons learned from athletics are to have a permanent rather than transitory effect, there must be a commitment to these precepts; that is, they must become part of his outlook on life. Only in this way can there be any consistency in his actions on and off the athletic field. There are too many examples of inconsistent behavior to believe otherwise. The laboratory situations are there, the leaders have their opportunities, generalization can take place. To have a permanent and positive influence, however, the athletic ideals must be so related, so harmonized with the individual's philosophy, and must become so much a part of the athlete's total being that they serve as motivating factors the rest of his life.

Individuals interviewed by the author were almost unanimous in expressing the opinion that sport had been a positive influence in their lives. They indicated the importance of thinking about the ultimate goal and not immediate gains for themselves. They emphasized the change in self-image when they had accomplished a feat which had been considered well-nigh impossible. They explained the changes that would occur within themselves when they faced up to an opponent and struggled with every ounce of muscle and spirit to gain mastery. They pointed to the humility gained when proud athletes are vanquished by worthy opponents. They talked often about fellowship and friendship, about overcoming pain and hurt, about giving that last dreg of endurance and strength. They pointed to the "real pro" who could never do less than his best.

Jerry Kramer, in *Instant Replay*, summarized his feelings in these words:

I know now that for me the main lure of football is the guys, my teammates, the friendship, the fun, the excitement, the incredibly exhilarating feeling of a shared achievement. When I look back upon the 1967 season, before I remember the block on Jethro Pugh, before I remember Bart's touchdown against the Cowboys, before I remember our victory in the Super Bowl, I remember a very special spirit, a rare camaraderie, something I can't quite define, but something I've tried to capture in this diary.[29]

In discussing physical fitness, it was pointed out that the intangible values were as important, or more so, than the more obvious, tangible results of greater strength, endurance, agility, and skill. The self-concept of a person is enhanced by his being strong, trim, good-looking, and vital. The increase in self-confidence, self-esteem, and self-realization through vigorous activity and attention to sound health precepts were frequently mentioned, as well as the increased zest for living, the

The Final Seconds

"The changes that would occur within themselves when they faced up to an opponent and struggled with every ounce of muscle and spirit to gain mastery." *By permission*, Eugene Bouley, referee at Springfield College.

greater productivity in work, and the resulting self-fulfillment. The ultimate end of personal development is sometimes regarded as a balanced and fruitful life achieved through the full development of his many dimensions—and one of these dimensions is physical fitness.

It would be completely unrealistic to claim that everyone who becomes involved in physical education activities and everyone who participates in sports benefits from the experience. A great deal depends upon the quality of leadership. There are coaches who are martinets; there is, in certain instances, emphasis on brutality; not all players or coaches try to live within the spirit of the rules; and it is possible to exploit both players and sports for selfish motives. Physical fitness itself may become a fetish, with narcissism as one of the outcomes.

Again it must be emphasized that good leadership is the key. Whether sound values are enhanced through transfer and generalization, whether desirable personality traits are developed through contagion and emulation, or whether individuals are hurt by inconsiderate, thoughtless, and low-quality leadership, it appears that the influence of the physical education teacher and the power of the coach will be a significant factor. If education is to be the goal, such leaders must be carefully selected.

8.11 INTERNATIONALISM AND SPORTS

The role of sports in international affairs is becoming more and more important. It has been stated that athletics have become an instrument of foreign as well as domestic policy. People in all countries are very much aware of the results of athletic competition between countries. The image of a nation is affected by the degree of excellence exhibited in international athletic competition by its citizens. The philosophy and attitudes of a society are frequently reflected in the way their athletes live and work in preparation for important contests. Most nations are deeply concerned with the image they project to other peoples of the world. They feel it is important to display their own citizens' strength, endurance, courage, and willingness to sacrifice for the achievement of a goal. It is therefore in the national interest to promote programs and to maintain an environment which will encourage excellence in all athletic endeavors.

More important, however, is the role of sports in fostering international understanding. Athletic activities are, for the most part, spontaneous, expressive, and exuberant. For this reason they tend to

Communicating Through Sports

"The philosophy and attitudes of a society are frequently reflected in the way their athletes live and work in preparation for important contests." *By permission,* Springfield College basketball team.

Two Countries Together in Sports (Learning together in India)

"More important, however, is the role of sports in fostering international understanding." *By permission*, Coach Steitz and The Springfield College basketball team.

remove emotional inhibition and other barriers to understanding. Through the medium of such activities children and young people can develop international friendship, which may seep into the adult world. Sports are great levelers; and in athletics the appreciation for individual performance can often transcend the differences of creed, race, and circumstances of birth. We know also that movement is a universal language, and communication between persons who do not know each other's native tongues is common in international games and dances.

Sports are useful in furnishing a rallying point, a focus for loyalties, and a source of national and community pride. Through the exploits of their athletes, communities and nations, regardless of size, can often achieve a sense of dignity and accomplishment otherwise denied them. Success in sports can create a confidence and a sense of inner strength which is helpful to young and struggling nations in their efforts to achieve the goal of freedom. Often, in the development of top-flight teams, whole communities share a feeling of participation in a common cause. It is for this reason that governments have, in many instances, been very concerned with the development of their Olympic teams.

There are problems with regard to the development of sports programs on an international as well as a local level. The same rules of sportsmanship and the same principles which should govern competitive athletics at the local level must be invoked in international competition. If such programs are to make for better international understanding, they must be conducted in an atmosphere of brotherhood and justice for all.

8.12 SPORTS AND SOCIAL CHANGE

Many of the social issues today are cause for concern and even alarm: the population explosion, the problems of ecology, campus unrest, revolution in our midst, cold wars and hot wars, the development of communes and hippie life style. It is not within the scope of this book to deal with these problems in any depth. It would take more than one volume to do justice to these topics and their relationship to sports. Nevertheless a few words appear to be appropriate.

When athletes, cheerleaders, and spectators become caught up in social causes and in dissent, sports are affected. In many educational institutions a substantial number of students now look upon athletics as something not worth giving themselves to, not worthy of the full effort of a mature person. Athletes themselves are divided: some insisting that discipline and self-discipline are not only learned in sports but necessary to any successful enterprise; others are equally certain that athletes, because of their visibility, have a responsibility to take an active part in the various campus causes.

Coaches and physical educators are also forced to reevaluate their positions. Should edicts with regard to long hair be enforced? Is it important to uphold law and order? Can loyalty and discipline be inculcated in sports? Has there been a self-defeating overemphasis on recruitment, subsidization, and authoritative organization? Should athletes be given time to participate actively in politics and in student government? These are the kinds of questions which must be examined and reexamined.

The author can only repeat what was said before. The coaching and teaching of sports furnish opportunities to influence large numbers of young people. There are intensely private and emotional situations in which coaches and physical educators can affect the behavior of athletes. Physical education teachers and coaches must keep abreast of current and changing social, political, and moral issues and utilize their positions and their opportunities to help mold good citizens and fine individuals. They must also relate their activities to the societal problems of the day.

REFERENCES

1. Allman, Fred L., Jr., "Competitive sports for boys under fifteen—Beneficial or Harmful?" *Journal of the Medical Association of Georgia*, February, 1967

2. American Association for Health, Physical Education, and Recreation, *Proceedings, First National Institute on Girls' Sports*, November 4-9, 1963. Washington: AAHPER, 1965

3. American Association for Health, Physical Education, and Recreation, *Values in Sports*, Report of a Joint National Conference, Interlochen, Michigan, June 17-22, 1962. Washington: AAHPER, 1963

4. Arnold, P. J., *Education, Physical Education, and Personality Development.* New York: Atherton Press, 1968, p. 108

5. Arsenian, Seth, "Development of values with special reference to college years," *Values in Sports*, Report of a Joint National Conference, Interlochen, Michigan, 1962. Washington: AAHPER, 1963, p. 59

6. Behrman, Robert M., "Personality differences between nonswimmers and swimmers," *Research Quarterly*, Vol. 38, No. 2, May 1967, pp. 163-171

7. Betz, Robert L., "A comparison between personality traits and physical fitness tests of males," unpublished Masters Thesis, University of Illinois, 1953, p. 66

8. Biddulph, Lowell G., "Athletic achievement and the personal and social adjustment of high school boys," *Research Quarterly*, Vol. 25, No. 1, 1954

9. Bishop of Portsmouth, "Beyond His Grasp?" *Outward Bound*, David James, editor. London: Routledge and Kegan Paul, 1964, pp. 212-217

10. Clarke, H. Harrison, and David H. Clarke, "Social status and mental health of boys as related to their maturity, structural, and strength characteristics," *Research Quarterly*, Vol. 32, No. 3, 1961, pp. 326-334

11. Cobb, W. Montague, "Race and runners," *Journal of Health and Physical Education*, January 1936

12. Copolillo, Henry P., *Football in Grade School: A Child Psychiatrist's Viewpoint*, December 1966

13. Cowell, Charles C., "The contributions of physical activity to social development," *Research Quarterly*, Vol. 31, No. 2, Part II, 1960, pp. 286-306

14. Cowell, Charles C., and A. H. Ismail, "Relationships between selected social and physical factors," *Research Quarterly*, Vol. 33, No. 1, 1962, pp. 40-43

15. Cratty, Bryant J., *Psychology and Physical Activity*. Englewood Cliffs, N.J.: Prentice-Hall, 1968, p. 186

16. Cratty, Bryant J., *Social Dimensions of Physical Activity*. Englewood Cliffs, N.J.: Prentice-Hall, 1967

17. Duffy, Elizabeth, *Activation and Behavior*. New York: Wiley, 1962

18. Frost, Reuben B., "Leaders for all," paper presented at the International Conference on Sport and Education, Mexico City, October 9, 1968

19. Gates, Georgina S., "The effect of an audience upon performance," *Journal of Abnormal and Social Psychology*, Vol. 18, 1923, pp. 234-244

20. Graubard, Stephen, and Gerald Holton, *Excellence and Leadership in a Democracy*. New York: Columbia University Press, 1962, p. 1

21. Hartshorne, H., and M. May, *Studies in the Nature of Character*. New York: Macmillan, 1928

22. Husman, Burris F., "Sport and personality dynamics," *National College Physical Education Association for Men, 72nd Annual Proceedings*, 1969, pp. 56-70

23. Jokl, Ernst, *The Medical Aspect of Boxing*. Pretoria: J. L. Van Schaik, 1941

24. Jokl, Ernst, and Peter Jokl, *The Physiological Basis of Athletic Records*. Springfield, Ill.: Charles C. Thomas, 1968, pp. 80-81

25. Kane, J. E., "Personality profiles of physical education students compared with others," *Psicologia Dello Sport, Proceedings of the First International Congress of Sport Psychology*, Ferrucio Antonelli, editor. Rome, 1965, pp. 772, 775

26. Kane, John E., "Personality and physical ability," *Proceedings of the International Congress of Sport Sciences.* Tokyo: The Japanese Union of Sport Sciences, University of Tokyo Press, 1966, pp. 201-208

27. Kay, A. W., *Moral Development.* New York: Schocken Books, 1968, pp. 247, 249, 251, 253

28. Kistler, Joy, "Student opinion as to values derived from physical education," *American Academy of Physical Education Professional Contributions,* No. 3, November 1954, pp. 71-72

29. Kramer, Jerry, *Instant Replay,* The Green Bay Diary of Jerry Kramer, Dick Schaap, editor. New York: World, 1968, pp. 283-284

30. Kroll, Walter, "Sixteen personality factor profiles of collegiate wrestlers," *Research Quarterly,* Vol. 38, No. 1, 1967, pp. 49-57

31. Ley, Katherine, "High school girl athletes need more opportunities to compete," *Shaping Up to Quality in Physical Education.* New London, Conn.: Croft Educational Services, 1968

32. Loy, John W., Jr., and Gerald Kenyon, *Sport, Culture and Society.* New York: Macmillan, 1969, p. 88

33. Malpass, Leslie F., "Competition, conflict and cooperation as social values," *Values in Sports.* Washington: AAHPER, 1963, p. 63

34. Martin, Lawrence A., "The effects of competition upon the aggressive responses of basketball players and wrestlers," unpublished Doctoral Dissertation, Springfield College, June 1969

35. McIntosh, Peter C., *Sport in Society.* London: C. A. Watts, 1963

36. Metheny, Eleanor, "Some differences in bodily proportions between american negro and white male college students as related to athletic performance," *Research Quarterly,* Vol. 10, No. 4, 1939, p. 41

37. Metheny, Eleanor, "Sports and the feminine image," *The International Olympic Academy.* Athens: Hellenic Olympic Committee, 1964, pp. 90-104

38. Ogilvie, Bruce, and Thomas Tutko, paper presented at the meeting of the North American Society for Psychology of Sports and Physical Activity, Las Vegas, Nevada, March 1967

39. Peck, Robert F., *et al.,* The Psychology of Character Development. New York: Wiley, 1960

40. Rice, Sidney A., "Sports fans are a menace," *Journal of Health, Physical Education, and Recreation,* Vol. 23, No. 5, May 1952

41. Rowan, Carl T., "The negro athlete," *Minneapolis Morning Tribune,* 12 articles, published in 1959

42. Ryan, F. J., "Some aspects of athletic behavior," *Track and Field Quarterly Review.* Ann Arbor, Michigan: United States Track Coaches Association, December, 1968, pp. 37-49

43. Schendel, Jack, "Psychological differences between athletes and non-participants in athletics at three educational levels," *Research Quarterly*, Vol. 36, No. 1, 1965, pp. 52-67

44. Seymour, Emery W., "Comparative study of certain behavior characteristics of participant and non-participant boys in Little League Baseball," *Research Quarterly*, Vol. 27, No. 3, 1956, pp. 338-346

45. Sherif, Carolyn W., Muzafer Sherif, and Roger E. Nebergall, *Attitude and Attitude Change*. Philadelphia: W. B. Saunders, 1965, p. 171

46. Singer, R. N., reaction to "Sport and Personality Dynamics," National College Physical Education Association for Men Proceedings, 1969, pp. 72, 76-79

47. Steggerdo, Morris, and C. E. Petty, "Body measurements on 100 negro males from Tuskegee Institute," *Research Quarterly*, Vol. 13, No. 3, 1942, pp. 275

48. Steinhaus, Arthur, "Summary and comments," *Exercise and Fitness*, The Athletic Institute, 1960, p. 234

49. "Oerter Follows Own Golden Rules," *Sunday Star*, Washington, D.C., November 10, 1968, p. D 3

50. Thomas, Clayton L., "Effect of vigorous athletic activity on women," paper presented at Springfield Academy of Medicine, Municipal Hospital, Springfield, Massachusetts, December 10, 1968

51. Werner, Alfred C., and Edward Gottheil, "Personality development and participation in college athletics," *Research Quarterly*, Vol. 37, No. 1, 1966, pp. 126-131

52. Westergren, Erik, "The motivation of physical education," *Psicologia Dello Sport, Proceedings of the First International Congress of Sport Psychology*, Ferrucio Antonelli, editor, Rome, 1966, pp. 870-879

53. Cooper, John M., Director of Graduate Studies, College of Health, Physical Education and Recreation, University of Indiana and former athlete, University of Missouri, Columbia, Missouri, personal interview, 1969

9 HANDICAPS, INJURIES AND RELATED PSYCHOLOGICAL ADJUSTMENTS

I find, by experience, that the mind and the
body are more than married, for they are most
intimately united; and when one suffers, the
other sympathizes.

Chesterfield

Whether we are dealing with someone who is perceptually handicapped, with an athlete who is recovering from injury, or with the pupil who is afflicted with an abnormality which prevents full function of some body part, we must be constantly aware of the emotional and mental effects of his plight and the need for attention to the psychological as well as the physiological factors involved. While in one sense the needs, drives, and protective mechanisms are the same in those who are handicapped as in those who are not, the circumstances in which the former operate are different and hence the degree of their emotional stability and the intensity of their psychological reactions are also different.

Coaches, physical education teachers, and trainers are constantly dealing with individuals who have sustained injuries, who have a difficult time competing in activities requiring considerable motor ability, or who are living with some form of permanent physical handicap. The opportunity to study behavior under such unusual circumstances, as well as the necessity to consider deviant behavior, presents itself over and over again in physical education environments. Let us look, therefore, at some of the handicaps that may need to be overcome and examine means by which the development of those afflicted can be enhanced, and in some cases the therapy improved.

9.1 THE PERCEPTUALLY HANDICAPPED

As was explained in Section 2.5, learning, interpreting, thinking, and skillful movement are all dependent on normal growth and maturation of the nervous system and proper neurological organization. The development of the perceptual apparatus is essential to the learning of motor skills and the ability to read well and think well. For those who, because of a genetic defect, or a disruption of normal nervous and muscular physiological processes, or some traumatic physical or emotional experiences, or lack of normal childhood activity, are unable to learn basic movement patterns or relate external movements to their own environment, special education is necessary. The condition of the child's abnormality must be assessed, and a program of basic movement fundamentals must be provided for his learning and development.

Barbara Godfrey and Newell Kephart, in their book, *Movement Patterns and Motor Education*, explain the role of motor activity in the educational process and indicate the hierarchical relationships of a sound physical activity program both in the elementary grades and the preschool years. They state in part,

We recognize that certain activities require the previous learning of more elementary and basic skills; consequently, more complex activites are not presented until the average child has attained the required basic skills. It is also recognized that the skills, attitudes, and knowledges which the child is acquiring are themselves organized in hierarchical fashion. The recognition of this hierarchy of activities and its accompanying hierarchy of skills is reflected in today's educational toys, each toy carrying a notation of the age level for which it is applicable as a learning tool.[14]

Neurological organization and integration sometimes do not reach the fullness of normal development. Whether this is the result of minimal brain damage, emotional trauma, or the lack of complete motor and psychological experiences, it is necessary at an early age to adapt physical education programs to specific needs. Many activites are unusually difficult for the atypical child to learn, and some of these children cannot establish motor patterns as readily as a normal child. Greater patience, more individual attention and individual activity, a greater variety of fundamental movement exercises, and more attention to motivation and encouragement are necessary.

Carl Delacato agrees with Godfrey and Kephart in their emphasis on complete neurological organization but goes even further in diagnosis and in careful programming of remedial exercises. He summarizes his fundamental concept as follows:

The basic premise of the neuro-psychological approach as outlined by the author is that if man does not follow this schema he exhibits a problem of mobility or communication. To overcome such problems one evaluates the subject via the neurological schema outlined above. Those areas of neurological organization which have not been completed or are absent are overcome by *passively imposing* them upon the nervous system in those with problems of mobility and are *taught* to those with problems of speech or reading. When the neurological organization is complete the problem is overcome.[12]

Delacato emphasizes the successive stages of motor development, the dependence of perceptual development and neurological organization on proceeding systematically through these stages, and the relationship of these processes to intellectual development. The remedial program he suggests is grounded on an analysis of the motor development of an individual and the determination of the stage in which he is operating. This program includes controlling the environment and function in order to assist the child in achieving normal neurological organization. Delacato explains:

Man has evolved phylogenetically in a known pattern. The ontogenetic development of normal humans in general recapitulates that phylogenetic process. We have been able to take children who deviated from normal development (severely brain injured) and through the extrinsic imposition of normal patterns of movement and behavior have been able to neurologically organize them sufficiently so that they could be placed within the human developmental pattern of crawling, creeping, and walking. Finally, with man's unique lateral neurological function added to this structure, talking, reading and writing developed.

If we can accomplish this with the severely brain injured, we should be able to organize those children who are not brain injured, but are only neurologically disorganized, with much greater results and with much less effort.[12]

Delacato's theories have not been accepted without serious challenge, however. *Time* magazine,* under the caption, "'Patterning' under attack" pointed out that a number of medical and health organizations had stated that "patterning" does not have the therapeutic value that has been attributed to it and that there is a lack of sound scientific evidence to support its proponents' claims. According to the article in *Time*, independent tests at the University of Chicago also failed to substantiate the validity of such therapeutic measures.

Lawther reviews some hypothetical concepts of child development and in particular the work of Doman and Delacato, some of which was done at the Institute for Achievement of Human Potentials. He points out that the theoretical basis on which they conduct their clinical work has been challenged but indicates that the numerous successes achieved by them should not be overlooked. The following quotation has real significance for students of motor development and special physical education:

Time, Vol. 91, No. 22, May 31, 1968, pp. 50-51.

Perhaps Delacato's successes are in part due to the greatly increased amount of stimulation, care, and affection which is lavished on these children—particularly, to the very great increase in quantity and variety of sensory input and sensory-motor experience which these children obtain under his programming.[18]

Regardless of whether we attribute the improvement in motor functioning and intellectual development on the part of these children to the highly structured training procedure or to loving care, attention, sensory stimulation, and a rich program of movement experiences, the physical educator must realize the significance of the "holistic" point of view as he plans his program of activities and seeks to meet the needs of the individual.

The importance of starting at the *functioning* level of the child rather than with his age or grade level must be emphasized. To assign a task which is too difficult, to make the activity too arduous, or to eliminate the satisfaction of achieving and the joy of success is disastrous when dealing with handicapped pupils.

It is also important to know that there are many scientists, therapists, physicians, and educators who are making the early development of children their life's work and who can give real assistance to the perceptually handicapped if proper referrals are made. The tragedy is that there are so many people, including parents and educators, who are ignorant of the symptoms which are indicative of special needs in this area and who are unaware of the kind of assistance which is available.

In working with the perceptually handicapped, one should try to order the tasks so that one will follow another in a given sequence. The more complex skills should not be introduced until the pupils have learned the gross motor movements. The intellectual counterpart of a motor act must also be taught, because, in the case of many handicapped and retarded pupils, inability to perform has led to inactivity, which in turn has limited their perceptual development. Unless minimum levels of motor proficiency serve as the basis for the learning of more complex skills and games, little success can be expected—and we must remember that even the minimum of success is of critical importance for such disadvantaged individuals. Without some kind of success life would be entirely devoid of fun and satisfaction, and the only possible result would be frustrations, aggression, apathy, depression, dependency, and other forms of escapism.

9.2 ADJUSTMENT TO PHYSICAL IMPAIRMENT

Physical education teachers and coaches are frequently called upon to deal with pupils who have some form of physical disability. Thus, they should know a few of the basic principles of psychology which may apply to the atypical student. Maladjustments due to physical disability often occur because of the way the afflicted individuals are treated by schoolmates, teachers, parents, coaches, and society in general.

The physically atypical individual has essentially the same needs, desires, motivations, conflicts, problems, and emotions as normal individuals. Very often the difference is mostly in degree. A physical handicap adds to the problems of adjustment which face most people, and for that reason the atypical individual is more likely to be maladjusted. There is more reason for such a person to feel fearful, rejected, discriminated against, and pitied than for one who has no handicap. He is more inclined to be lonely, sensitive, depressed, and defensive. He is often faced with the fact that he cannot be successful in what he wants to do, be it the passing of a football, the pitching of a baseball, or entering the field of physical education.

If individuals faced with temporary or permanent physical impairments are to make a good adjustment to their situation, they must focus on the positive aspects of life rather than the negative aspects. Thoughts must be directed to possible accomplishments, to increasing skills which are still available, to learning to live within the limitations which exist.

There are some general principles which may be helpful to those who are working with the atypical and who wish to understand them and assist them psychologically:

1. A physical education teacher must concentrate on the pupil and not the disability. He will then learn to know and treat him as a person and not as a handicapped individual.

2. Every effort must be made to organize programs for the handicapped so as to compensate for possible gaps in educational backgrounds, for absences due to the need for special treatment, and for the difficulties encountered with respect to regular attendance in inclement weather.

3. Handicapped individuals should be encouraged to understand their own condition. Too often they are either discouraged because they think they are worse off than they really are or unrealistically optimistic and hopeful so as to later suffer a "let down" when faced with reality.

4. Most handicapped individuals desperately want to conform, and resent segregation. Every effort should be made to provide opportunities for them to work and play with normal children of their own age.

5. Tasks must be kept within the range of the pupils' ability. Repeated failures can cause too much anxiety and even emotional damage to those who are already burdened with mental and physical problems.

6. Adolescence brings with it special problems for the handicapped. At this age they are especially sensitive to corrective devices, braces, and abnormalities. They are faced with all the problems which normal children have at this age, and these are accentuated by their disabilities.

7. Efforts to conceal handicaps and defects sometimes lead to compensations, both physical and mental. Psychologists generally agree that physical impairments are among the important causes of pronounced adjustive reactions.

8. The person who is atypical resents being pitied but needs understanding. The manner in which he is treated by schoolmates, friends, and teachers is one of the significant factors in the degree of his adjustment or maladjustment. Handicapped individuals are usually more than normally bitter toward thoughtless remarks and unkind acts.

9. The handicapped person must be helped to understand the consequences of his response to his condition. He must choose between withdrawal and participation, daydreaming and facing reality, responses which lead to a solution and those which increase the problem.

10. Motivation which leads to enthusiastic participation must be the goal in programs for the handicapped. Where possible they should share in the planning. They should be oriented to the purposes and reasons for each activity and the anticipated results.

All aspects of psychotherapy become important in dealing with handicapped individuals. Because participation and resocialization are so important, attention must be given to recreational and occupational therapy as an adjunct to physical therapy. The needs to feel wanted, to belong, to be a person of worth, and to be a contributing member of society become especially acute when an individual has a physical impairment or a mental handicap. Once again we must emphasize that the handicapped person should be treated as a *person* first and foremost and that there should not be an inordinate attention on the affected part.

Arthur Daniels and Evelyn Davies, reporting on experiences of the handicapped, tell of a student who was a polio paraplegic and who was encouraged by a physical education teacher to try to learn to swim:

John learned to swim and later he took a course in archery. He knew his way around the physical education department now and he had some friends. One day he asked his adviser, "Why is it I never had a chance to learn anything like this in high school? Why did I have to wait all these years to find out I could do some things like everybody else? Why did I always have to go to study hall when the other kids went out to play?" The adviser just shook his head. He couldn't give John a single reason why it had been necessary for him to take the psychological and social beating all through the elementary and secondary school years. There wasn't any.[11]

Physical disability in some instances serves as a stimulus to withdrawal and in others may bring about more aggressive behavior. Just as motivation for the normal individual is the product of a number of factors, so also is the motivation of the handicapped person. The same injury, the same handicap, may elicit an excellent adjustment from an emotionally stable person and a totally inept response from another individual.

Howard Rusk and Eugene Taylor, in their book, *New Hope for the Handicapped*, discuss adjustments to handicap and conclude with the following optimistic statement:

Regardless of the various viewpoints expressed by the psychiatrists and psychologists, those who have worked closely with the physically disabled know that having once made the emotional adjustment to their disabilities, they possess a depth of understanding, patience and tolerance which is rarely found among those who have not endured some soul-torturing experience. They have been forced to discard the superficial and to find the fundamentals.[24]

Physical educators working with the physically handicapped must not rely too much on gimmicks and superficial motivating devices; rather, they must assist the handicapped individuals to develop genuine motivations toward achievement, toward self-improvement and self-fulfillment. The motivational techniques used must, of course, take into account the age of the impaired individual and the motivating forces which are typical of the group to which he belongs. The relative permanence of the disability, the depth of emotional trauma, the intellectual and physical assets which exist, and the circumstances surrounding the person's life, will all have a bearing on the psychological treatment which is required.

9.3 PERSONAL INJURIES AND PSYCHOLOGICAL ADJUSTMENTS

Coaches and trainers are constantly faced with the problem of dealing with athletes who have been injured. They realize that there are individuals who magnify injuries as well as those who attempt to conceal them. There are hypochondriacs on the one hand and stoics on the other. There are also those who have mature and rational attitudes toward injury or the prospect of it. The actions of a coach and trainer in connection with a player's injury and their attitude toward the injury can have long-lasting and important effects, both with regard to the success of a team and the future welfare of the player.

There are instances where a coach minimized or ignored an injury which the athlete considered significant and as a result of the resentment caused by this affrònt the athlete subsequently put in a performance which was below par and appeared to lack spirit. There are also instances where too much sympathy and attention for a relatively minor injury caused an athlete to miss so much practice and play that he was unable to recover the lost ground during the entire season.

The attitudes which athletes have toward injury are largely the result of the sum total of their experiences. The pain threshold, the fears instilled by parents and others, the apathetic or oversolicitous reactions of coaches, the attitudes of physicians toward injury, the emotional responses of teammates and peers, and the maturity and emotional stability of the athletes at the time of their injury are some of the central factors affecting responses to injury and pain. There are undoubtedly innate differences in the ability to disregard pain and even in the intensity of the discomfort brought on by injury.

Pain may be the result of several factors. Physical injury is of course usually the basic cause. In addition, there may be psychological troubles which produce sensations of pain. A stomach-ache often accompanies anxiety and worry. Recalling a traumatic incident may bring back a recurrence of the pain. Headaches occur frequently as a result of tension or circulatory maladjustment. Josephine Rathbone and Valerie Hunt throw some useful light on this problem when they say:

Also, pain may be caused not by true injury or memory of it, but by muscle tension. For example, headaches may be due to tension in the neck muscles. This type of pain may be the result of ischemia (deficiency of blood flow in a part). This same explanation covers many backaches. Since muscle tension often accompanies anxiety, it can be said that some headaches and backaches, at least, are due to psychic causes.

It is also known that persons with psychoneuroses, who react more violently to all stimuli and fears, appear to have more pain than those who are less highly strung and phlegmatic. The signs other than pain associated with visceral disease—sweating, vasomotor changes, and muscular rigidity, for example—can also be "learned," as it were, and will reappear with or without pain when a repetition of the provocation occurs.[23]

Injuries to an individual can affect his self-confidence, cause sweating and blushing, produce nausea and stomach pains, bring about indigestion and lack of appetite, and can increase blood pressure, heart rate, and respiratory volume. At the same time, apprehensions may increase abnormally, insomnia and restlessness are common, muscular spasm occurs more frequently, and emotional problems surface more readily.

Robert Moore points out that it is possible to *seek* injury for psychological reasons. There are those, he says, whose early psychological experiences cause them to be more injury prone than normal. He mentions as examples boys who have great athletic potential but are afraid to be aggressive and remove themselves from conflict by injury; he describes the athletic and ambitious father who pushes his less able son into sports for which the latter is not equipped; he tells of the overaggressive athlete who lacks good control but rushes blindly into the fray with resulting injury; he contrasts this athlete with the overtimid player who sustains injury because he hesitates and loses momentum as he is about to be tackled; he includes in his examples the athlete who feels he is invulnerable and demonstrates a counterphobic reaction. All these types of athletes may have a higher than normal risk of being injured[20].

Calvert Stein, writing about the psychological implications of personal injury,[27] classifies the reactions of an injured person into primary and secondary reactions as follows.

Primary or immediate reactions:

1. fear of self-annihilation
2. fear of harm to others
3. anger at another person or object
4. anger at one's self
5. apprehension over personal damages and costs
6. fear of blame and punishment

Secondary psychological reactions:

1. a feeling of foolishness or embarrassment
2. an altered image of oneself
   a)   as a whole and undamaged person
   b)   as a strong and healthy specimen
   c)   as a responsible person

The totality of circumstances which surround an injury combine to create the attitude of the patient and to influence his adjustment to the occurrence and the many kinds of discomfort involved. In physical education situations, the combination of sensory stimuli may involve blood, protruding bones, excitement in the voices, facial expressions of the surrounding people, appearance of deformity, inordinate sympathy, abnormal position of the limb, and pain in the affected part. These are superimposed on the residual of past experiences of all kinds. An athlete who has had a serious injury to his knee may be particularly sensitive to additional damage to that part of his body; a person who has had his knee "lock" many times because of a "floating cartilage" may take an additional occurrence of this kind in stride; a tired or stale player will be incapacitated from a relatively minor injury much more quickly than when he is fresh and rested; an individual who is experiencing repeated failures in his efforts to perform will believe that he is seriously hurt long before he will admit it when everything is going well; and it is a common phenomenon to see players who are being defeated succumb to injury much more readily than when they are winning.

Stein discusses this topic further under the heading "Residual Emotional and Physical Complications" when he says:

Other reactions to personal injury include weakness from disuse, numbness or cramps from long tensed muscles, pain from corrective procedures such as traction, pressures from casts and appliances, drainage tubes, catheters, etc., distress from unusual positions, digestive and excretory disturbances both incident to and resulting from the injury as well as related to the treatment, loss of familiar companionship, interruption, if not termination of usual program, anxiety over routine responsibilities at home, work, or school, additional worries about costs, disfigurement, the question of recovery, and an often-unrecognized fear that the doctors may not have found and corrected everything. The fear and revulsion over possible deformity, however slight, and of visible blemishes, is ever present . . . [27]

In view of the prominent involvement of psychosomatic factors, coaches and physical educators dealing with handicapped students and injured athletes should have a basic understanding of the diverse ways in which students are affected by handicap or injury and some of the adjustment mechanisms which are or should be set in motion. For, all injuries and diseases are functional-organic, all therapies have their physical and psychological components, and all handicaps need appropriate personality adjustment.

9.4 SUMMARY OF ADJUSTIVE REACTIONS

Adjustive reactions take place in both the normal and the abnormal individuals. The same mental adjustments which are described here in connection with the handicapped and injured may be found to some degree in persons not so afflicted. Adjustment reactions are in many instances helpful to sound mental health and it is only when they are relied on to an inappropriate or excessive degree that they become abnormal and injurious to emotional health. Most adjustment mechanisms function to alleviate anxiety or decrease tension. They are therefore commonly termed "defense mechanisms" or "escape mechanisms." Such adjustments are responses to needs which cannot be readily satisfied. The individual then resorts to special devices or methods in an attempt to attain his objective. He does not wish to lose his sense of security, belonging, success or self-esteem and therefore, often unconsciously, reacts in ways which will protect him from further frustration, tension, and anxiety.

The matter of adjustive reactions is generally not completely understood. Such reactions are usually responses to unresolved conflicts and threats to a person's self-esteem or security. Adjustments are made to the environment and to other people and often include the substitution of pleasant feelings for unpleasant ones. As such adjustive or defense mechanisms become more frequent and as the individual becomes more dependent upon them, the danger of their adverse effect on emotional health increases. As more and more reliance is placed upon the adjustive mechanisms they tend to become more unconscious and involuntary. Very often such defensive reactions originate as voluntary and creative responses to particular frustrating situations. This brings about some relief from anxiety and results in pleasant feelings which the individual remembers. When another problem or conflict arises, it becomes more tempting to resort to a similar adjustment. Meanwhile the obstacle or person causing the frustration may remain in the unconscious and the solution will be only temporary. Defense mechanisms therefore tend to be delusory and prevent individuals from conscious, mature evaluations and from creatively solving their problems. Adjustive reactions, however, can minimize the disruptive force of a disturbing situation and act as a stabilizing influence on the individual. They should not be used regularly as an escape from reality or as a substitute for facing up to a problem and attempting to solve it in a logical and mature manner.

Some of the common mechanisms which athletes and students resort to in situations related to physical education are as follows.

1. *Compensation.* To overcome a feeling of deficiency because he has only one arm, an athlete may work exceptionally hard to make the football team. His need for the approval of peers and superiors may be so great that it drives him to extreme effort. In many instances this has "paid off" in terms of successful achievement and self-fulfillment.

In a slightly different way, a feeling of inferiority may result in "grandstanding," boasting, bullying, or rebelling. These are methods of attracting attention which the person in question has been unable to obtain in more legitimate ways. Sports history is filled with cases in which the player who is "benched" becomes a disciplinary problem instead of a loyal supporter.

Coaches sometimes compensate for a feeling of inferiority by being extremely authoritarian or by driving their players almost beyond endurance. History is replete with the names of great men who have been motivated to great achievement as a way of compensating for some weakness or deficiency. When compensation leads to strong motivation and sound achievement it is adjustive and desirable. When it leads to further frustration or too much anxiety it is harmful and often results in antisocial behavior.

2. *Rationalization.* Individuals who feel guilty or who recognize that their own behavior is below accepted standards will often find reasons which they give as justification for their actions. An explanation which attributes more worthy motives to them is substituted for the real reason for acting as they did. Handicapped persons often resort to rationalization when they are unable to attain their goals.

A moderate amount of rationalization is normal and in some instances may be a helpful protective device. When it becomes a substitute for an honest assessment of a limitation and is used regularly, however, it becomes disruptive. The athlete who is always ready with an alibi for poor performances, the coach who can "explain" every defeat, the disabled person who talks himself and others into believing he is incapable of performing a certain task when actually he is not, and the student who takes the "sour-grapes" attitude when he fails to attain his goals, are all examples of rationalizing.

3. *Projection.* The student who fails a course and blames the professor, the halfback who runs into the wrong hole and blames the blockers, the golfer who blames the club for a poor shot, and the coach who blames the team to cover up his own inadequacies, are all utilizing *projection* as their method of defense.

An individual finds failure more acceptable if he can project the cause, if he can attribute his own weakness to someone else, if he can blame someone or something which he feels free to attack, if he can find a scapegoat for his own inadequate behavior. As with other adjustments, it may be helpful for anyone and necessary for the physically impaired individual to utilize projection occasionally. This, too, can become an escape from reality and eventually lead to emotional breakdown.

4. *Displacement.* Displaced anger and aggression is a common phenomenon. A mother gets angry on account of her husband's behavior and vents her feelings on her child; a ten year old boy is punished and in turn strikes his younger brother; a basketball player loses his temper when a foul is called and slams the ball at the floor; the man who becomes angry at his boss directs his aggression toward his children; these are all common examples of displacement.

Coaches sometimes utilize this reaction in the hope that it will produce positive results. Football players might be stimulated to anger by the insulting or stinging remarks of the coach made in the hope that they would become more aggressive in their blocking and tackling and thus become more effective.

Handicapped individuals have much more frequent occasions than other people to be frustrated by their inability to perform certain tasks. They then sometimes vent their feelings on another person, a chair, a ball, a tool, or some other object. Striking lockers with fists after a humiliating defeat, hurling a tennis racket as a result of serving doubles in a critical situation, slamming a jacket down after having been removed from a game, throwing a bat after striking out, and charging an opposing guard in basketball because he was covering too closely and effectively, are examples of this type of reaction.

5. *Dependency.* Feelings of inadequacy and the inability to cope with problems which present themselves often result in a need for help of one kind or another. Most people desire assistance from a powerful source when faced with difficult decisions and serious problems. In some instances they may go to their superior, on whose advice they always rely; at other times they may seek out a friend, in whom they have great confidence, and talk things over; under still other circumstances they may turn to God, to the Bible, or to some other source of strength and comfort.

Coaches have often been approached by players for personal advice, the handicapped talk over their problems with the therapist, patients pour their hearts out to physicians, and clergymen are sources of encouragement, counsel, and strength for a large number of people.

Dependency usually entails a certain amount of submissiveness and acceptance of a greater authority or power. It is the contrary of the self-sufficiency found in the person who believes he can personally do everything and needs no help from anyone else. Both extreme dependency and a complete independence are detrimental to emotional stability and health. To be able to rely on the assistance of a greater power generates a feeling of security and equanimity that relieves tension and makes possible the acceptance of the inevitable. Those who become too dependent on others, however, accept their inadequacies and their condition to such an extent that they cease to struggle, lose their initiative, and become submissive.

Obviously the middle road is the best for individuals with physical disabilities. They must face reality and accept the situation as it is, but they must not relapse into complete dependency, submissiveness, and apathy.

Great athletes tend to be among those who are too self-sufficient and independent. They have great confidence in themselves and tend to believe that if they struggle hard enough and persevere long enough they can overcome every possible obstacle. Some of this spirit and desire to achieve on one's own is characteristic of champions. Nevertheless it is necessary to recognize real limitations and not invite frustrations by persisting in trying to accomplish the impossible.

6 *Identification.* Boys and girls grow up "identifying" themselves with their respective heroes or idols, who may be great athletes, movie stars, famous soldiers, glamorous characters in stories, coaches or teachers. Often it is a parent or a successful brother or sister who serves as the hero or example. Identifying themselves with the objects of their admiration, they often imitate the actions, the speech, and the mannerisms of the latter. This desire to imitate has often influenced the choice of a career.

Individuals may identify with a prestigious club, a great football team, a college, or great historical characters. They live, for a time at least, in the reflected glory of such a group. The important thing to them is to be a part of something which is well thought of, famous, and carries with it a great deal of prestige.

Identification, as an adjustment mechanism, may have its benefits. It gives support to the insecure, it bolsters the person who feels inadequate. Nevertheless, this practice, too, can be carried to an extreme which is harmful. If too much effort is expended trying to imitate another person, if the concern for personal development is lost, if a person tries to be someone other than himself, if personality traits of another are introjected into oneself, there is apt to be a loss of realism, and a lack of completeness in the individual's development. For, each man who seeks self-realization must be himself and cannot be successful wearing another's mantle.

For the weak and handicapped, however, a certain amount of identification can be helpful. To know that one is part of a strong and secure organization, to feel the support of a resourceful and renowned physician, to receive therapy in a famous clinic, all contribute to the security and emotional health of an individual who has feelings of inadequacy.

In athletics certain character traits may be developed or brought out by identification with terms which are steeped in tradition and success. In certain eras of sport, players were enjoined to "remember you are a Yankee," "act and play like a Green Bay Packer," "Don't forget you are wearing the uniform of Notre Dame," and so on. Such enjoinders often did have the effect of motivating athletes to perform with great courage, demonstrate tremendous poise, and play as if victory were always possible if not assured.

Care must be taken, however, that such intangibles of spirit and such psychological factors be blended with enough realism to make for stable individuals, for it is necessary to live life as it is, and not merely act it.

7. *Daydreaming and Fantasy.* When individuals are anxious or worried they often indulge in daydreaming. They may be escaping into a world of fantasy. Permanently crippled individuals try to experience vicariously some of the things about which they hear and read. They dream of themselves as participants in great adventures and exploits. They pretend they are great athletes, great hunters, great statemen. Daydreaming occurs often when individuals are faced with tasks which are too difficult. It may also take place when activities are not challenging enough. It is engaged in by almost everyone to some degree. It provides relief from conflict and frustration, and an escape from unpleasant situations, boring classes, and uninteresting lives.

It is important, however, to face life realistically. To dream of great accomplishments and fine adventures can be the beginning of high achievements and self-fulfilling endeavors. To achieve a proper balance between fantasies which cause one to lose touch with reality and the complete lack of any dreams for the future is the desirable goal. Such a balance should lead to challenging and adventurous lives which bring about optimum growth and development in all aspects of the individual. It is related to the concept previously discussed under "level of aspiration."

It is not unusual on an athletic squad, to observe individuals who have difficulty concentrating very long on a talk by the coach during a "skull session," In the author's experience the "subs" were generally those whose span of attention seemed short or who indulged in most daydreaming. Some of them were thinking ahead to the days when they would be stepping into the shoes of the current stars. Others were beginning to realize and accept the fact that they would never be "regulars." In the former case, the daydreaming was undoubtedly a motivating device which could ultimately lead to stardom. In the latter case, the dreaming was most likely a form of psychological adjustment to some degree of frustration or failure.

8. *Regression.* Regression is a return to reactions which are typical of a younger age. It is a commonly found adjustive reaction and may take many forms. The individual who resorts to crying or lamentations about his fate in order to get what he wants is displaying childish behavior. A person who resorts to temper tantrums or exhibitionism to obtain attention is generally regressing. Living in the past instead of facing up to the problems of the present, running home to get away from problems and to obtain solace from parents, and exhibiting an inordinate interest in awards, trophies, and championships are examples of regressive behavior.

Regression can also be adjustive. An individual can obtain relief by crying, by pouring out his tale of woe to sympathetic parents, by visiting an old friend, or even on occasion by reviewing a scrap book portraying past achievements. Severely injured or handicapped persons occasionally have a real need for such memories, and individuals who have nothing which they can remember with pleasure have more difficulty maintaining emotional balance than those who do. Nevertheless, the person who resorts to regressive behavior too frequently is apt to be lacking in some aspects of mental health. The healthy person lives in the present and future, not in the past.

9. *Repression and Suppression.* Everyone represses or suppresses some of his feelings of guilt, fear, or dangerous desires on certain occasions. Painful and uncomfortable experiences may be intentionally or unconsciously forgotten. Many people refuse to admit the presence of negative thoughts and unpleasant frustrations. When something is willfully and consciously dismissed the phenomenon is called *suppression*, when it is unconsciously forced out of our thoughts it is termed *repression.*

An athlete who has been hurt by a thoughtless and unkind act on the part of the coach or another player may repress his feelings with regard to it. This may affect both the rapport and the intimacy of communication which previously existed. A coach's display of partial-

ity, his benching a player when there is no valid reason, unfair
disciplinary measures, or his lack of understanding for a youthful prank
may cause athletes to have unpleasant or painful feelings which the
latter may find necessary to either suppress or repress.

Some form of repression is probably present in most adjustive
mechanisms. A minimal degree is natural and healthy, but when it
becomes excessive it adds to the difficulty of viewing problems in their
proper perspective and facing them realistically. In some instances,
however, repression may assist in the control of dangerous desires and
may reduce the pain of unpleasant experiences. Like most adjustive
mechanisms, it has its legitimate uses and may, in desirable amounts,
assist in the rehabilitation of the handicapped.

10. *Withdrawal.* A person may withdraw from activity rather than
subject himself to failure, ridicule, or unpleasantness. This type of
behavior is a real problem with many pupils in physical education
classes or with athletes who are in the early learning stages of a sport.

The boy who withdraws from the playground because he cannot
perform well, the embryonic shortstop who intentionally fails to reach
a grounder because he may fumble it, the young man who does not go
to parties because he does not know how to dance, and the disabled
person who goes into seclusion to hide a deformity are all examples of
individuals who are attempting to remove themselves from potentially
distressing situations.

Withdrawal is a particularly serious problem in working with many
of the individuals who are mentally or physically handicapped.
Employees at state hospitals report that this is the most difficult
problem to overcome when trying to conduct a good program of
recreation. Leaders must resort to many devices and tricks to lure
withdrawn individuals into participatory roles.

Coaches are generally quite alert to the problem of withdrawal as
it is reflected in the play of their athletes. They much prefer the person
who tries things regardless of the risk, who suffers minor failures but
bounces right back to try again, over the individual who is so overly
conscientious and concerned that a misplay or a small failure causes
him to withdraw. In other cases a coach may expend considerable
effort in trying to find out why a potentially great athlete fails to
report for the team. More often than not he finds that behind this
withdrawal is the fear of repeated injury or a previous painful
experience in the sport.

Withdrawn persons often need the most help. They have given up
the struggle and need something special to motivate them to try again.
Individual attention, firm but understanding handling, unusual devices

to interest them, small successes from which they may derive joy and pleasure, and experiences which will help them regain confidence, are examples of things which the understanding and experienced leader will try to provide.

9.5 PSYCHOSOMATIC DISORDERS

The degree to which physiological health is influenced by psychological factors is indicated by the large number of maladies which appear in lists of psychosomatic disorders. Stomach ulcers, cancer, colitis, asthma, allergies, indigestion, headaches, backaches, hypertension, some types of arthritis, colds, and cardiac problems have all been attributed, at least partially, to psychological disorders or nervous tension.

It is not the province of the coach or physical education teacher to act in the capacity of a psychiatrist. He can, however, do much to encourage positive mental health and prevent emotional problems. By helping those with whom they work to recognize their real capabilities as well as their limitations, by providing hurdles of appropriate magnitude, by presenting challenges rather than frustrating situations, by helping students to attack one problem at a time, and by making proper referrals, a therapist, teacher, or coach can do much to prevent emotional disorders and to promote optimum mental health.

9.6 SUMMARY

Whether one is a physician, therapist, coach, or teacher, the goal is essentially the same, to assist individuals under his influence to reach their potential, to help them achieve self-fulfillment. With that in mind each must search for the factors which motivate, the weaknesses that hinder, and the causes of both desirable and undesirable behavior. This is a challenging task, for each person is motivated by a different combination of elements, each must adjust to a different set of needs, each has undergone experiences which necessitate a different approach.

There are athletes who are searching for a model worthy of emulation; there are pupils who desperately need a means of escape from a conflicting situation; there are many who are trying to adjust to a frustrating set of circumstances; some will have an urgent need to give themselves to a worthy cause; and more than a few have a deep need for a medium through which they can express themselves. Leaders must be ready to overlook the insignificant, to listen to those in real need of sympathy, to give an "out" to the person who has recently completed a poor performance, and to serve as a supporting pillar when athletes and pupils are injured, weakened, frustrated, anxious, or fearful.

Appropriate adjustive mechanisms of the right intensity can contribute to sound emotional health. Prolonged and inordinate appeal to defense and escape reactions can be harmful. With sound counseling, good referral practices, and understanding leadership much can be done to enable potential neurotics to lead normal and productive lives. A sound mixture of sympathy and firmness combined with an understanding of normal adjustive reactions will assist coaches and physical education teachers to give the proper guidance to all pupils and players so that the latter would learn to know themselves and discover meaning in what they do.

REFERENCES

1. American Association for Health, Physical Education, and Recreation, *Programming for the Mentally Retarded*, Report of a National Conference, October 31-November 2, 1966. Washington: AAHPER, 1968

2. Ashcraft, Samuel C., "The handicapped in the regular classroom," *NEA Journal*, Vol. 56, No. 8, 1967, pp. 33-34

3. Beisser, Arnold R., *The Madness in Sports*. New York: Appleton-Century-Crofts, 1967

4. Brooks, Fowler D., *Child Psychology*. Boston: Houghton-Mifflin, 1937

5. Cantor, Alfred J., *Ridding Yourself of Psychosomatic Health Wreckers*. West Nyack, New York: Parker, 1965

6. Catell, Raymond B., "Some psychological correlates of physical fitness and physique," *Exercise and Fitness*, Athletic Institute, 1960, pp. 138-151

7. Clarke, H. Harrison, and David H. Clarke, *Developmental and Adapted Physical Education*. Englewood Cliffs, N.J.: Prentice-Hall, 1963

8. Clifton, Marguerite A., "The role of perception in movement," *The Academy Papers, No. 1*, The American Academy of Physical Education, March 1968, pp. 21-27

9. Connor, Francis P., "Crippled and health-impaired children," *NEA JOURNAL*, Vol. 56, No. 8, 1967, pp. 37-39

10. Cratty, Bryant J., *Developmental Sequences of Perceptual-Motor Tasks*. Freeport, N.Y.: Educational Activities, 1967

11. Daniels, Arthur S., and Evelyn A. Davies, *Adapted Physical Education*. New York: Harper and Row, 1965, pp. 71-72

12. Delacato, Carl H., *The Diagnosis and Treatment of Speech and Reading Problems*. Springfield, Ill.: Charles C. Thomas, 1968, pp. 7, 77-78

13. Espenschade, Anna S., "Perceptual-motor development in children," *The Academy Papers, No. 1*, The American Academy of Physical Education, 1967, pp. 14-20

14. Godfrey, Barbara B., and Newell C. Kephart, *Movement Patterns and Motor Education.* New York: Appleton-Century-Crofts, 1969, p. 4

15. Hochberg, Julian E., *Perception.* Englewood Cliffs, N.J.: Prentice-Hall, 1964, pp. 1-118

16. Johnson, Warren R., "The problems of aggression and guilt in sports," *Psicologia Dello Sport, Proceedings of First International Congress of Sport Psychology,* Ferrucio Antonelli, editor, Rome, 1965, pp. 187-189

17. Klafs, Carl E., and Daniel D. Arnheim, *Modern Principles of Athletic Training.* St. Louis: C. V. Mosby, 1963

18. Lawther, John D., *The Learning of Physical Skills.* Englewood Cliffs, N.J.: Prentice-Hall, 1968, p. 18

19. Lehner, George F. J., and Ella Kube, *The Dynamics of Personal Adjustment.* Englewood Cliffs, N.J.: Prentice-Hall, 1955

20. Moore, Robert A., *Sports and Mental Health.* Springfield, Ill.: Charles C. Thomas, 1966, pp. 105-108

21. Ogilvie, Bruce C., and Thomas A. Tutko, *Problem Athletes and How To Handle Them.* London: Pelham Books, 1966

22. *Physical Activities for the Mentally Retarded,* Report of Project on Recreation and Fitness for the Mentally Retarded and Lifetime Sports Education Project, American Association for Health, Physical Education, and Recreation

23. Rathbone, Josephine, and Valerie V. Hunt, *Corrective Physical Education.* Philadelphia: W. B. Saunders, 1965, p. 120

24. Rusk, Howard A., and Eugene J. Taylor, *New Hope for the Handicapped.* New York: Harper, 1949, p. 224

25. Siegal, Arthur S., "A motor hypothesis of perceptual development," *American Journal of Psychology,* Vol. 66, 1953, pp. 301-304

26. Stafford, George T., *Sports for the Handicapped.* Englewood Cliffs, N.J.: Prentice-Hall, 1939

27. Stein, Calvert, "Psychological implications of personal injuries," *Medical Trial Technique Quarterly.* Mundelein, Ill.: Callaghan, 1962, pp. 18-19, 21-22

28. Sullivan, Walter, *Disturbances of Your Peace of Mind.* New York: Paulist Press, 1950

29. Wolf, Stewart, "Psychosomatic aspects of competitive sports," *The Journal of Sports Medicine and Physical Fitness,* Vol. 3, No. 2-3, 1963, p. 157

10 SUGGESTIONS TO TEACHERS AND COACHES

*And so the coach's work is really refined
pedagogy as the results of his teaching are put
to a test every Saturday.*

Knute Rockne[22]

Educating through sports, through physical activity, this is the subject matter of this book. To be an effective educator through sports requires a thorough knowledge of the subject matter, namely the sports, a mastery of pedagogical techniques, an understanding of the learner, the art of communication, the ability to influence, and commitment to the complete development and self-realization of all individuals. This is a challenging, monumental, and demanding task and one that is worthy of the very best efforts to which a teacher or coach can give himself. This chapter is concerned with translating concepts, theories, and opinions into practical suggestions and helpful hints. The words of athletes, teachers, and coaches are liberally sprinkled throughout to add interest and emphasis to the items listed.

10.1 TEACHING SPORTS

1. In the early years of a child's life, parents and teachers should provide opportunities for all possible natural and developmental movements. Rings for grasping, space for crawling, objects to be reached, bars for pulling, resistance for kicking, and other devices should be provided to encourage the child to learn. As maturation and growth proceed and self-motivation develops, the natural movements in the natural sequence will usually be learned.

2. There should be as little "pressure" as possible in the early learning stages. Practice should be at normal speed, under circumstances

which are not emotional, and should not be in a highly competitive situation. Good execution, complete understanding, and a gradual increase in tempo are usually to be encouraged.

3.   Optimum results are generally obtained when learning is enjoyable and satisfying. For this reason a positive attitude on the part of the teacher and a liberal application of praise, whenever it can sincerely be given, are urged.

4.   The goal and objectives of each lesson should be clear as practice and learning proceed. While the objectives of the teacher may include much more than those of the pupils, the task of each should be understood and should serve as a challenge and a goal.

5.   When an individual's entire being is bent on learning an activity, greater intensity of effort and therefore more complete achievement are likely.

6.   Every teacher should know and use many teaching methods. Some will serve best in one set of circumstances and others in another. The age of the learner, the nature of the activity, the personality of the teacher, the interest of the group, and the objectives of the lesson are some of the factors to be considered. There is no one "best method."

7.   The "whole" and "part" methods of teaching should be intelligently and appropriately interspersed. Players and pupils must perceive the whole scheme into which the parts are to be integrated. They must not, however, be asked to grasp a "whole" which is so complex and inclusive that they cannot meaningfully deal with it while they are trying to learn.

8.   When it becomes apparent that more practice is needed on an element of a complex skill or a phase of a total game, it is part of good teaching and coaching procedure to organize the practice so as to remedy that particular deficiency or weakness. In speaking of coaching basketball, Everett Dean said,

Actual parts of the offense, such as two-man and three-man plays should be lifted and used as fundamental drills. By following this plan, there is concomitant learning by the players, such as the learning of the play itself, the timing, the fundamentals necessary to execute the play, learning one another's playing habits, condition, and so on.[11]

9.   When attempting to correct faults and overcome weaknesses, the teacher-coach must concentrate on one thing at a time. The pupil can only give attention to a limited range of movement at a particular moment. Patience and persistence are required.

10. Correct performance of fundamentals and good habits should become so ingrained that they are automatic. It is only when the execution of basic movements has been automatized that the necessary amount of attention can be given to deciding what to do.

11. A buoyant, enthusiastic, confident, and optimistic attitude is conducive to rapid learning and good performance. The teacher-coach carries much of the responsibility for creating an environment that encourages such attitudes, which, once present, tend to be contagious.

12. The utilization of many kinds of audio-visual aids as teaching devices is increasingly recognized as an important advance in education. Video tapes, film strips, closed-circuit television, motion pictures, and demonstrations assist pupils and performers in the perception of their task and keep them informed of their progress.

13. When competition is introduced in fundamental drills, there is usually an increase in fun and enjoyment. As these drills become simulated game situations, the likelihood of transfer increases.

14. Learning by doing is still a basic tenet of all education. For this reason scrimmage under game conditions must not be neglected when preparing a team for a season.

15. Drills are an effective way of automatizing basic movements. Individual differences in the need for drills, however, must be recognized. One should not continue to drill an entire group because a few need it. Williams, Dambach, and Schwendener state:

Always have an adequate reason for drilling; do not drill for the sake of discipline, or for exercise, or other traditional reasons but for the sake of gaining skill in some motor problem that relates to a larger activity which vitally appeals.[24]

16. Each activity brings with itself its own special problems. The teacher-coach should know the basic principles of teaching and learning which apply to all program elements and then become expert with regard to those which are pertinent to the specific activities which he is teaching and coaching.

17. Everyone who teaches should familiarize himself with the basic principles connected with the learning curve. There must be patient treatment of the beginner as he tries to gain insight and learn a new facet of a sport. Rapid improvement after the initial stage of learning and then a decrease in the rate of improvement as expertise and proficiency are attained should both be anticipated. Motivational devices and teaching methods should be adjusted to the stage of learning the student is in and the appropriate stimulation for continued progress.

The Perfect Layout

"Correct performance of fundamentals and good habits should become so ingrained that they are automatic. It is only when the execution of basic movements has been automatized that the necessary attention can be given to deciding what to do." *By permission*, James Voss, Washington State University.

Show and Tell in India

"Demonstrations assist pupils and performers in the perception of their task and keep them informed of their progress." *By permission*, Benjamin Davis and Lawrence Buell, Springfield College.

18.   Efficiency in the organization of classes and practices should be
continually evaluated with a view to eliminating unproductive activities
and substituting those which make for increased learning and greater
motivation. The words of Paul Weiss seem appropriate here:

We all gain when the comparatively inept are converted into the efficient, the
indifferent are turned into the cooperative, and skill is made to conspire with
commitment and good judgment.[23]

19.   When an individual has achieved a reasonable degree of proficiency
in the basic motor skills (walking, running, climbing, hanging, jumping,
throwing, etc.) he is ready to learn more complex and intricate ones.
Running must be differentiated into the sprint, the distance run, the
charge of the fullback, or the driving run of the pole-vaulter. The
pitcher, the catcher, the quarterback, the javelin thrower, and the
basketball player must each learn his specialized throw. Little refine-
ments of gross activity patterns should be added when the basis of
fundamental bodily movements has been established.

20.   Pupils tend to learn most rapidly when they are in a state of
"readiness." This state is a function of maturation, of the amount of
learning which has already occurred, and of motivational factors.
Teachers of sports should become expert in not only judging the state
of readiness but also controlling the total environment so as to facilitate
learning.

21.   When a motor skill which is basic to several different motor
patterns in several different sports is being taught, this fact about the
skill should be indicated by the teacher. The probability of transfer is
increased when teachers and coaches assist pupils to generalize and to
recognize similar elements in different situations. The best stance for a
fast start in any direction, the possibilities of increasing peripheral
vision, the summation of forces in many hurling situations, and the
shortening of the radius to increase the speed of rotation, are examples
of principles which apply to numerous motor activities. The general
character of the principles should be understood by those involved in
the teaching of physical education.

22.   There is considerable evidence that mental practice can play a role
in facilitating the learning of physical skills. The teacher should
therefore encourage and assist the learner to analyze his mistakes and
his performances and to determine the causes of both failures and
successes. This mental analysis, however, should not replace traditional
practice but should supplement it. On the other hand, in cases where
athletes are becoming too anxious and tense, it may be wise to

discourage such introspection, especially when they are preparing for a contest.

23. Exploration and discovery are an important part of all learning. It is particularly important, that, in the early stages of skill learning, the pupils should be given opportunities to discover things for themsleves. Challenges can be presented, tasks imposed, and goals displayed. The pupil should then have the opportunity to try developing his own method of accomplishing the given purpose. At the higher-skill levels teaching must be more specific and there must be greater emphasis on performance according to exact mechanical and biological principles.

24. Motives initiate, direct, control, and stop action. Teachers and coaches contribute to the environment which combines with past experiences to provide the stimuli for whatever behavior results. Motivation is the key to rapid learning and outstanding performance. Every great teacher and all great coaches are students of the art of arousing a team or stimulating the learner so that performances may as nearly as possible approach the limit of potential. As Knute Rockne said, "It is not what a coach knows, it is what he can teach his boys, what he can make them do"[22].

25. Personality development proceeds along with the development of motor skills. Good teachers and coaches are cognizant of what is happening with respect to all aspects of the student even as they are presenting new techniques and new strategies in sport.

The outcomes of educational situations are usually much more diverse and comprehensive than the goals. While fundamental movements and game tactics are being learned, pupils are becoming aware of many facets of their being, learning how to interact with others, testing themselves, and relating to superiors, peers, and subordinates. Teachers and coaches must keep this in mind as they arrange practice situations and guide pupils through drills, maneuvers, scrimmages, and contests.

26. When assisting pupils in the development of creativity, more than freedom is required. Spontaneity comes when techniques have been mastered and imagination can run rampant because fundamental movements have become automatic and the necessity for concentrating on procedure has been eliminated.

27. Persistent behavior problems may have an origin that is complex and deep. It will be necessary to treat the causes and not just the symptoms. This will necessitate understanding, patience, and sometimes professional assistance.

28.   Both planning and execution are important. The best-laid plans are worthless if not implemented. Perfect execution is impossible without careful planning.

29.   If certain skills and habits are to be used in several situations, they should be taught in more than one situation. They can be practiced in several sports or in more than one situation in the same sport.

30.   When a teacher is trying to help a pupil break a bad habit, he should try to do so by helping the latter to substitute the correct technique. It is not enough to tell him that he is wrong; he must be shown what is right.

31.   The circumstances of physical education should be controlled so that all members of the group can have a chance to taste success. This may well mean modifying the rules, using a smaller ball, shortening the distance, or adjusting the size of the equipment.

32.   The law of exercise, the law of readiness, and the law of effect should be thoroughly understood by all teachers and coaches. In many instances careful interpretation and rational application of the principles are necessary. These laws must not be thought of as inflexible, immutable, and universal, but rather as basic principles to be intelligently applied.

33.   It is generally agreed that individuals and teams learn and improve the most by competing against others who are slightly better than they are. This rule must not, however, be so rigidly applied that the joys of success are seldom experienced.

34.   Training for leadership and followership must not be overlooked. Sports abound in opportunities where athletes and pupils can develop these qualities. Planning must include the provision of situations where as many students as possible can enjoy experiences which help the pupils become both good leaders and good followers.

35.   Calisthenics should be performed with a specific purpose and should not constitute a major part of a lesson. It is true, however, that a great deal of exercise can be given to a large number of people in limited space with few leaders by this method. However, the psychological effects as well as the physiological outcomes should be carefully weighed.

36.   There is far more self-expression in physical education than is generally realized. Dramatization and expression can occur, not only in dance, but in gymnastics, basketball, tennis, diving, football, baseball,

and many other activities. The freeing of an individual to move as he himself is best able, sometimes to music, sometimes in imitation, and sometimes to express his own interpretation of an act, can be art, and creative self-expression. A solid tackle, a beautiful tee-shot, a well-executed half-gainer, the completed "iron-cross," clearing the bar in good form, or hurling the discus to a new record can all be both artistic and expressive. While individuals perform these and similar feats, they are actually communicating to others who, because of similar experiences, are able to understand.

10.2 COACHING HINTS

From the written word and the spoken word have come many morsels of sound advice. Young coaches may learn from reading and listening to some of these, while older coaches may be stimulated to recall and to renew their faith in well-known principles.

1. Walter Schwank said in an interview with the author:

I believe if one were to single out a single quality that is absolutely necessary for great performances and for winning, it would be "confidence," Confidence, to a large extent, emanates from the coach. He has to drive himself and work hard, but he also has to exhibit a great deal of confidence himself and seek to build confidence in his players. A good way to begin is to work with the team leaders in order to be sure that they believe they can win. They will then inspire others.[45]

2. Optimism and buoyancy should be cultivated on and off the field. Cheerfulness, a sense of humor, and faith that the goals can be reached will do much to make practices enjoyable and seasons successful.

3. In sports such as swimming, track and field, and wrestling it is important for each individual to "feel" the support of the team. Teammates should "walk to the marks" with the performer, help him get ready, pat him on the back as he moves forward for the beginning of the contest, and in every way possible let him know he is not alone.

4. Physiological condition is related to psychological conditioning. Some sports demand greater stamina than others. However, if an athlete feels he is not in top physical condition, he is probably not ready psychologically. As Coach Berquist, the University of Massachusetts baseball coach, said, "It disturbs me when I realize that some practices include too little conditioning. If a player is not in condition, he is really not ready to play the game"[26].

5. Peak performances are the product of the right combination of a number of things. Careful planning, superb physical condition, genuine

motivation, perfection of techniques, knowledge of tactics and strategy, high morale, mental preparation, belief in the worthiness of the effort, a sharing of enthusiasm, concentration on the accomplishment of the task at hand, and confidence that with supreme effort it can be done, all combine to call out the full resources of individuals and teams and to produce performances that approach the limits of the athletes' real potential.

Hamlet Peterson, veteran Luther College coach, included in his list of motivating factors the inculcation of individual responsibility, the acceptance of challenges, individual and team pride, opportunities for athletes to test and prove themselves, the avenging of a humiliating defeat, the excitement of fellow students and faculty, inspiring leadership, and emotional arousal of the team. The last could be achieved by developing a desire to win for an injured and well-liked teammate, by reading challenging items in a newspaper, through the natural rivalry in the "big game," through the presence of individuals "important" to the team, or the inspirational play of a great star[42].

6. Coaches must not hesitate to repeat and repeat again. Overlearning will stabilize an athlete's performance in the excitement of a close contest or when fatigue begins to set in. The automatization of important motor skills will carry an individual through the agony of exhaustion or the bewilderment of too many extraneous stimuli which otherwise might cause him to perform poorly.

7. A coach should use a wide variety of teaching techniques. By so doing he will reach players with different backgrounds and learning habits and will reinforce the learning of each athlete. Classroom teaching, practice on the field, demonstrations, mental practice, and audio-visual aids combine to make for effective teaching and learning.

8. Films depicting high-level performances should be carefully selected. They should depict form and techniques worthy of emulation and appropriate for learning by the athletes to whom they are shown. Occasionally films may be included with high entertainment value, but most of them should contain illustrations of things to be learned.

9. Statistics are valuable for purposes of analysis and study by coaches. Care must be exercised not to burden the players with too many of these, especially during the game and between halves. It is generally better, at these times, to concentrate on immediate and crucial objectives.

10. Athletes must be helped to realize their own capabilities. Coaches can assist by judicious praise, by presentation of objectives and goals

which are appropriately high, by comparing an athlete's performances with others who are only slightly better, and by telling others, in the said athlete's presence, of his potential. He may be helped to tap unsuspected resources if his capabilities and his ambitions are carefully guided and nurtured.

Larry Gluckman, a member of the 1968 crew team at Northeastern University, threw light on this phenomenon as he recounted his experiences. He said:

Here at Northeastern when we get ready to row we go to Ernie's office and sit there. He gives us his strategy and he usually—being the optimist that he is—says, "I know Northeastern can come up with their best performance and I know you're capable of winning." So you feel the same way. Confidence is knowing you can win. It comes from realizing from your practices what your potential is and what your limits are.[33]

11. The great coach assists players in developing the right kind of self-concept. If they see themselves as "losers," they are more apt to play that way. If they see themselves as "winners," that is usually the way they will perform. Stan Marshall, in telling about one of the best football teams he had ever coached, said:

This team was made up of winners. They looked upon themselves as winners. They had been winners in high school. Their self-image was that of a winning team. Because of their long background of winning, they saw themselves as a successful team. I believe, as a general rule, winners continue to win.[40]

12. Coaches should be very careful about ignoring athletes immediately after competition. Even critical comments are often better than just being ignored. Irv Schmid, long-time soccer and assistant track coach at Springfield College, put it in these words:

I have had the experience of being patted on the back when I won and the coach not even being at the finish line when I lost. This bothered me and stuck in my mind as something I would never do. I don't think now I'm guilty of not saying anything to a player after he has finished a game. I may criticize, but I also give praise. However, I again say that when I was running, the hardest thing for me to take was no comment when I was not a victor and all kinds of praise when helping the team to win.[44]

13. Coaches should encourage each individual to discover how he might best prepare himself mentally for a contest. Each individual is different and must not be expected to react in exactly the same way as others. A few examples from outstanding athletes are:

(a)   Butch Stolfa, a former football star at Luther College, said, "Like many athletes, I tended to become quiet and irritable before a football game. After getting taped, dressed, etc. for a game, usually earlier than other players, I always moved to some inconspicuous area of the dressing room away from other squad members. I wanted to be alone with my thoughts; to lie down, relax as best I could, and mentally and spiritually prepare myself for the game. Always my mind reviewed certain anticipated situations with a short, silent prayer to 'psych myself for the contest!' ''[46]

(b) Charles Roys, a great former catcher at Springfield College, used these words: '''Psyching oneself for a contest' is a rather individual reaction, partially removed from the motivating factors of the coach. As a player and coach, the following seemed to have influenced me prior to a peak performance: (a) personally deciding that the forthcoming game was extremely important to the institution, the team, and to me as an individual; (b) the knowledge that important people were to be in the audience seemed to be inspiring, i.e., my parents, close friends, professional scouts; (c) the rewards of winning always appealed to me more than the lessons of defeat. The stronger the opposing team the more enthusiastic I became''[43].

(c) Warren Williamson, wrestling coach at South Dakota State University, wrote: "I am not a great believer in 'psyching,' at least not to the extreme or in some of the ways I hear it is being done. I have seen this hurt performances and also have seen it hurt individuals mentally following losing efforts. These effects are sometimes carried for a lifetime. I prefer a more stable preparation developed around an understanding of one's ability and potential and what is expected of him. The competition itself will 'psyche' the dedicated athlete in most every instance''[50].

(d) Ross Merrick, formerly a star basketball player and coach, summed it up thus: "Getting an individual 'psyched up' for an individual performance is, in my estimation, much more difficult than getting a group properly motivated for a team game. It seems to me it is easier through 'group action' in a team sport to get individual players peaked for a contest. It seems to take off the pressure that you get in individual type competition''[41].

(e) Erv Huether, varsity baseball coach at South Dakota State University, sums it up nicely in these inspiring words: "All mankind possesses capabilities to perform far in excess of their fondest expectations. With this fact in mind, the good competitor is prepared to rise to his greatest performance each time he steps into the arena of strife"[34].

14. A carefully planned and meticulously maintained bulletin board can be very helpful. Charts indicating a team's level of performance, clippings to emphasize or deemphasize certain points about the opponents, inspirational poems and slogans, important rule changes, humorous items to alleviate tension, and important hints with regard to play are types of material that make for an interesting and useful bulletin board.

15. Coaching is a "year around" profession. Everything players do between seasons has a bearing on their performance during the season. Periodic letters to all the players, continual follow-up with regard to the academic work of the athletes, keeping in touch with their vacation activities, learning to know their parents and friends, and being available for counsel with regard to personal problems—these are all included in the many responsibilities and functions of the coach. They are also related to the education and development of the athlete.

16. One of the secrets of successful coaching is conducting practices and dealing with athletes in such a way that they are motivated to work hard at tasks which for many are only drudgery. Drilling on fundamentals, conditioning when tired, overlearning plays and team movements, coming to practice day after day, and preparing difficult assignments are often neither pleasant nor enjoyable. The development of the kind of self-discipline that causes athletes to work hard to improve and to achieve excellence, even though this involves doing things they dislike, is one of the ingredients necessary to accomplish great things and achieve long-range goals. James Bonder terms this attitude "a voluntary submission" and explains it in part by saying:

The quasi-autocratic relationship is not a difficult one, for players willingly subscribe to it . . . Players realize and accept without question the necessity for the coach to make all major decisions. It is a willing submission and conformity on the part of players. Whatever players do and however hard they try, they cannot win by tipping the scales of authority in their favor. They can only win by losing gracefully to the authority. They realize success is dependent upon strict obedience. For some unexplainable reason, players do not resent the strictness of these demands. They recognize that belonging to a team means surrendering something.[6]

Obviously the circumstances should be factors in a consideration of whether to adopt dictatorial or democratic methods. In emergency situations, where immediate decisions are necessary, there is little time for prolonged consultation, nor can such consultation be effective. The coach must, in such instances, issue sharp commands and the players hasten to obey. At other times, however, and in more leisurely situations, other leadership techniques are recommended. "Terry" Jackson, a former all-American soccer player and currently a varsity coach, put it this way:

I definitely feel that the coach does have an influence on the boy. The type of coach who has the most influence is the one who is a coach, *but a person also*, the one to whom the boy is not afraid to come and talk. I don't think the coach who is a dictator has as much influence as the other kind.[35]

17. On trips and on game days, coaches must be particularly concerned about attitudes, spirit, and the psychological aspects of game preparation. With departures from routine, different sleeping accommodations, long trips, meals prepared and served in strange places, and time hanging heavily on their hands, the team members can easily become mentally upset, overanxious, or too relaxed. Coaches can do much to prevent detrimental reactions by the right mixture of cheerfulness, optimism, concern, and friendliness. Captains and veterans also play an important part in creating and sustaining desirable attitudes.

18. New players should be given experience early in the season. Many a contest has been won or lost on the strength and readiness of substitutes. Many substitutes need time for self-testing and the development of confidence.

19. Teams which are on a "losing streak" need more than criticism. Confidence is even more necessary. It will be more difficult to prepare for peak performance if their self-image becomes one which shakes their confidence in themselves. George Van Bibber said about an important game in which he played and where Purdue snatched victory in the fourth quarter from a favored Michigan team:

The most important motivating factor for the whole team was the drive of personal and team confidence gained through the total effort that preceded the game. The team was not to be denied a victory it felt it deserved.[47]

20. Teamwork consists in working together in the way that is best for the team. In some cases it may mean shooting almost every time you have the ball; in others it may be not shooting at all. In certain situations it may be concentrating on defense; in others it may be focusing on offense. On one occasion teamwork may involve sharply rebuking a teammate, while on another it may require constant encouragement. Teamwork can be doing something which is unpleasant

but necessary, receiving glory modestly, sharing praise with teammates, or submerging oneself for the good of the whole. It most often is exhibited in accomplishing some unnoticed but important task which leads to the accomplishment of a team objective.

Many players do not learn the full meaning of teamwork until it is too late. It is the responsibility of the coach to teach them.

21. It is extremely important that substitutes have good spirit. They must somehow be made to feel that they are making a worthwhile contribution. Because it is more difficult for a substitute to maintain his enthusiasm and eagerness, the coach must make a conscious effort to encourage him so that he becomes a productive squad member.

22. Great athletes have the ability to make hard plays look easy. Even while operating at peak levels they appear completely relaxed. Morehouse and Rasch explain it in these words:

... The outstanding characteristic of the expert athlete is his ease of movement, even during maximal effort. The novice is characterized by his tenseness, waste motion and excess effort. That rare person, the "natural athlete," seems to be endowed with the ability to undertake any sports activity, whether he is experienced in it or not, with ease. This ease is an ability to perform with minimal antagonistic tension.[18]

23. Many athletes "try too hard." We see this when the runner "ties up" and shortens his stride, when the free-thrower "tightens" as he is about to shoot, when the quarterback passes wide off his target, when the golfer "chokes" on an important putt. Energy is wasted, coordinations diminish, and antagonistic muscles refuse to relax. Athletes can improve in their ability to relax, and coaches can assist them in this endeavor. A confident, ready, free, and eager attitude is the goal.

24. Staleness may be physiological, psychological, or a combination of both. Staleness is seldom found on winning teams, but its cause and effect have not been fully ascertained. The phenomenon is, to a certain extent, circular. Stale teams lose, and losing is often a causal factor in staleness. Staleness generally manifests itself in a lack of eagerness, an abnormal irritability, a loss of appetite, headaches, and sometimes allergic reactions. The stale athlete fatigues easily, moves more slowly than usual, appears to resent suggestions, is absent minded, and no longer looks forward to practice. Shorter practices, more rest, a victory, an excellent personal performance, or an exciting social event will often alleviate staleness. Careful scheduling of contests, coaches' attention to the personal problems of players, and good conditioning based on sound health practices should serve as effective preventive measures. Beyond these, medical or even psychiatric assistance may be necessary.

25.   The wise coach is constantly alert for signs on the part of athletes of insecurity and the feeling of lack of acceptance by peers. Fear of loss of status on account of inadequate performance, inability to sleep due to anxiety with regard to his future in a sport, and a gnawing apprehension that he may be a failure can give rise in an athlete to excess tension, pressing, staleness, and possibly eventual psychosomatic disturbances.

26.   Coaches must be thoroughly familiar with the phenomenon of "momentum." It may develop through an unusually auspicious beginning for one team or another; it may result from an exceptional feat on the part of a single athlete; it may begin with the cheering of the crowd; it may come as a result of "closing the gap" when behind; it may be initiated by unexpected success. Momentum will work for a contestant or a team in some instances and against it in others. To stop the opponent's momentum, to gain the initiative, and to maintain momentum when it is on "your" side—this is an important goal. Knowing when to substitute and when not to is a partial answer. Being mentally prepared is another. To regain the initiative once it is lost, and when the opponents have achieved momentum, takes courage, determination, and often special tactics. Changes in strategy and play are often desirable in such situations.

When asked whether the phenomenon of momentum operated in track and field, Bob Giegengach replied,

Yes, it can happen in track also. There must be something operating when suddenly on a given day everyone performs so well. Some kind of unity appears to be present when everyone senses, after one or two events, that it is going to be a big day. I like, in the opening event, to put as much power to work as possible, even if it means meeting the opponents "head to head" where they are the strongest. If one can "destroy them in the beginning," everything seems to go well from then on.[30]

And Carmen Cozza indicated that it operated in football when he said,

Yes, it happens in all sports. Sometimes it seems like a game of "surges." It works both for you and against you. Poise, timing, and execution seem to be right when you have momentum and lost when it is working against you.[28]

Speaking of momentum in a different way Weber states:

A team gets rolling through winning several football games and this has a bearing on the frame of mind for the games to follow.[49]

27.   Many coaches speak of goal-setting as the most important and long-lasting motivational device. A few excerpts from experienced

athletes and coaches are:

The coaches' job is to set realistic goals and step-by-step strive to achieve them. This involves careful evaluation of personnel and the personality of each individual. It involves building team morale and individual morale.[27]

Setting a goal for the season, such as a conference championship, an NCAA bid, a scoring championship, a school record, etc., are means of motivating individuals to play up to capacity or even overachieve.[51]

The psychological limit must somehow be overcome through careful coaching, understanding and motivation. The challenge must be real and accepted by the participants.[38]

Coaches and players, like students in the classroom, seem to achieve pretty much what is expected of them. Expectations are both seasonal and situational. All the forces which influence an athlete, coaches, friends, peers, press, alumni, and parents determine what these expectations will be. In some cases where the coach is a strong personality, his influence dominates all others.[36]

There seems to be a common goal—a basic desire to excel or to win. It appears to be a progressive, self-feeding sort of thing and it has one great physical characteristic which is observable, and that is a *supreme concentration*. To all things extraneous to the task at hand, the team is oblivious.[31]

It is important to set a goal. An athlete loves to achieve the impossible, to be the first to reach a new goal, to establish a record. There should be a gradual development of mind and body so that the athlete is "ready" at game time, not two days before.[32]

28. When athletes have established "their own best way" to prepare themselves mentally for a game, the coach should interfere as little as possible. To ridicule an individual for his peculiarities in this regard may counteract many positive things which have been done to prepare him mentally. Matthew Maetozo said:

All who are associated with athletes must realize that they may possess certain precontest idiosyncracies and superstitions. Each individual usually prepares for a contest in a fixed way. He must follow a fixed routine or he will not feel, psychologically, that he is ready. I have known an athlete who felt more confident and competent defensively after obtaining a new glove. He *thought* that this increased his range and ability.[39]

29. Herb Bartling, formerly a star performer in football and basketball and a psychology major, felt it was important to emphasize differences in various situations:

"Psyching oneself for a contest" is exceedingly complex. I would suggest that this mental preparation varies from one type of sport to another, from one position to another, and from one individual to another. We have individual differences here as in anything else. Thus, where one person might need to "psych down," another might need to "psych up." My own problem was always one of expending too much emotional energy prior to a contest.[25]

30. There are those who feel that the best way of achieving peak performances is not to be too concerned about the outcome but concentrate on the satisfaction that comes from having "given one's all" in the attempt. Perhaps the familiar words of Grantland Rice, "It matters not whether you won or lost but how you played the game," may have the greatest meaning for many. Joy Kistler said much the same thing as he responded,

When the superb effort appears to be necessary, the best way to prepare is the "joy of effort" concept. One is most likely to eliminate the factor of "fear of failure"—and this is so necessary to supreme performance—by concentrating on the *pleasure* involved in trying to do a bit better than ever before.[37]

31. The importance of forgetting the self for the good of the team came through over and over as coaches and athletes were interviewed. Concentrating on the task and not on one's own success or failure seems to be the key. "Sox" Walseth had this to say:

In a team sport such as basketball, the good of the team must be paramount in each player's mind, not an individual's success or failure. In other words, there must be a strong feeling that accomplishing the goal of winning this particular game is *the* most important thing and not individual performances. If the motivation of each player is one hundred percent for the team to do as well as possible, you will have a good effort.[48]

32. Several coaches indicated that they utilized incentives, rewards, awards of various kinds. They were generally quick to point out, however, that these were symbolic and served to add interest and zest to practices and to relieve the monotony of long and strenuous seasons. All felt that they should not and could not replace the deeper and more lasting motivations. Kent Finanger included in a long list of motivational techniques the following observation:

I emphasize positive motivation, team goals, and team unity. But I also utilize "rewards" of various kinds: steaks, names on blackboard, certificates, cokes, and other forms of incentives. We work on building individual and team pride as well as pride in school. We emphasize dedication, togetherness, and willingness to work.[29]

33. Coaches should explore fully the underdeveloped potentials of athletes. While estimates vary as to the degree to which individuals achieve their potential, most experienced observers believe that there is a great deal of latent ability in most persons and that development falls far short of what is possible. Darrell Mudra emphasizes this when he states:

The second concept that underlies the perceptual approach is the idea that everyone on the team has talent worth developing ... You don't know which players are going to make a big contribution to your squad, and because ability is sufficiently general, you work with them all.[19]

10.3 THE UTILIZATION OF PSYCHOLOGY

It is apparent that psychological concepts have much that is of value to the coach and the physical education teacher. A caution may, however, be in order. Psychology cannot replace hard work, perseverance, careful planning, effective leadership, and carefully conducted classes and practices. Psychology should be a part of all this. It is not a supplement, but an integral facet of teaching, of drilling, of learning, and of developing.

Psychological concepts must be appropriately applied. A knowledge of the principles underlying motor learning, an understanding of effective motivational techniques, the ability to assess and utilize diverse personality traits, and an appreciation of the emotional problems of individuals—these are all needed by the person who aspires to be the master teacher or the great coach.

Allowances and adjustments for individual differences, sensitivity to problems of mental health, and the desire to make the activities of physical education meaningful in the lives of the pupils will contribute to physical education. The values derived from associations with athletic leaders who have as their major goal the self-fulfillment of every student and every athlete can never be accurately measured. Their influences continue to spread, like a ripple of water, through all who are touched by their teachings and their lives.

REFERENCES

1. Allen, George H., *Pass Defense Drills*. Reading, Mass.: Addison-Wesley, 1968

2. American Association for Health, Physical Education, and Recreation, *Knowledge and Understanding in Physical Education*. Washington: AAHPER, 1969

3. Arnold, P. J., *Education, Physical Education and Personality Development*. New York: Atherton Press, 1968

4. Auerbach, Arnold "Red," *Basketball for the Player, The Fan and The Coach*. New York: Pocket Books, 1953

5. Bernard, Harold W., *Psychology of Learning and Teaching*. New York: McGraw-Hill, 1965

6. Bonder, James B., *How to Be a Successful Coach*. Englewood Cliffs, N.J.: Prentice-Hall, 1958, p. 3

7. Bowen, Wilbur P., and Elmer D. Mitchell, *The Practice of Organized Play.* New York: A. S. Barnes, 1929

8. Bresnahan, George T., W. T. Tuttle, and Francis X. Cretzmeyer, *Track and Field Athletics.* St. Louis: C. V. Mosby, 1960

9. Coombs, John W., *Baseball.* Englewood Cliffs, N.J.: Prentice-Hall, 1939

10. Cousy, Bob, *Basketball is My Life.* New York: J. Lowell Pratt, 1963

11. Dean, Everett S., *Progressive Basketball.* Englewood Cliffs, N.J.: Prentice-Hall, 1950, p. 47

12. Friermood, Harold T., and J. Wesley McVicar, *Basic Physical Education in the YMCA.* New York: Association Press, 1962

13. Hammer, Bill, *Football Coach's Complete Handbook.* Englewood Cliffs, N.J.: Prentice-Hall, 1963

14. Knapp, Clyde, and Patricia H. Leonard, *Teaching Physical Education in Secondary Schools.* New York: McGraw-Hill, 1968

15. Lambert, Ward L., *Practical Basketball.* Chicago: Athletic Journal Publishing Company, 1932

16. Madsen, Charles H., Jr., Wesley C. Becker, and Don R. Thomas, "Rules, praise and ignoring: elements of elementary classroom control," *Journal of Applied Behavior Analysis,* Vol. 1, No. 2, 1968

17. Moore, Roy, "An analysis of modern theoretical approaches to learning with implications for teaching gross motor skills in physical education," unpublished Ph.D. Thesis, University of Iowa, 1949, Microcard

18. Morehouse, Laurence E., and Philip J. Rasch, *Scientific Basis of Athletic Training.* Philadelphia: W. B. Saunders, 1958, pp. 40-41

19. Mudra, Darrell, "The coach and the learning process," *Journal of Health, Physical Education, and Recreation,* Vol. 41, 1970, p. 29

20. Piaget, Jean, *The Construction of Reality in the Child.* New York: Basic Books, 1954

21. Rhoda, William P., "Student attitudes and opinions toward the University Service Course Program for Men," *Physical Educator, Vol. 15, 1958, pp. 141-142*

22. Rockne, Knute K., *Coaching.* New York: Devin-Adair, 1931 pp. 209, 218

23. Weiss, Paul, *Sport: A Philosophic Inquiry.* Carbondale, Ill.: Southern Illinois University Press, 1969, p. 48

24. Williams, Jesse F., John I. Dambach, and Norma Schwendener, *Methods in Physical Education.* Philadelphia: W. B. Saunders, 1932, p. 131

25. Bartling, Herbert, Acting Director, Counseling and Testing Center, Eastern Illinois University, Charleston, Illinois, and former athletic star, South Dakota State University, response to questionnaire, 1969

26. Bergquist, Richard E., Baseball Coach, University of Massachusetts, personal interview, 1969

27. Bies, Orval, Track and Field Coach, St. Olaf College, response to questionnaire, 1969

28. Cozza, Carmen, Football Coach, Yale University, personal interview, 1969

29. Finanger, Kent, Director of Athletics and Basketball Coach, Luther College, Decorah, Iowa, response to questionnaire, 1969

30. Giegengack, Robert, Track and Field Coach, Yale University, and Coach of United States Track and Field Team, Olympic Games, Tokyo, 1964, personal interview, 1969

31. Gilbert, Paul, Professor of Physical Education, Colorado State University, response to questionnaire, 1969

32. Ginn, Ralph, member of Physical Education faculty and former Football Coach, South Dakota State University, response to questionnaire, 1969

33. Gluckman, Larry, Captain of Crew, Northeastern University, personal interview, 1969

34. Huether, Ervin, member of Physical Education faculty and Baseball Coach, South Dakota State University, response to questionnaire, 1969

35. Jackson, Albert T., Soccer Coach, Wesleyan University, personal interview, 1969

36. King, Clark, Director of Physical Education for Men, Virginia Military Institute, response to questionnaire, 1969

37. Kistler, Joy, former Director of Health, Physical Education and Recreation, Louisiana State University, response to questionnaire, 1969

38. Long, James, Director of Health, Physical Education and Recreation, Oregon State University, response to questionnaire, 1969

39. Maetozo, Matthew G., Director of Health, Physical Education, and Recreation, Lockhaven State College, response to questionnaire, 1969

40. Marshall, Stanley, Director of Health, Physical Education, and Recreation, South Dakota State University, personal interview, 1969

41. Merrick, Roswell D., Assistant Executive Secretary, AAHPER, Washington, D.C., response to questionnaire, 1969

42. Peterson, Hamlet, former Director of Athletics and Coach, Luther College, Decorah, Iowa, response to questionnaire, 1969

43. Roys, Charles N., member of Physical Education faculty and Baseball Coach, Springfield College, response to questionnaire, 1969

44. Schmid, Irvin R., member of Physical Education faculty and Soccer Coach, Springfield College, personal interview, 1969

45. Schwank, Walter, Professor of Physical Education and former Coach, University of Montana, personal interview, 1969

46. Stolfa, Anton, Director of Physical Education and Athletics, Davenport Public Schools, Davenport, Iowa, response to questionnaire, 1969

47. Van Bibber, George, former Director of Physical Education and Coach, University of Connecticut, response to questionnaire, 1969

48. Walseth, Russell M., Basketball Coach, University of Colorado, response to questionnaire, 1969

49. Weber, Robert J., Director of Physical Education and former coach, State University of New York, Cortland, New York, response to questionnaire, 1969

50. Williamson, Warren, member of Physical Education faculty and Wrestling Coach, South Dakota State University, response to questionnaire, 1969

51. Witham, James, former Director of Athletics and Coach, Northern Iowa University, response to questionnaire, 1969

MISCELLANEOUS REFERENCES

MISCELLANEOUS REFERENCES

1. Durant, John, editor, *Yesterday in Sports*. New York: A. S. Barnes, 1956

2. Eichenlaub, John E., *College Health*. New York: Macmillan, 1962

3. Falls, Harold B., Earl L. Wallis, and Gene A. Logan, *Foundations of Conditioning*. New York: Academic Press, 1970

4. Franks, B. Don, editor, *Exercise and Fitness—1969, Proceedings of a Symposium Honoring Dr. Thomas Kirk Cureton, Jr.* Chicago: Athletic Institute, 1969

5. Friermood, Harold T., *The YMCA Guide to Adult Fitness*. New York: Association Press, 1963

6. Frost, Reuben B., "Some psychological implications for olympic sports," *Report of the Fifth Summer Session of the International Olympic Academy.* Athens: Hellenic Olympic Committee, 1965, pp. 136-149

7. Gallico, Paul, *Farewell to Sport*. New York: Pocket Books, 1945

8. Garrison, Karl C., and Stanley J. Gray, *Educational Psychology*. New York: Appleton-Century-Crofts, 1955

9. Goodenough, Florence L., *Developmental Psychology*. New York: Appleton-Century, 1934

10. Hall, Calvin S., *Psychology*. Cleveland: Howard Allen, 1960

11. Hartley, Eugene L., and Ruth E. Hartley, *Outside Readings in Psychology*. New York: Thomas G. Crowell, 1958

12. Hartmann, Heinz, *Ego Psychology and the Problem of Adaptation*. New York: International Universities Press, 1958

13. Hebb, D. O., *The Organization of Behavior*. New York: Wiley, 1949

14. Hein, Fred V., Dana L. Farnsworth, and Charles E. Richardson, *Living.* Oakland, N.J.: Scott, Foresman, 1970

15. Hollander, Zander, *Great American Athletes of The 20th Century.* New York: Random House, 1966

16. Jokl, Ernst, *International Research in Sport and Physical Education.* Springfield, Ill.: Charles C. Thomas, 1964

17. Keele, Cyril A., and Eric Neil, *Samson Wright's Applied Physiology.* New York: Oxford University Press, 1965

18. Meanwell, Walter E., *The Science of Basketball.* Madison, Wis.: Democrat Printing, 1924

19. Morgan, Clifford T., *Physiological Psychology.* New York: McGraw-Hill, 1943

20. Morgan, William P., "Psychological considerations," *Journal of Health, Physical Education, and Recreation,* Vol. 39, November/December 1968

21. Nash, Jay B., *Building Morale.* New York: A. S. Barnes, 1942

22. Pettit, Bob, with Bob Wolff, *The Drive Within Me.* Englewood Cliffs, N.J.: Prentice-Hall, 1966

23. Plimpton, George, *Paper Lion.* New York: Pocket Books, 1969

24. *Psicologia Dello Sport, Proceedings of the First International Congress of Sport Psychology,* Ferrucio Antonelli, editor, Rome, 1965

25. Rosenblith, Judy F., and Wesley Allinsmith, *The Causes of Behavior II.* Boston: Allyn and Bacon, 1961

26. Ryan, Dean, "What does psychology have to offer coaches and trainers?" *Proceedings, 68th Annual Conference, National College Physical Education Association for Men, January 1965.* Washington, D.C.: AAHPER 1965, pp. 34-38

27. Scott, M. Gladys, "The contributions of physical activity to psychological development," *Research Quarterly,* Vol. 31, No. 2, Part II, 1960, pp. 307-320

28. Silvia, Charles E., *Lifesaving and Water Safety Today.* New York: Association Press, 1965

29. Sliepcevich, Elena M., Summary Report of a Nationwide Study of Health Instruction in the Public Schools, 1201 Sixteenth Street, N.W., Washington, D.C., 1964

30. Steinhaus, Arthur, "Fitness beyond muscle," *The Journal of Sports Medicine and Physical Fitness,* Vol. 6, No. 3, 1966, p. 191

31. Veenker, George F., *Basketball for Coaches and Players.* New York: A. S. Barnes, 1929

32. White, Paul Dudley, and Curtis Mitchell, *Fitness for the Whole Family.* Garden City, N.Y.: Doubleday, 1964

33. Adams, George, Physical Education major and member of football team, Springfield College, personal interview, 1969

34. Arguin, Ralph, Physical Education major and member of soccer team, Springfield College, personal interview, 1969

35. Arnold, Lloyd C., National Director, YMCA Health and Physical Education, personal interview, 1969

36. Balis, Tony, Cocaptain, soccer team, Wesleyan University, personal interview, 1969

37. Belk, Lyle, Basketball Coach, North Dakota State University, response to questionnaire, 1969

38. Bischoff, David, Associate Dean, School of Health, Physical Education and Recreation, University of Massachusetts, personal interview, 1969

39. Bitgood, Paul, Professor of Physical Education and former Coach, Rochester University, personal interview, 1969

40. Bradley, Bruce, member UCLA Water Polo Team and U.S. Olympic Water Polo Team, Olympic Games in Mexico City, 1968, personal interview, 1969

41. Brockmeier, Winfred, Director of Athletics and Football Coach, Wausau Public Schools, Wausau, Wisconsin, personal interview, 1969

42. Brown, Lyle, Basketball Coach, University of Rochester, Rochester, New York, personal interview, 1969

43. Brynteson, Paul, member of Physical Education faculty and football coach, South Dakota State University, response to questionnaire, 1969

44. Buckley, Chester, Professor of Physical Education and former Coach, St. Cloud State College, response to questionnaire, 1969

45. Bundgaard, Axel C., Director of Athletics and Physical Education, St. Olaf College, response to questionnaire, 1969

46. Cataldi, Peter, Professor of Physical Education, Syracuse University, personal interview, 1969

47. Childs, Harold, Professor of Health Education and former gymnast, Springfield College, personal interview, 1969

48. Chinappi, Tony, catcher on University of Massachusetts baseball team, personal interview, 1969

49. Chipman, LeRoy, Physical Education Instructor and Basketball Coach, Hartwick College, Oneonta, New York, response to questionnaire, 1969

50. Christensen, Jack, Physical Education Instructor and Coach, Rochester Public Schools, Rochester, New York, personal interview, 1969

51. Cieplik, Raymond, member of Physical Education faculty and Soccer and Baseball Coach, Springfield College, personal interview, 1969

52. Clausen, M. Richard, Director of Physical Education and Athletics and former Football Coach, University of Arizona, response to questionnaire, 1969

53. Cobb, Robert, Professor of Physical Education, University of Maine, personal interview, 1969

54. Cormier, Brian, Director of Health and Physical Education, Central YMCA, Springfield, Massachusetts, personal interview, 1969

55. Dicicco, Anthony, Physical Education major and soccer goalie, Springfield College, personal interview, 1969

56. Dooley, Aubrey, Track and Field Coach, South Dakota State University, response to questionnaire, 1969

57. Dunn, Edward, member of Physical Education faculty and Varsity Football Coach, Springfield College, personal interview, 1969

58. Eldridge, Stephen, Wrestling Coach, U.S. Coast Guard Academy

59. Ellershaw, Lawrence, Former Director of Health and Physical Education, Central YMCA, Springfield, Massachusetts, personal interview, 1969

60. Forbush, Al, Director of Health and Physical Education, New Haven YMCA, New Haven, Connecticut, personal interview, 1969

61. Forsyth, Harry, member of Physical Education faculty and Baseball Coach, South Dakota State University, personal interview, 1969

62. Foster, Graham, Physical Education Instructor and Coach, Roslyn Public Schools, Roslyn, New York, personal interview, 1969

63. Gibbons, William, Football and Wrestling Coach, Brookings High School, Brookings, South Dakota, response to questionnaire, 1969

64. Graham, George, Physical Education Instructor and Football Coach, Rochester Public Schools, Rochester, New York, personal interview, 1969

65. Hoffman, Ronald, Director of Physical Education and former Coach, St. Lawrence University, personal interview, 1969

66. Joyce, Arnold, Physical Education Instructor and Swimming Coach, Virginia Military Institute, personal interview, 1969

67. Kiphuth, Delaney, Director of Athletics, Yale University, personal interview, 1969

68. Kjeldsen, Erik K. M., Coach of Gymnastics, University of Massachusetts, personal interview, 1969

69. Knudson, Thomas, Physical Education Instructor and Basketball Coach, Bridgewater State College, response to questionnaire, 1969

70. Lander, Donald, Physical Education Instructor and Coach, Rochester Public Schools, Rochester, New York, personal interview, 1969

71. Ley, Catherine, Director of Physical Education for Women, New York State University at Cortland, personal interview, 1969

72. LeSueur, Paul, Physical Education major and member of Soccer Team, Springfield College, personal interview, 1969

73. Marking, James, member of Physical Education faculty and Basketball Coach, South Dakota State University, response to questionnaire, 1969

74. Maynard, Douglas, Cocaptain, Soccer Team, Wesleyan University, personal interview, 1969

75. McClone, Robert, Fitness Director, New Britain YMCA, New Britain, Connecticut, personal interview, 1969

76. McKeon, John, Physical Education Instructor and Soccer Coach, East Stroudsburg State College, response to questionnaire, 1969

77. Melleby, Alexander, Director of Health and Physical Education, YMCA of Greater New York, New York City, personal interview, 1969

78. Moriarity, Philip, Swimming Coach, Yale University, Connecticut, personal interview, 1969

79. Morrell, Robert, member of Track Team, Springfield College, personal interview, 1969

80. Moser, Charles, Director of Athletics and Football Coach, Abilene High School, Abilene, Texas, personal interview, 1969

81. Neumann, John, member of Physical Education faculty and former Coach, Springfield College, Springfield, Massachusetts, personal interview, 1969

82. O'Brien, Kenneth, Track and Field Coach, University of Massachusetts, personal interview, 1969

83. O'Connel, Ward, Diving Coach, Yale University, personal interview, 1969

84. Pisano, Al, Physical Education Instructor and Lacrosse Coach, New York State University at Cortland, personal interview, 1969

85. Ricci, Benjamin, Professor of Physical Education and Director of Exercise Physiology Research, University of Massachusetts, personal interview, 1969

86. Robinson, Roger I., Physical Education Instructor and Football Coach, New York State University at Cortland, personal interview, 1969

87. Rogers, Joseph R., Jr., Swimming Coach, University of Massachusetts, personal interview, 1969

88. Sanborn, Wayne, Physical Education major and member of Football Team, Springfield College, personal interview, 1969

89. Scro, Moe, Physical Education Instructor, Roslyn High School and Football Coach, Adelphi University, personal interview, 1969

90. Selin, Carl, Director of Physical Education and Athletics United States Coast Guard Academy, personal interview, 1969

91. Shattuck, Alden M., Physical Education major and member of Soccer Team, Springfield College, personal interview, 1969

92. Shaw, Jack, Director of Health, Physical Education and Recreation, Syracuse University, personal interview, 1969

93. Thompson, Harry, Director of Outdoor Education Project, Glenwood Landing, Long Island, and former Director of Physical Education, personal interview, 1969

94. Vancisin, Joseph R., Basketball Coach, Yale University, personal interview, 1969

95. Vessichelli, Robert, member of Football and Baseball Teams, Roslyn High School, Roslyn, New York, personal interview, 1969

96. Wales, Ross, Bronze Medal winner, Butterfly Stroke, United States Swimming Team, Olympic Games, Mexico City, 1968, and Captain of Princeton University Swimming Team, personal interview, 1969

97. Walsh, Edward, Director of Physical Education and Coach, Manhasset High School, Long Island, New York, personal interview, 1969

98. Waterman, Bert, Wrestling Coach, Yale University, personal interview, 1969

GLOSSARY

GLOSSARY

ADJUSTMENT MECHANISM. A behavior by which an individual protects his self-esteem and which helps to restore homeostatic balance.

AMBIENT. Encompassing, on all sides.

ANTIGRAVITY REFLEX. A reflex that counteracts the pull of gravity, that tends to maintain the human body in the upright position, and in which the large extensor muscles are stimulated to contract.

ANXIETY. An uneasiness and feeling of foreboding often found when a person is about to embark on a hazardous venture; it is often accompanied by a strong desire to excel.

APATHY. Listlessness; absence of emotion even under normally stimulating situations.

ASSOCIATIONIST. One who espouses stimulus—response associationism as the principle theory of learning.

CARDIOVASCULAR. Pertaining to the circulatory system (heart and blood vessels).

CATHARSIS. A purging, cleansing, or freeing; sometimes applied to a theory of play or a theory of aggression. Inherent is the idea that activity can purge the organism of tensions and anxieties.

CEREBELLUM. A part of the brain located behind the cerebrum and above the pons; controls and coordinates much motor activity.

CEREBRAL DOMINANCE. Also termed hemispheric dominance. The theory that one hemisphere of the cerebrum dominates the motor activities of an individual and that when this dominance is lost, motor coordination becomes more difficult.

CONCEPT. A principle or meaningful idea, often based on a pattern of items.

COUNTERPHOBIC. Opposing or working against fear.

CUE. A signal to begin, a stimulus that guides behavior.

DRIVE. A basic impulse, an inner urge; it can initiate, direct, or inhibit behavior.

EMOTION. A state of physiological and psychological imbalance accompanied by feelings of anger, fear, affection, joy, despair, etc.

ENDOCRINE GLANDS. Glands producing internal secretions which pass directly into the bloodstream and are carried by the blood or lymph.

ERGOGRAPH. An instrument for measuring and recording the amount of work done.

EXTEROCEPTOR. A sense organ which responds to stimuli coming from outside the body.

FEEDBACK. All the information which comes through exteroceptors and proprioceptors and which keeps the organism informed as to his physical condition, his current status, and his progress. It includes information as to bodily movements and the position of the various body parts.

FIXATION. A rigidness in behavior; a preoccupation with a task; a state resulting from complete frustration with an important assignment or the blocking of goal oriented behavior.

FRUSTRATION. A psychological state which usually results from the blocking of the achievement of an important goal. It may also be caused by inner conflict. It may, if prolonged, result in apathy and dependency, and sometimes anger.

GENETIC. Pertaining to the origin or genesis of something; related to heredity.

GESTALIST. Pertaining to the beliefs of the Gestalt psychologists who hold that learning occurs through insight and that what the learner perceives is a pattern or configuration. The learner reacts to a total situation and not isolated stimuli.

HOLISM. The philosophy that all aspects, all facets, and all dimensions of the human organism are reciprocally interrelated and that educators must realize that the whole man is affected by all experiences.

HOMEOSTASIS. A stable state of physiological conditions; an internal state of chemical and energy balance.

HOSTILITY. A feeling of ill will, unfriendliness, and antagonism toward an individual or object.

HYPOTHALAMUS. The subthalamic region of the midbrain which is thought to contain the mechanisms for the control of emotions (anger, fear, etc.).

INCENTIVE. Something that exerts an influence toward a specific action; reward; extrinsic stimulus.

INDIVIDUATION. The separation of a part of a gross motor act from the total movement pattern and making it an entity unto itself. It can then be made part of another motor act.

ISOMETRIC. Retaining the same length; applied to the forcible contraction of muscles when the lever arm does not move.

KINESTHESIS. The awareness, on the part of each individual, of the position and movement of the various parts of the body as well as the body as a whole.

LABYRINTHINE. Pertaining to the inner ear and especially the complex apparatus which contains the mechanisms for the control of balance and the perception of body position.

MENARCHE. The onset of menses or the beginning of menstrual function.

MENTAL PRACTICE. The intellectualization of motor movements; the mental rehearsal of each part of a movement pattern without actually going through it physically.

METABOLITE. The product of the chemical processes which occur in the human body; the substances produced by metabolism.

MOMENTUM. Impetus; the surge which comes when a team is suddenly stimulated by a leader or a happening in an athletic contest.

MORO-RESPONSE. Also called the "startle reflex"; the response of an infant to a sudden jarring or change in position. Its persistence beyond several months of age often indicates abnormality.

MORPHOLOGIC. Pertaining to structure or form.

MOTIVATION. That which initiates, directs, or stops behavior; something which impels one to move, to act, or to desist; any need, urge, emotion, or drive that prompts an individual to action.

MOTOR PATTERN. A series of acts, related and integrated so as to accomplish a given motor task.

MOTOR SKILL. A movement which has been learned; usually applied to a relatively complex movement and one in which the individual has attained a high degree of competency. Various basic movements may have been integrated into a unit of action, performed with precision and skill.

MOVEMENT PATTERN. A pattern laid down in the cortex, which when called upon by certain stimuli, will produce a desired and somewhat complex action response. A skill which has been learned and which is really a combination of many movements that may be called out by specific stimuli.

NEED. A state or condition urgently requiring relief.

NEUROLOGICAL INTEGRATION. The process by which nerves grow, develop, and move toward their ultimate sites so that they may perform the many tasks that are theirs. The integration of the nerves with the many other systems of the organism is essential for coordinated and effective functioning.

NEUROSIS. A nervous disorder characterized by abnormal psychological behavior, including compulsions, fears, anxieties, and other personality difficulties.

OSSEOUS. Composed of or pertaining to bone.

PARAPLEGIC. Paralyzed in the legs and lower half of the body.

PERCEPTION. The fusion of all new internal and external environmental stimuli with past experiences; the organization, discrimination, and interpretation of these to the end that they take on meaning.

PERCEPTUAL MOTOR. A term currently applied to all purposeful skeletal movement; used particularly to apply to early development of motor coordinations and the achieving of proficiency in the basic bodily movements.

PONS. The portion of the central nervous system which connects the medulla oblongata (bulbar region) with the cerebrum and the cerebellum. ("Pons" means bridge.")

PROPRIOCEPTOR. A sense organ which receives stimuli from the internal part of the organism, particularly from joints, muscles, tendons, soles of the feet, etc.; proprioceptors keep the organism informed of bodily movement and position. Feedback comes largely through these sense organs.

PSYCHOANALYTIC THEORY. Psychological theory which deals with the awareness and understanding of self and the conflicts within each individual. Sigmund Freud, with his concept of the "id," the "ego," and the "superego," is thought by most to be the father of the psychoanalytic theory. Sometimes used as a theory to explain play.

PSYCHOSIS. A severe personality disorder in which the individual is generally out of touch with reality; usually characterized by progressive deterioration of mental capacities.

PSYCHOSOMATIC. Pertaining to the relationship of mind and body and to their functioning as a unit.

PYRAMIDAL FIBERS. Nervous fibers going from the motor areas of the body and running up the spinal chord to the brain. They constitute the pyramidal tracts of the spinal chord.

QUADRICEPS FEMORIS. The muscles on the anterior side of the thigh; so called because of the four heads of this large muscle; the principal extensor of the lower leg.

REALIZE. To make real or at least apparently real; to achieve one's potential.

REFLEX. Generally a movement that is performed involuntarily as a result of a stimulus transmitted from a sense organ through a spinal ganglion to an efferent nerve and then to a muscle. Reflexes can be much more complex.

RELAXATION THEORY. The play theory which emphasizes the need for relaxation from the stresses and strains of modern life. Not only is a change of work necessary, but many parts of the organism become far too fatigued because of too little recreation.

RIGHTING REFLEX. The reflex which causes animals to be able to right themselves when thrown blind-folded up in the air. In the case of a cat, there will be a "head-neck" reflex, a "neck-body" reflex, and a "body-leg" reflex interacting to enable the animal to land on its feet.

SELF-ACTUALIZATION. Integration of one's actions and motives; accepting oneself as a person; pursuing an altruistic goal; developing one's capacities toward the goal of reaching one's potential; complete involvement in a cause larger than self.

SELF-FULFILLMENT. The achieving, in a partial measure at least, the goals which have been set; receiving the rewards of altruistic action; fulfilling the promise of one's youth; advancing toward the achievement of one's potential.

SELF-IMAGE. Self-concept; the way in which one sees himself; the way in which a person believes other people see him.

SELF-REALIZATION. Making actual one's goals; harmonizing one's achievement with one's abilities; achieving inner serenity; finding a cause to which one can give himself completely.

SERVO-MECHANISM. The apparatus in the human organism that provides feedback to the central nervous system with regard to all environmental stimuli. It includes the adjustment to incoming stimuli and the constant awareness of position, movement, and current status.

STATUS. Position of a person with respect to others in his group; may refer to economic or social status.

SURPLUS-ENERGY THEORY. A theory of play usually attributed to Schiller and Spencer which emphasizes the importance of activity which has nothing to do with furthering the life processes of the organism. Each person has some time and some energy for activity which has no material or ulterior motive.

TACTUAL. Pertaining to the sense of touch or "feel."

TENSION. An emotional state characterized by upset equilibrium, high blood pressure, sleeplessness, etc.; usually results from the blocking of drives toward a goal.

TRANSFER. Refers to the transfer of what is learned in one situation to another. In physical education, it may be the ability to throw, or jump, or run. In behavior, it may be the transfer of what is learned in a game situation to a serious life struggle.

URGE. A motivation which impels a person to a certain behavior. It may be an inner drive or an eagerness for some reward. It is an impulse to action resulting from past experiences combined with current stimuli.

INDEX

INDEX

ABCDE79876543210